The Byron Women

MARGOT STRICKLAND

The Byron Women

WITHDRAWN

ST. MARTIN'S PRESS
New York

Copyright © 1974 by Margot Strickland

All rights reserved. For information, write:
St. Martin's Press, Inc.
175 Fifth Avenue, New York, NY. 10010

Printed in Great Britain

Library of Congress Catalog Card Number: 74–33912
First published in the United States of America in 1975

Contents

Acknowledgements

I should like to thank the following people for their sympathetic help in the course of my research on this book : Mrs Olive Ordish, Mrs Jean Haynes, the Earl of Lytton, the late Malcolm Elwin, John Grey Murray, Professor G. Wilson Knight; Lord David Cecil, Miss Dorothy Marshall, Peter Warne and Miss Eileen Lynch of the Hertfordshire Records Office, Miss Lucy I. Edwards, Mrs. Elma Dangerfield and the Byron Society, Sister Joseph Mary, P.C.J., the Countess of Halifax, Sir John Trelawny, Richard Bebb, Gerald Sanctuary, Francis Carr, Mrs Genevieve Voelcker, Corbett Woodall, Mrs P. M. Whigham, Mr E. Brandreth of Harpenden Public Library; also the following institutions : Canterbury Cathedral Archives and Library, Nottingham City Museum and Libraries Committee, the Keats-Shelley Memorial Association, the Pierpont Morgan Library, New York, the Trustees of the British Museum, Cambridge City Library, the Beaney Institute, Canterbury.

Although I have not seen the Lovelace Collection of Byron Papers, I am grateful to the owner of that collection, the Earl of Lytton, for his permission to use the passages quoted in books based on the Lovelace Papers. These include : The 2nd Earl of Lovelace, *Lady Noel Byron and the Leighs* (1887) and *Astarte* (1921); E. C. Mayne, *Life and Letters of Lady Byron* (1929); Doris Langley-Moore, *The Late Lord Byron* (1961); Malcolm Elwin, *Lord Byron's Wife* (1962) and *The Noels and the Milbankes* (1967); Maboth Moseley, *Irascible Genius* (1964); Clara Thomas, *Love and Work Enough* (1967).

The late Mr Elwin, as one of the only two recent writers to have examined the unpublished letters and documents relating to Elizabeth Medora Leigh, wished to dissociate himself from the assumption that Elizabeth Medora Leigh was Byron's daughter.

M.S.

Illustrations

Foreword

The spirit shadowing this book must be Byron's. With the possible exception of Caroline Lamb, it is unlikely that any of the eight women whose lives are recounted would be much remembered were it not for him, and it is a measure of his multi-faceted brilliance that they should all be so different. Confronted by a Byron, women do not behave logically but biologically. Byron, however, was much more than an extraordinarily handsome and talented young poet, over whom the women of the day swooned with monotonous regularity. A study of some great men suggests that sexual drive and powerful leadership are strongly linked.

Byron was in every sense a leading man. He was a prophet, an agent for change and a spokesman for a generation a century and a half in advance of his time. His ideas on truth, liberty and world citizenship were revolutionary. 'There must be a universal republic,' he forecast, meaning that the principle of 'my country, right or wrong' would become secondary and be replaced by what Graham Greene calls 'the greater loyalty'. Revolution in England would have accelerated political and social change, but the expected revolt slowed into evolution. Byron's dramatic instinct led him to identify with the people, but his tragic exit from the scene was essential – he could never have become the common man's legislator. Everything that Byron did and wrote, studied in context, contributes to human understanding. His poetry reflects his life and his life was an epic poem of great grandeur. In going to Greece to die, Byron was spiritually going home.

It is accepted, the author believes, that Byron and his half-sister Augusta were lovers and, as Byron himself believed, perfectly naturally so, following an emotional relationship recurrent in family life since the ancient Greeks. Theirs was a classic Oedipus/Electra complex, their story a Greek drama performed in Regency costume. Most social workers will confirm that such a relationship is certainly not unknown today. Had not Byron been so courageous as proudly

9

to proclaim his feelings, and had he not been in a public position where they were sure to be noticed, the relationship would have excited little interest. It has been hinted that Byron's and Augusta's father was more than ordinarily fond of his full sister,[1] an affection unremarked upon but for subsequent generations' fascination with the Byron legend.

It may never be known whether Medora was or was not Byron's child. He appeared to believe her to be so, as did Annabella, their daughter Ada, Medora herself and various others. There was a sufficiency of Byron blood in her veins if she were not to ensure a likeness to both Byron and Colonel Leigh. A marked resemblance to one or the other is genetically unconvincing as proof, since Augusta was a Byron, her husband Colonel Leigh was Augusta's first cousin, and his mother a Byron. But Colonel Leigh was frequently absent from home and during the relevant period Augusta seems to have been mostly in London with Byron. In addition, a woman in love as Augusta undoubtedly was, would be likely to avoid cohabitation with a man other than her lover, even if that man were her husband. By the time Medora's paternity was called in question, it would not be easy for Colonel Leigh, father of seven, to recollect with accuracy his movements at the time Medora was conceived. It is significant that few of Medora's relatives appear to have tried to convince her that she was not Byron's daughter. Most seem to have accepted it, though this in no way proves that she was. Byron did not accept paternity lightly; no man in his position ever does. In Claire's case, he assured himself that Claire had had no relations with Shelley during the relevant times, before accepting Allegra as his daughter.

Medora's autobiography was published posthumously to refute Harriet Beecher-Stowe's allegations in an American journal that Medora was Byron's daughter. Later, in her book, *Lady Byron Vindicated*, Mrs Beecher-Stowe openly and with relish stated that incest was the prime cause of the separation and Byron's departure from England. The transatlantic champion of coloured people was militant in her defence of Lady Byron, who throughout her book figured as a sainted martyr, while Augusta Leigh was described as

---

[1] Doris Langley-Moore, 'The Great Byron Adventure' (*Sunday Times*, February-March, 1959).

'the partner of his sins'. Based on conversations she had had with Annabella some years before, it was written and published, she declared, as a result of Teresa Guiccioli's book, published in 1869.[2]

Ever since Byron's death 150 years ago, there has been a see-saw of public opinion concerning the rights and wrongs of the separation drama. In his book *Astarte*, Ralph, Earl of Lovelace, brought up by Lady Byron, discussed his grandfather's marital relationship with the greatest sympathy and understanding. After Byron's death, Moore's biography, disliked by Teresa, Augusta and Annabella, gave the impetus to a world-wide public controversy. Moore invited Lady Byron's comments and her 'Remarks' were first privately circulated and later published in a bid for the public's elusive sympathy, which has obstinately remained with Byron. In the present work it is assumed that Annabella was basically truthful. Memory is selective and it is only human to select episodes which place the writer, even a woman as heroically upright as Annabella tried to be, in a sympathetic light. There may have been pressure on her to distort, emphasize, colour, omit, but she was no Caroline Lamb. By her nature, it is believed, she could not embroider or fabricate what had no foundation in fact. Harriet Beecher-Stowe reported that Byron had told his wife, 'The world has made up its mind that "By" is a glorious boy; and the world will go for "By", right or wrong.' The reader must draw his own conclusions.

Of the many documents and letters studied, none were so moving in their tenderness, concern and distress as those of 'Moome' to Augustus Lamb. In the chapter on Caroline, his mother, no attempt has been made to retell yet again the disgraceful episodes in her tragic life; it was preferred to dwell on a less familiar aspect of a woman described as having 'a touch of genius'.[3] She did not know it, but she was a captive Celtic woman artist, struggling to free herself from oppressive Anglo-Saxon male domination. History and genetics suggest that the Celt and the Anglo-Saxon, while invincible joined against a foe, are ethnically incompatible and incapable of living together peaceably. So it was with Caroline and William Lamb. It is not entirely in relation to Byron that Caroline is growingly remembered. Her tragedy was that her talent, though considerable, was flawed, but she prophesied that her name would

---

[2] *Lord Byron, jugé par les témoins de sa vie* (Paris, 1868; London, 1869).
[3] Lord David Cecil, *Melbourne* (Constable, 1939).

be kept 'in capitals', and her poem 'A New Canto' is printed as an Appendix to this volume.

The most successful woman is unquestionably Teresa, tender, passionate, Catholic and continental. All Englishwomen everywhere in search of their particular Byron should make a serious study of Teresa.

October 1973   Margot Strickland
Lemsford, Herts.

Augusta

'Devoted in the stormiest hour.'

Epistle to Augusta (Stanza 8)

The Honourable Augusta Mary Leigh was born in 1783, the daughter of Captain John Byron and the former Marchioness of Carmarthen, who was already the mother of three children when she eloped with 'Mad Jack', as he was known. A divorce was obtained, enabling them to marry shortly before Augusta's birth. Captain Byron was reportedly still under twenty-one years old and Augusta's mother died shortly after the child's birth. The constantly insolvent Captain Byron later captivated and married the Scottish heiress Catherine Gordon who became Lord Byron's mother. Three years later Captain Byron died in France, and thus Augusta was orphaned at eight years old. Although she had rarely seen her father who was ever on the run from creditors, Byron was to write later, 'Augusta and I have always loved the memory of our father.'

Until she was four years old Augusta lived with her bad-tempered stepmother and afterwards with her maternal grandmother, the Countess of Holderness at her Derbyshire Manor. Under her grandmother's wing, the shy Augusta became accustomed to life in aristocratic households and was at ease in this type of society from her earliest years, effortlessly absorbing the rules of etiquette and the subtleties of the English class system. Her older half-sister and half-brothers were never to be as intimate with her as Byron became, though they showed themselves affectionate relations. When she was aged fifteen, Lady Mary Osborne, Augusta's half-sister, who was five years older, wrote of her genteel and gentle manner and that 'Her very pretty face . . . makes her . . . very striking and interesting at first sight . . . she has a fine complexion and fine colour, but is rather freckled.'

As an orphan she was dependent on kind relations for home,

clothes and company and was most at home with her mother's family. 'She has been very happy lately, having had so much Carmarthen company,' wrote Lady Mary Osborne, 'and almost broke her heart to come away.' Spending seven years near the Derbyshire coal-fields made an indelible impression on her mind. She was often at Castle Howard in Yorkshire and at Kiveton, near Worksop, as a guest of her mother's first husband. Lady Holderness died when Augusta was seventeen, after which Augusta found herself in the unhappy and vulnerable position of a homeless gentlewoman accustomed to the best society, but with only modest means.[1] Her stepmother retained her interest in Augusta and wrote to her when she was eighteen, 'Your brother is at Harrow school, and, if you wish to see him, I have no desire to keep you asunder.' Byron described his mother as diabolical. 'You, Augusta, are the only relation who treats me as a friend,' he wrote, and although Augusta was anxious to please Mrs Byron, she sometimes failed to meet that exacting lady's requirements. 'I left my mother', Byron reported to Augusta, 'in a monstrous pet with you for not writing.'

Drawn together through their common plight of an insecure childhood, Byron and Augusta quickly found a mutual sympathy, expressed in letters as they were rarely able to meet. She knitted him purses; he confided in her. She was often concerned about him and, hearing disquieting reports when he was at the critical age of sixteen, wrote to John Hanson, the family solicitor, asking him to call on her, 'feeling particularly anxious to have some conversation with him about Lord Byron who she has not seen this twelvemonth.' Byron was grateful for her affectionate interest and wrote to his 'amiable Augusta' from Harrow, 'My sources of amusement are Books, and writing to my Augusta, which, wherever I am, will always constitute my greatest pleasure.' When Byron fell into debt at Cambridge she was, for the only time in her life, in a position to try to rescue him financially.

For a well-born young lady marriage was essential and a choice of spouse for Augusta presented a severe problem. She was attractive, with dark hair and eyes, a generous mouth and a pleasing disposition, but she was too poor to attract suitors of birth and means

[1] She had an income of £350 a year from Lady Holderness.

and was doubtless considered fortunate when she became engaged to her cousin, Colonel George Leigh, whose mother was a Byron. The match was fostered by her dominating kinswoman, Elizabeth, Countess of Melbourne,[2] but disapproved of by Mrs Byron. Augusta was twenty-one but the rakish Colonel was in no hurry. 'That you are unhappy, my dear sister,' wrote Byron, 'makes me also. . . . Can't you drive this Cousin out of your pretty little head?'

Three years elapsed before Colonel Leigh was persuaded to the altar and they were married on 17 August 1807, his father objecting to the marriage on account of Augusta's low income. Augusta was twenty-four years old, which was considered rather a late age for a bride at that time. Georgiana (so named because Byron expected the child to be a son), the eldest of what was to be a large family, was born the following year. Byron sent his 'best thanks for making me an uncle . . . but the next *must* be a nephew.'

Augusta was unquestionably better connected than her husband. Her mother had been a Baroness in her own right and her grandmother a Countess. Lt. Col. Leigh of the 10th Dragoons was limited financially and socially. Moreover he was of that breed of feckless Englishmen who cheerfully gamble all their income away at the racecourse and spent much of his time in the entourage of the Prince of Wales to whom, through Augusta's connections, he had had the good fortune to be appointed an Equerry.

They made their home at Six Mile Bottom, a hamlet in a hollow near Newmarket where Col. Leigh was attached to the Prince's stud. There were two houses of consequence there: the Hall and the Lodge. The Leighs lived at the latter which Col. Leigh bought in 1810. It was a low-ceilinged property and Augusta found it crampingly small after the great houses to which she was accustomed. She was marooned there with her small children, her husband often away, enduring the life of a captive mother for several years. A second, mentally-retarded, daughter was born in 1811 and Augusta wrote to Byron, 'Oh! that I could immediately set out to Newstead. . . . I can't tell you *half* the happiness it would give me to see it and *you*; but my dearest B. it is a long journey . . . you can so easily come here. I have set my heart on it. Consider how very

[2] Lady Melbourne's grandfather was connected by marriage to the 2nd Earl of Holderness.

long it is since I've seen you.' Then came the lifelong refrain:
money worries. 'Probably you have heard of the many changes in
our situation. . . . in a pecuniary point of view it is materially
altered for ye worse,' Augusta told him. In 1811 Colonel Leigh had
incurred the Prince of Wales's displeasure over some double-dealing
in the sale of a horse, and the pressures upon Augusta were beginning to become unbearable. To offer some relief, Byron invited
Augusta to make her home at Newstead. But Augusta found herself
pregnant with her third child, born the following June, and she
could not contemplate the dislocation involved in leaving Col.
Leigh. Byron and Augusta did not meet that year.

In 1813 another of the Leighs' innumerable financial crises
occurred, and Augusta temporarily abandoned her troublesome
family at Six Mile Bottom to stay with her old friend, the Hon. Mrs
Thérèse Villiers, in London, where Byron was established at Bennet
Street. She was described at this time by the Irish poet Tom Moore
as 'very attractive . . . affectionate . . . childish . . . ready to laugh
at anything.' Byron had become the lion of the season, the rage of
London's fashionable salons, and Augusta was his constant companion at the many social events they attended together. Neither
brilliant nor well-dressed, she had early learned to make herself
agreeable in the highest strata and was able unerringly to guide him
through the social labyrinth. She knew exactly who was who, whom
to know and, more important, whom not to know – essential information for gentlefolk of limited means intent on social survival
in England's pleasant but class-ridden land.

During July, Byron wrote to Lady Melbourne, 'My sister is in
town, which is a great comfort, for never having been much
together, we are naturally more attached to each other.' It was
during this period that their fraternal affection developed into an
intense passion. When siblings fall in love with one another it is
usually the result of an emotionally deprived childhood. Byron had,
following his success, developed a conquering assurance, under
which he was still the unhappy little boy Augusta had known,
whereas she had become that most desirable of creatures to an un-
encumbered bachelor, the pretty young wife and mother, virtuous,
devoted and safely married. Their reunion after several years without meeting was a joining of two people completely in tune with one
another. They were inseparable and spent most of July and August

together, sometimes in London, occasionally at Six Mile Bottom where 'The Lodge', little more than a cottage, was a delightful refuge from London formalities. In the summer garden Byron sat under a laburnum tree and wrote. As the summer wore on they became ever more conscious that divided they could not endure to be, and decided that they must go away together and live abroad.

But though that scheme was shelved by Augusta, torn between her adoration for Byron and her devotion to her children, she could not bring herself to relinquish him as yet. Byron confided to Lady Melbourne his desire to take Augusta to Sicily with him but she advised against it : 'It is a crime . . . and a cruelty . . . depriving of all future peace and happiness a woman who has maintained a good reputation.' Augusta returned to the country, to her three children and the man who cared more for the pleasures of the turf than the company of the woman who had waited three long years to become his wife. Byron frequently visited her there and later that year Augusta sent him a lock of her hair wrapped in a piece of paper on which she had written her name and the legend, *'Partager tous vos sentimens, ne voir que par vos yeux, n'agir que par vos conseils, ne vivre que par vous, voila mes voeux, mes projets, et le seul destin qui peut me rendre heureuse.'* In those few French phrases Augusta expressed her love for Byron more eloquently than she ever did afterwards: 'To share all your feelings, to see only through your eyes, to act only on your advice, to live only by you; these are my desires, my plans and the only destiny that can make me happy.' Byron added to her words his own, 'La chevelure of the *One* whom I most loved. X.' He was twenty-four, Augusta twenty-nine.

Augusta was pregnant when Byron was at Newstead in January, but he sent for her to join him as he wished her to see the Abbey before it was sold to pay his considerable debts. They had intended to discontinue a dangerous relationship which threatened to engulf them, but Augusta was unable to refuse him and made the two-day journey to Newstead Abbey, where they were happily snowbound for three weeks. It was in this year, at the peak of their happiness together, that they carved their names on a tree-trunk in the grounds of the Abbey.

But already Byron's self-dramatizing poetry had caused gossip to spread in society. 'The Bride of Abydos' concerned a romance between a pair believing themselves to be brother and sister, and one of Augusta's nephews at Eton suffered a good deal of schoolboy ragging on the subject of his aunt Augusta's intimacy with her brother.

Byron was at that time involved in romances with various women, either in person or by correspondence, but Augusta was constantly on his mind. 'She was not to blame,' he defended her to Lady Melbourne; 'She was not aware of her own peril until it was too late.' A week before her confinement Byron was with Augusta again and on her child's birth in the Spring, he went immediately to see it. He assured Lady Melbourne, 'Positively she and I will grow good and all that,' presumably alluding to his intention to discontinue the relationship.

In August Byron was in Hastings, and Augusta was the only woman in a party which included Byron's cousin and heir George Byron, and the Rev. Francis Hodgson who, after Byron, was Augusta's most faithful correspondent. They stayed there ten days, during which time Byron finally decided that he must marry. Marriage would offer emotional and financial stability, both of which he conspicuously lacked.[3] Augusta suggested her friend, Lady Charlotte Leveson-Gower, to whom a proposal on Byron's behalf was penned by Augusta; it was immediately rejected.

Byron and Augusta were next together at Six Mile Bottom where the children were much in evidence in so small a house. Medora was Augusta's fourth child, but it was her second name and rarely used in the family, where she was known by her first name, Elizabeth or Libby. She was a pretty dark-haired girl who resembled Byron. During this visit to Augusta, Byron wrote a formal proposal of marriage to Annabella Milbanke, a young heiress who had also earlier rejected him, passing it over the dinner table for Augusta's comment. She thought it charmingly expressed but Byron doubted the wisdom of sending it. 'It is a pity it should not go,' Augusta persuaded, 'I never read a prettier one.' 'Then it shall go,' decided Byron and the letter was posted.

At this stage both felt that Byron's marriage was a necessity in ensuring that his future should be calmer and free from debt, although Byron later declared that he would have given up everything for Augusta. That she adored her half-brother cannot be

[3] As early as 1808 he admitted 'a golden dolly' was essential.

questioned. Her elegant mother's abandonment of a devoted husband,[4] three children and a considerable position as Marchioness of Carmarthen, for the young and penniless Jack Byron, a union of which Augusta was the issue, had set a romantic precedent. So also had the same Captain Byron's deep affection for his full sister with whom he lived in France until his death. Augusta was extremely interested in her forbears.[5]

Byron found Augusta's endearing foolishness irresistible, tinged as it was with a fond maternal streak. She was fun to be with, uncomplicated emotionally, made no scenes and did not argue. That the affection between them should have become a deep and abiding love was inevitable, given their natures and circumstances. In September Augusta was at Newstead again and wrote, 'Of future plans I really can say nothing they are in such a glorious state of uncertainty.'

Byron's courtship of Miss Milbanke by correspondence proceeded but while she eagerly awaited her first sight of Byron for over a year, he lingered several days at Six Mile Bottom with Augusta and her children. From there he wrote to Lady Melbourne, smitten with doubts again while in Augusta's happy company, 'I am not sure that I shall go now.'

When he finally went, he talked incessantly about Augusta. He told Annabella that 'no one would possess so much of his love as she did,' and a fortnight later, having conquered Annabella's preciseness with passion, he returned to his sister. The two women exchanged letters and thus began the extraordinary triangular correspondence which was to last for some years. Augusta wrote to the Rev. Francis Hodgson, 'Thank you a thousand times for yr kind congratulations on the *approaching* marriage, which I hope will secure my dearest B's happiness.'

The women's letters expressed affectionate regard for each other, appropriate in that they were about to become closely related. Annabella's were sincere, Augusta's devious. The former had noth-

[4] Out of respect for his wife's passion for Capt. Byron, he facilitated the divorce.
[5] In an Oedipus complex 'the child identifies himself with the parent of the same sex and thus adopts the latter's behavioural tendencies.' In woman this is known as an Electra complex. (H. Maisch, *Incest*, trans. C. Bearne, André Deutsch, 1973).

ing to hide, the latter much. Annabella was anxious to be liked by Augusta, knowing Byron's great affection for his sister, and various schemes were set in motion for the women to meet. These Augusta managed to avoid, staying discreetly at Six Mile Bottom. In December a puzzled Annabella wrote to Byron, disappointed that Augusta could not accompany him on a proposed visit. Augusta did not wish to go with him for several reasons, the chief of which may have been a desire to avoid close contact with the girl about to marry Byron. There was, however, a subtler one : the rich, clever but provincial Miss Milbanke was and ever would be Augusta's social inferior, and had therefore to be kept at a distance.

On his way to the marriage with Annabella, Byron inevitably stopped at Six Mile Bottom yet again, enjoying a family Christmas there whilst his bride daily awaited him. The gathering was small and Col. Leigh ailing and complaining, but Augusta was in good looks and spirits, as happy to have Byron with her as he was to be there, surrounded by romping small children.

Once again Byron doubted the wisdom of his approaching marriage, now only days away. He wrote a letter breaking the engagement but Augusta foolishly persuaded him to destroy it and to continue with the fore-doomed match. Having urged the reluctant bridegroom on towards his marriage with a provincial but potentially wealthy blue-stocking, Augusta began to realize that her own deepest feelings could not so easily be stifled. A letter from her reached Byron the very morning after his marriage night.

Augusta began this letter to her newly-married brother, 'Dearest, first, and best of human beings.' Pouring out her feelings about his marriage, she confessed she was tormented 'as the sea trembles when the earth quakes'. Byron proudly read this letter out aloud for his wife's admiration.

Throughout the honeymoon Byron constantly praised Augusta. 'I only want a woman to laugh,' he complained to his earnest young wife. 'I can make Augusta laugh at anything. No one makes me happy but Augusta,' was his recurring theme.

Annabella courageously decided to confront the problem of Augusta by inviting her to join the honeymoon couple, and Byron seemed pleased by the idea. Augusta declined, the niceties of the English class system dictating that Augusta's social position, although she was materially poor, would be lowered should she be the guest of the Milbankes. The women were exchanging letters almost daily. Byron's behaviour had become so bad that Annabella cried out, 'Augusta – will you be my only friend?' Byron had already intimated to his wife that he and his sister had been lovers.

Augusta's reaction was typically evasive and insincere. 'Not even I can know him better than you do,' she told Annabella, yet in another letter she could not resist a reference that she knew would be relayed to Byron : 'I am so glad he is spoiled . . . he would have it that no one could spoil him but *me*.' Aware that Byron was bored in Annabella's family circle where the only diversions were provincial parlour games, she wrote mischievously, 'Only think of Byron playing drafts! I never should have suspected him.' Continuing to make fun of her new sister-in-law, Augusta continued, 'He has now so many occupations – waking, dining, playing drafts with Mama . . . but I am vain enough to think he does not forget Guss.'

A few weeks later Byron and Annabella left the bride's parental home for Six Mile Bottom where Annabella was to be Augusta's guest for the first time. Augusta did not wish them to come, and made various excuses in order to avoid having them, but finally the visit could be postponed no longer. They arrived,. only to find a cowardly Augusta hiding upstairs; she could not bring herself to touch Annabella.

On their first evening Byron began his obscene taunting of both women. 'Now I have *her* . . . I can do without *you* – in all ways,' he told his wife. Throughout the three-week-long visit Byron behaved appallingly, moving Augusta to express admiration for Annabella's stoicism. 'I think I never saw or heard or read of a more perfect being in mortal mould than she appears to be,' she wrote to the Rev. Francis Hodgson. In the claustrophobic intimacy of the Lodge, Augusta 'seemed fearful of every word he uttered,' reported Annabella, 'fearful of checking him . . . but was careful not to respond.' Annabella observed, '[Byron's] signs of passion . . . were so marked that she must have been conscious of them.' Augusta was clinging to a precarious self-discipline. Young and attractive, sexually starved and neglected by her husband, adored by Byron whose love she fully returned, she found herself in an agonizing situation. To be in the same house with Byron was sufficient to charge the atmosphere, but he referred thoughtlessly to her 'inflammable temperament'.

Two or three days after their arrival a parcel was delivered from a London jeweller containing a pair of brooches made to Byron's order, one containing a lock of his hair, the other Augusta's, each brooch engraved with three crosses. 'Do you remember our signs at Newstead?' asked Byron fondly of his sister, alluding to the symbols of their attachment, and the brother and sister immediately pinned the brooches on.

Annabella's defence was a generosity which further bewildered Augusta, striving to control her senses and keep her wits. 'You are kind to me because you do not know me,' she told Annabella. Remorseful and aware of her weakness, she told Annabella, 'He can never respect *me*,' and when Byron called her his best friend she cried, 'Oh I fear I have been your worst,' for as the elder of the two she assumed responsibility for their mutual attraction. Annabella noted that towards the end of their visit, Byron lost interest in Augusta[6] and turned back to his wife. Their child Ada was probably conceived during this time.

It was a relief to both women when Byron and Annabella left for London and their expensive home at 13, Piccadilly Terrace, but a week later Augusta joined them. Augusta had that year been appointed a Woman of the Bedchamber to the ageing Queen Charlotte and from now on she was to spend periods of time in apartments at St James's Palace. Already at ease in society, she now obtained entry into Court circles, her impeccably aristocratic background through her mother's family qualifying her for the position. Her life was henceforth to veer between rural, domestic isolation at Six Mile Bottom and the formalities of a tedious Court which lacked the gaieties surrounding the Prince Regent. The seventy-one-year-old Queen Charlotte had for years suffered agonies over her periodically ill husband, George the Third, whose reason finally broke down in 1811. A foreigner herself (she had been Charlotte of Mecklenburg-Strelitz), she tended to surround herself with German ladies whose command of English was minimal. The Court etiquette was excessively strict : ladies were not allowed either to cough or sneeze in the Royal presence and on occasion not even to move. Augusta was largely cut off from her friends and relatives; her duties were those of a supernumerary, long hours being spent in the unproductive business known as attending. But the appointment carried

[6] She was menstruating.

the advantages of several hundred pounds a year and a London home.

'You are a fool for letting her come,' Byron told his wife on Augusta's arrival, but Annabella saw her role as that of reformer – later she confessed the impossibility of separating them. Augusta afterwards wrote to her sister-in-law, 'I never would have entered your house – perhaps I did wrong . . . to do so. . . . Dearest A *intentionally* I have never wronged you.'

The burden of being unable to confide in anyone but each other itself formed a curious bond between the sisters-in-law. Augusta later wrote that 'Concealment appeared a duty under the circumstances,' and Annabella admitted, 'I erred in encouraging you myself.' Byron continually stressed his dissatisfaction with Annabella throughout his wife's pregnancy and Annabella was thankful when the opportunity arose to visit her favourite uncle who was dying. Of this visit she wrote, 'I felt that death-bed a relief from the horror of an incestuous household.'

By June, the atmosphere at Piccadilly Terrace had become intolerable and Augusta returned to Six Mile Bottom, closely followed by Byron, who was grateful to escape the confines of a household fully occupied with the approaching *accouchement*. He made clear that it was fun to be with Augusta again : 'Goose left a mousetrap in the apartment allotted to me, the consequence of which is that . . . I have nearly lost a toe,' he told his wife. Augusta and her family relaxed him as nobody else could : 'Goose is taking a quill from her wing to scribble to you. . . . the children here looking shockingly – quite green – & Goose being as red as ever you have no idea what a piece of patchwork might be made of the family faces' – thus he presented a picture of happy domesticity to Annabella, their self-styled 'guardian angel'. But Augusta, tempted though she must have been, steadfastly refused herself to him and Byron returned to Piccadilly offended with her.

At this time Byron had been appointed to the Committee of Management of the recently burned down Theatre Royal, Drury Lane. A number of distinguished persons had been found to help raise a large sum of money for its rebuilding. The men were witty and good company, the complaisant actresses attractive, and Byron took full advantage of his position to enjoy their favours, 'as much to vex Augusta as you,' he taunted his wife. Nevertheless, in July of that year he drew up his will, making Augusta and her family his sole inheritors. His behaviour grew daily worse, but Annabella wrote to Augusta hopefully that she was beginning to understand him : 'His misfortune is an habitual *passion* for *excitement* . . . he loves or hates us together,' and then a cry from the bewildered heart to the only woman who could share her extraordinary situation, 'O Augusta, will it ever change for me?' But Augusta must by now have known that Annabella was incapable of handling Byron, nor was there hope for a marriage of which she herself had been one of the two chief architects.

Byron's financial affairs were in disarray, a bailiff was sleeping in the house and Annabella implored Augusta to return. 'You will do good I think,' she told her and Augusta was back in Piccadilly Terrace in November. Annabella's child was expected the following month but Byron was unsparing of the two women's feelings, boasting openly of his passion for his sister. His proximity must have made her wretched. 'Ah,' she told Annabella, 'you don't know what a fool I have been about him.' Augusta 'threw her hair back from her forehead with trembling hand,' recalled Annabella of this scene; in a fever not so much of guilt as frantic sexual desire, she had to suffer Annabella's chaste kiss on the forehead as she left the room.

Byron had serious political and financial matters on his mind. These probably exacerbated his treatment of his wife, which became so abusive that Augusta and Mrs Clermont, Annabella's maid, with Byron's manservant Fletcher, had difficulty in guarding Lady Byron adequately. George Byron was sent for by Augusta as additional aid, and came for an indefinite period, but this did not prevent Augusta sitting up with Byron night after night; this was 'avowedly to prevent an act of outrage towards me,' wrote Annabella afterwards, but such behaviour was unlikely to dampen their mutual attraction.

Annabella and Byron's daughter was born on 10 December 1815, and was named Augusta Ada. For a time she was known as Augusta junior and her aunt was invited to be the child's godmother. But Byron's behaviour was such that a Dr Baillie was consulted on the state of his mind and it was decided that Annabella and Ada should leave. Although Dr Baillie warned Augusta against remaining alone with her brother, she elected to stay, fearful that Byron might harm himself. She had indeed prepared to go and had ordered fires to

be lit in her apartments in St James's Palace, but Byron's solicitor
prevailed on her not to desert her brother. The night of Annabella's departure, Byron took Augusta to the theatre at Drury
Lane.

Immediately letters flew back and forth between the departed
wife and the remaining sister. 'It is my greatest comfort that you
are in Piccadilly,' the unhappy Annabella told Augusta. The latter
sent Annabella regular bulletins about Byron and sometimes the
news was good : 'B stayed at home yesterday evening – no brandy
and took his medicine,' but often Byron 'grew *fractious*', railing at
everyone, and occasionally Augusta wounded the fugitive wife : 'He
talked of you quite coolly,' she told her.

Augusta found herself in a very difficult situation, for London was
seething with rumours about Byron, his wife and his sister. If
Augusta left her brother it would be tantamount to an admission of
her guilt. If she stayed, her reputation was equally endangered. She
courageously chose to stay and, by remaining, shared with Byron
the humiliation of public ostracism. Quietly enduring the many
slights, she somehow succeeded in retaining her social position, and
returned to her apartments in St James's Palace. Here, on Easter
Sunday 1816 she and Byron had a farewell meeting at which he
wept bitterly. 'Wherever I go,' he wrote to his wife from Mivart's
Hotel, 'and I am going far . . . be kind to her . . . to her children . . .
it is sorrow to her to have waters now, or the earth hereafter,
between her and her brother.' They parted in tears, never to meet
again, though Augusta's friend Mrs Villiers wrote to Annabella, 'He
may propose to her to go abroad to him . . . & Col. Leigh is quite
capable of acquiescing in it.' For the Colonel was aware that his
wife was to be Byron's beneficiary.

Byron and Augusta ceaselessly wrote to each other. Although he
was now exiled, Byron's constant flow of autobiographical verse
continued to shock and excite the reading public. Caroline Lamb
implored him not to publish the 'Stanzas to Augusta' and Byron
paid heed and instructed his publisher to withhold them for the
present.[7] In 1816 Augusta wrote to the Rev. Francis Hodgson, 'I
quite dread the poems – so afraid of their renewing unpleasant
recollections in the public mind & containing bitterness towards her

---

[7] They were not published until six years after his death.

who has already suffered too much whatever you hear pray tell me whatever I say pray *burn*.'

In the summer of 1816 Augusta was far advanced with another pregnancy. Despite the damage it must do to Augusta's reputation, Annabella insensitively decided to end relations between them. Informing Augusta shortly after the birth of her son Frederick, 'Before your confinement I would not risk agitating you,' she proceeded to demolish her : 'There are reasons . . . founded on your conduct . . . which indispensably . . . impose on me the *duty* of limiting my intercourse with you.' Annabella was discovering that in spite of all the machinations against him, public sympathy obstinately remained with Byron and people were whispering, 'There was no error *in the heart*.' Poor Augusta, never much cared for by anyone other than Byron, was at Six Mile Bottom breast-feeding yet another infant; she told Annabella, 'I cannot say I am *wholly surprised*.' From the maelstrom of her own shattered emotional life, aggravated by the present difficulties of numerous children, a stupid husband and means so straitened that the modest house at Six Mile Bottom had recently been put up for sale, she was yet able to write bravely to Annabella, 'We are all perhaps inclined to magnify our trials.' With dignity she continued, 'The tide of public opinion has been so turned against my brother that the least appearance of coolness on your part towards me would injure me most seriously and I am . . . compelled to accept the "limited intercourse" which is all you can grant.' Augusta revealed the frantic state she had been in, trying to resist Byron's caresses while she achingly desired him : 'You ought to consider that *I* . . . may have had provocation.' Augusta's long frustration and the stresses and strains of her situation in the glare of public life resulted in severe depression and a corroding sense of guilt. Still on call from the Palace, she was ordered to attend the Prince Regent's fête. A distressed gentlewoman ever in debt, she yet needed to maintain a certain style at Court, and Mrs Thérèse Villiers helped her with her choice of clothes. 'I never saw anything to equal her dejection . . . apparently insensible of being in society,' was the latter's comment. Augusta at one point burst out with the remark, 'I'm sure *I'm* not prepared for the next world so I hope this will last.'

Augusta was not deeply religious but was tortured by the belief that she was being punished for the misdeed of having loved her brother too well. Her life constrained to the limits of English society, she had read little and travelled not at all. She was not to know that her situation was neither unnatural nor uncommon in the history of human relations, and a real fear of God and His retribution haunted her.

Mrs Villiers was not an entirely loyal friend, for she now became a confidante of Lady Byron, vicariously enjoying the drama inherent in the lives of the two A's as she went between them with highly informative letters. 'I have seen upon her [Augusta's] table a thick unsealed letter addressed by her to him,' she excitedly told Annabella. In turn she told Augusta, 'Annabella is your guardian angel,' and Augusta meekly assented.

Byron was now in Italy but continued to send Augusta thoughtlessly inflaming letters : 'I have never ceased, nor can cease to feel for a moment that perfect and boundless attachment which bounds and binds me to you . . . renders me utterly incapable of *real* love for any other human being – for what could they be to me after you.' The day after he wrote this letter he expected her to be entertained by his account of an amorous escapade in the course of which he had fallen into the Grand Canal and proceeded to his assignation dripping wet. Poor frustrated Augusta was in daily receipt of letters which contrasted sharply with her own penurious existence, surrounded by children, an uncaring husband and mounting bills.

Augusta was slyly revenged upon Annabella's lofty moral stance by sending them all on to her at her own insistence. However, the letters had the unfortunate effect of determining Annabella and Mrs Villiers to extract a confession from Augusta. 'I agree with you,' Annabella told Mrs Villiers, 'in thinking an interview particularly desirable.' The object was to complete Augusta's 'reformation'.

Augusta, trembling with fear and guilt, met Annabella and Mrs Villiers in some rented rooms near Knightsbridge and a satisfactory confession was obtained. Byron, from the time he was 16, had been an anxiety to her on account of his sexual habits. Mrs Villiers wrote smugly afterwards, 'I think I am justified in saying . . . her eyes are really opened as to the enormity she has been led into.' Other meetings were arranged, since confession to incestuous relations after Byron's marriage was desired, but this was strongly denied by Augusta. Having relived for the other women a private and precious relationship, Augusta was then made to feel remorse for giving

Annabella a sleepless night. Annabella hoped she was 'bringing her
to realize the horror of her crime', but after another tortured interview Augusta pleaded for release. Mrs Villiers had doubts as to
Augusta's reformation, commenting that her 'horror of the crime
[was] . . . not too great.'

Between these ghoulish interviews, Annabella arranged a small
dinner-party at which the company consisted of four women, all of
whom had one subject in common : Byron. The guests were Mrs
George Byron, Mrs Villiers and Augusta.

From the continent Byron sent Augusta gifts to distribute around
the family : 'I mean to buy some pretty granite and spar play-
things for the children.' He hoped she might travel to Italy for a
few months. Considerate of her husband's constant lack of money,
he offered to pay all her expenses : 'The greatest obstacle would be
that you are . . . necessary as a housekeeper.' It is the married
woman's lot in a love affair ever to be, as Byron put it 'admirably
yoked' to the husband and the home. He did not help by speculating
on what might have been : 'We might have lived so single and so
happy. . . . I shall never find anyone like you – nor you . . . like me.
We are just formed to pass our lives together. . . . We – at least I
am . . . removed from the only being who could ever have loved me,
or whom I can feel unmixedly attached to. . . . My voice and my
heart are ever thine. . . . We are the last persons in the world who
ought or could cease to love one another. . . . I always loved you
better than any earthly existence, and I always shall, unless I go
mad.' This he signed 'XB'. When this letter was sent to Annabella,
she wrote furiously to Mrs Villiers, 'they are *absolute love letters.*'

Augusta's return to Six Mile Bottom after the series of confes-
sional interviews was met with fresh financial problems. Byron's
emotional letters continued to arrive and Augusta begged Annabella's advice. 'She wants to know how she can stop them,' wrote an
outraged Annabella who had believed she and Mrs Villiers had
'purified' Augusta. Enclosing yet another of Byron's letters to her,
Augusta, mortified by guilt and desire, wrote of 'the grief it is to me
of him having such ideas – *IF he really has* them.'

While Byron was at Venice he received an unhappy letter from
Augusta, strongly enough worded to cause him concern. Aware as
he was of her constant money troubles, her extreme misery yet
suggested to him some other unspecified reason. Byron answered, 'I

can't make out whether your disorder is a broken heart . . . or what your melancholy or mysterious apprehensions refer to. . . . I know nothing about what you are in the doldrums about.' With a masculine lack of understanding he continued, 'I should think all that could affect *you* must have been over long ago. But Augusta was still in her thirties and was yet to bear another child. She was unable to bring herself to go into detail about the cause of her despondency. Her seventh and last child was born the following January. A few weeks before her confinement Augusta was shocked by the news of Byron's imminent return to England. She wrote in a panic to Annabella, 'Luckily I do not die easily – or think this stroke would about finish me.' Annabella answered jealously, 'It can scarcely be doubted that you are his principal object in England,' and warned Augusta not to receive Byron but Augusta defied this edict. 'What reasons could I give for not seeing him?' she asked, doubting if he would actually come. To Byron she wrote that she would not, however, see him alone and Byron answered, 'Very well . . . you will never see me more.'

It was a false alarm. Byron's Italian mistress Teresa was ill and he decided against coming, reproaching Augusta, 'You will probably never see me again as long as you live. Indeed you don't deserve it, for having behaved so *coldly, when I was ready to have sacrificed everything* for you.' Augusta, however, had little choice but to stick to her home, husband and children. Had she eloped with Byron as he implied he wished her to do, it would have meant a life of exile in a foreign country and desertion of her children to a feckless husband.

A year and a half later Byron fluttered his English womenfolk again with the promise of a journey home. He wrote to his sister, 'Perhaps we may meet in Spring,' but once again it came to nothing and the following year Byron died on Easter Monday in Greece. His valet Fletcher wrote to Augusta:

I am sorry to be under the Painfull Obligation of wrighting you the Most disegreeable letter that I ever to this unfortunate moment Had ever to write, not only for *me* or *you* But for all the world in General. How Shall I be able to proceed or Pronounce the fatal word which My Duty Demands from *me* has a faithfull Servant – but Proceed I must though it costs me tears of Blood – in the first place in the 15th Febry. My Lord was attacked with a convulsive fit. . . . he breathed his last without even a sigh or a grone. . . . Now Hond Madam . . . My Ld tole me you had been verry ill and I hope Madam you are quite Recovd and that your Amiable Familey his all Quite well his the Prayers of your Most Obt and Humble St. – I must conclude By my prayers for you to receive this fatal news with the consolation of being serting My Lord His much happier than any of us.

Augusta was outwardly composed and wrote little betraying the great grief she felt nor did anyone witness, as in Lady Byron's case, uncontrolled weeping and wailing. Her deep understanding of Byron's sensitivity made her, according to Edward J. Trelawny, the only individual who really understood the truth regarding Byron's lame foot, for she wrote to thank Trelawny for parrying inquisitive investigations about it for a proposed biography.

When the 'dear remains' arrived at Tilbury in June, Augusta spent a day on board the vessel and made all the funeral arrangements. She looked upon Byron's embalmed body and of this awesome experience wrote to Francis Hodgson, 'The melancholy comfort that it bestowed on me *never* can be expressed. . . . It was awful to behold what I parted with . . . now cold and inanimate, and so altered . . . not a vestige of what he was.' With relative calm she composed the wording of Byron's memorial tablet at Hucknall Torkard where he was taken and buried in the family tomb.

The shock of Byron's death was swiftly followed by the embarrassment of his memoirs which were legally Augusta's property. She had never seen them and betrayed no fear of what they might reveal, though several of their readers considered them unfit for publication and Augusta was advised that they should be burned. 'God knows what will happen to-morrow at twelve – for there must be some very mysterious proceedings,' she wrote, 'I am *quaking*.' Preoccupied as ever with her problematical family she added distractedly, 'I am as well as possible . . . ye elder children better ye younger fallen sick.' With due ceremony the memoirs were burned at the offices of John Murray at 50 Albemarle Street, in the presence of Murray, Byron's solicitor and several others. Augusta was the only woman present. Col. Doyle, one of Annabella's advisers, pronounced solemnly, 'On the part of Mrs Leigh, I put them into the fire.'

A few months after Byron's death, Augusta fell a victim once again to her own sexuality. This time the object of her affections was Henry Trevannion, a young Cornish kinsman whom she had not seen since he was a boy and who had now grown into an attractive man. Augusta was forty-one and the mother of seven children, the youngest of whom was four years old. While her child-bearing years were over, there is no reason to believe her less charming or attractive than formerly, and it is at about this age that a woman's sexual impulses are strongest. Augusta was the child of a couple who had eloped passionately in love, the woman some years older than the man. Her affectionate and sensual nature had found fulfilment only in her love for Byron. She had given Byron up, withstood scandal, kept her position at Court and held her family together devotedly. She had suffered years of self-sacrificing frustration sexually and socially, hampered by her brood of harassing children. Now Byron was dead, she was at last free from his tormenting letters. She was not free, however, from her own compulsions. Henry Trevannion was a Byron;[8] he was personable and sensual. Augusta was trapped by her desire for the young man, who exercised a considerable hold over her. It is a situation where the younger man invariably has the upper hand. Tormented by fear and guilt, for Henry Trevannion was the reverse of honourable, and wishing to avoid a scandal, Augusta found the solution to her problem on her own doorstep, when Henry became attracted to her daughter Georgiana, then a shy girl of seventeen, who probably became pregnant.

Suddenly Augusta was writing to Annabella, 'You will perhaps be much surprised to hear there is a proposal of marriage to Georgey!' She continued glowingly, 'I had known his family . . . before my marriage. . . . We renewed our acquaintance about two years ago – and I asked after the *hero* of my present tale . . . forgetting how the years must have made them [the children] into men! . . . He was introduced to me . . . about last July twelvemonth and I've seen much of him since from liking him and finding him so far superior to the *common herd*.' Annabella might well be surprised at the suddenness of the proposal. Marriages were usually carefully arranged according to rank and wealth. Although Augusta had expectations from Byron's will (still to be settled), her pressing

[8] Mrs Sophia Trevannion, née Byron, was Lord Byron's grandmother.

financial difficulties rendered advantageous marriages for her children a vital necessity. With her social connections she had no reason
to suppose that Georgiana would lack suitors. Henry Trevannion,
a student of law, had little money and no position. The truth was
that Augusta, motivated by fear of scandal and the necessity to
dispose of the young man, had embarked on a repetition of the
Byron disaster by planning another marriage, this time involving
her own daughter.

Colonel Leigh, though neglectful and absorbed in gambling, had
nevertheless overlooked a good deal in his wife's conduct : he must
have been aware of Augusta's devotion to Byron and of the publication of openly passionate poetry dedicated to her. The only time he
had evinced concern was when Byron was about to marry and he
feared he would lose his share of Augusta's expected inheritance
from her brother. This new situation, however, concerned his eldest
daughter and he strongly opposed the match. For the first time
during their marriage he exerted himself and tried to prevent his
daughter's marriage to a scoundrel described by the infatuated
Augusta as 'the only person I know worthy of Georgey'.

Henry Trevannion was only a second son and his father a
widower contemplating remarriage, so his financial prospects were
dismal. Augusta betrayed herself when she wrote to Annabella that
she was 'without the slightest idea until lately that Georgey was
likely to attract him or indeed anybody – She is such a *quiet* being
. . . not brilliant in any way.' A woman in her forties is often unaware of her daughter's attractions and jealous of them when they
supplant her own.

To accomplish the marriage with the necessary speed,[9] Augusta
had to raise money. In the hope of a loan she wrote to a surprised
Annabella, asking for £2,000. Exaggerating wildly she wrote of the
lovers' *'unheard of Misery'*. They were, she said, 'both looking like
ghosts, & as for *the Law* there will be no studying of that while this
state of things lasts.' Annabella, somewhat taken aback, complied
with her usual saintly generosity and the pair were swiftly married,
with the bride's father conspicuously absent and Augusta and
Medora her only relations present.

[9] No real reason has been discovered for this hasty marriage. It may have
been the traditional one. They were married a few weeks after the engagement.

Augusta wrote afterwards to Annabella, 'Our Marriage thank God is happily over & in parting with dearest Georgey I feel that I could not to *anyone* in the world with such perfect confidence *as* to Henry Trevannion. I have seen him *daily hourly* for three months – in Moments of Sickness, Sorrow, anxiety and suspense . . . (which Shew the real Character) & his has only risen in my estimation!'

When Byron died Augusta inherited everything. His wife and daughter, and his heir George Byron, received nothing. Although Augusta wished to help the new Lord Byron, now married, he was offended and refused (accepting financial help from Annabella instead) and an estrangement ensued. But Augusta managed to allow Byron's manservant Fletcher £70 a year for a time, and gave the devoted servant several trunks full of his clothes.

The sum decided upon to compensate John Murray for the loss of Byron's memoirs was 2,000 guineas, but it was suggested that responsibility for payment be shared between Augusta and Annabella, the former's poverty being well known. Augusta's pride was piqued : '*Mine* was the act of destroying the MS., *mine* and *mine* ALONE ought to have been the consequences . . . the more so as Lady Byron says she did NOT CONSENT to the destruction.'

But it was known that Augusta would never be able to raise the money and Byron's legacy quickly disappeared. What was the reason for her permanent state of near destitution? Estimated by Annabella at upwards of £100,000, the legacy was in fact much less. She did not live stylishly, she did not attempt to play the grand hostess, and her apartments at Flag Court in St James's Palace though not luxurious were rent free; the country house at Six Mile Bottom, now given up, had been small and not costly to maintain. But her sons were profligate and constantly threatened disaster, continually having to be bought out of scrapes, while Georgiana and Henry Trevannion quickly produced three children and had to be supported. After Byron's death, blackmailers descended on his family and Augusta borrowed foolishly to pay them off.

Augusta was unable alone to face these difficulties and was certain to take what seemed at the time the easiest way out. 'Decision was never my forte,' she wrote. When she did make a decision it was invariably the wrong one. 'Half-measures will always be her bane,' Annabella summed her up.

Augusta, occupied with her Court duties and young children, had

B

not seen her married daughter Georgiana and third daughter
Medora for over a year when they, together with Henry Trevannion,
returned from a stay in France. Augusta was quite unaware of the
dramatic events which had preceded the trio's removal from Canterbury, where they had been living in a house of Annabella's, to France
where fifteen-year-old Medora's child by Henry Trevannion had
been born and had died. Augusta was puzzled by Medora's dis-
inclination for the children's dances which she had formerly enjoyed
but it was some time before she knew the full extent of what had
happened. Augusta was even then quite unable to see Henry Trevannion objectively. 'He has been QUITE what I expected of him,
and my greatest comfort,' she wrote. The unstable young man confessed to his 'Dearest Moe', as he called his mother-in-law, that he
had taken laudanum in a moment of desperation. 'I promise you
not to do so again,' he told her, adding, 'Would to God that had
been all!' Henry Trevannion and Medora were again left alone
together in Augusta's St James's Palace apartments whilst Georgiana
was occupied with her young children. Augusta foolishly deluded
herself that nothing was amiss and continued her social activities.
Inevitably Medora became pregnant again. Augusta was aghast at
this new development but she showed her *tendresse* for Henry Trevannion in a letter to the young man in 1831 : 'My dearest . . . You
know how I have loved and regarded you as my own Child . . . I
can never cease to do so. . . . Show me only how I can comfort and
support you – confide in me dearest . . . as I have opened my heart
and feelings to you, you will comfort me! . . . and as you are dear!
MOST dear! *Much* MUCH is in your power! Heaven bless comfort and guide you!'

Henry Trevannion must have turned on his mother-in-law, for,
about the same time, she wrote again, 'You say *you do not respect
me*. . . . It is a hateful world where more important interests than
mere worldly ones are at stake but . . . it becomes a serious consideration.' There she was for a moment the practised Court lady,
aware of what could and could not be tolerated in society. Augusta
continued, 'You are tried, SEVERELY tried I feel. . . . Do not
accuse yourself, dearest . . . oh! how I *have* loved you! How I will
always love you! and God bless you dearest.'

To the poor Medora, pregnant for the second time and still under
seventeen, she wrote sternly, 'Upon painful subjects one is apt to

express oneself strongly. . . . *On my knees I implore you*! to use every *effort of your* soul to cope with these temptations which assault you! . . . Think of others upon which *shame* and *disgrace* must fall . . . of the broken heart of your father.'

Augusta was the type of woman not truly maternal towards her own children. She bore seven, but only her lovers Byron and Trevannion aroused her protective instinct and they received more maternal affection than did her clamorous family.

Her religious belief was perfunctory, based rather on superstition than on faith. Her letter to Medora desperately sought comfort in one of life's rituals. 'I confidently hoped . . . you to be confirmed this Easter! . . . I hoped to prepare you sufficiently myself. . . . Such a ceremony . . . could be postponed till you felt your mind and heart disposed for it.'

Trevannion and Medora later fled to France and Augusta's burdens now included Georgiana and three grandchildren in addition to her own remaining four, for the retarded child had mercifully died. Augusta never saw Medora again, but her departure was not the end of that particular drama.

When Augusta was forty-six she visited Newstead Abbey again and wrote to the Rev. Francis Hodgson afterwards, 'I did so enjoy being in the dear beloved Abbey the air – the Water – & all the Elements wore a different aspect far superior to what they are elsewhere!' And to a woman friend she wrote, 'I was still there in *imagination* and *memory*.' Curious to learn more of the Abbey's legendary hauntings, she reported she had heard that 'a sort of *Black Mass* regularly appeared – flung itself across the foot of the bed and vanished! ! ! !'

In 1832 the Countess Teresa Guiccioli, Byron's last mistress, paid Augusta a visit. Some years earlier Augusta had received Teresa's handsome brother, Pietro, who had moved her by his evident reverence for her brother's memory. Byron had written that his mistress's decision to call on Teresa had put her 'in a flutter' but Augusta was quite composed and received the Italian in Flag Court. Teresa described Augusta afterwards as 'the most good-natured amiable person in the world', but Augusta left no record of the impression Teresa made upon her. Augusta was uninterested in foreigners and never travelled out of England.

In a society as restricted as England's, it was inevitable that she should constantly come across Ada, Byron's daughter, now an adult. But she was ever saddened by Lady Byron's implacable objection to their meeting formally, and was careful never to speak to the girl who had been fondly named after her.

Augusta's life was still largely passed among London's fashionable society, although limited by her lack of means to its fringes. Her quarters were still in Flag Court, St James's Palace, where, with her daughter Emily, a dog and several birds, she lived comfortably, although always in debt, on a pension from the Royal Family.[10] She frequently attended social events during the season and wrote to her faithful correspondent Francis Hodgson of one such occasion :

On Saturday I was persuaded to accompany a friend to dine ten miles out of town . . . it was to a Lion and Lioness Hunter's Mansion – Shirley Park; great friends of Miss Jane Porter (the authoress); and *our* object was to see *her.* Imagine an immense long room *full* when we arrived; the American Minister and his wife, and somebody else and *his* wife, *attaché* of this embassy; Mr Wilkinson, a renowned traveller in Egypt and thereabouts, and a particular friend of Lord King; Mr & Mrs Haynes Bayley : a Pole, who has written several works in English, and is celebrated in his way. This was the cream of the party; and *I* was to be gazed at as the Sister of Lord Byron ! I wished so *you* could have heard all the tributes of every sort to *his* memory, at which it was impossible not to be gratified. Mr Wilkinson is a very agreeable and pleasing young man. Asked me if I had lately seen Lady King [Byron's daughter, Ada, later Countess of Lovelace]. I said, 'No, I am *very* sorry to say, not for a long time,' except at the Exhibition, where I went twice to look at her picture; and then we went on upon the picture, and I enquired after the health of the original, and if he had seen the baby; and he praised Lord K very much; and I said it had pleased me very much to hear of her marriage with one so highly spoken of by everybody. We never approached the subject of her mother. This is the second running against of such intimates that I have lately had. I met the other evening, at a very tiny party . . . Mrs Somerville, the scientific Mrs S., the intimate friend of Ada, to whom Mde de M. presented me and said, 'You know Mrs L, that your niece has called her son Byron?' 'Yes,' said Mrs S., 'Byron King' and I exclaimed, 'I am very glad to hear that' and asked

[10] Queen Charlotte died in 1818.

after her health and the child and again we steered clear of Milady B.

Augusta made numerous efforts to secure her children and grand-children's financial future but was incapable of orderly thought or prudent action. Sir John Hobhouse in 1846 relinquished his execu-torship of Byron's will in despair at the innumerable Deeds she had set up, for that relating to Medora was only one of many more than the Estate was able to discharge.

In 1848 Augusta was conscience-stricken about Medora and wrote to Annabella for news : 'God knows whether my poor child is alive or not,' to which Annabella distantly replied, 'Mrs Leigh must be well aware that she would have to be legally informed of her daughter's death.' Leaving a son and a daughter, Medora died in France when she was thirty-four years old.

Some years after Medora's death, Lady Byron became obsessed with a great grievance about Augusta over which she had brooded ceaselessly. Though confessions of incest had once been painfully extorted from Augusta in the presence of Mrs Villiers, another ordeal by confession was thought necessary to be inflicted upon the ageing Augusta : that she had fomented Byron's hatred of his wife after the separation. Annabella had made a great friend and con-fidante of a powerful young preacher, the Rev. Robertson of Brighton, a noted orator who was particularly successful with women, and he encouraged Annabella to seek one final meeting with Augusta.

The opportunity arose with an appeal from Emily Leigh, Augusta's youngest and most stable daughter, to her godmother Lady Byron, appealing for money on her mother's behalf. Annabella seized the chance to obtain the much-desired interview. 'You have more than once asked me to see you,' she wrote to Augusta; 'I will comply with . . . that wish. . . . We may not longer have it in our power, Augusta, to meet again in this life.' But Annabella made it clear that Augusta need have no hopes of further financial succour : '*No other expectations* must be entertained by you for a moment. . . . On any other terms . . . I cannot see you again,' concluding with her occasional touch of the tragedy queen, 'unless summoned to your death-bed.'

Augusta pondered for several days, keeping Annabella in a state of suspense, but finally agreed to the summons, although protesting for the second time in her life at being interrogated before a third party, for the Rev. Robertson was to attend Lady Byron.

The meeting was to take place at an hotel in Reigate and Augusta was instructed to travel by train. This was an affront to a woman of Augusta's social standing and an added nervous and physical strain, since she had only journeyed once before by this means and was now aged sixty-eight. She travelled alone, a widow now, for Col. Leigh had died in 1850.

Annabella had prepared a list of questions to be put to the nervous old lady : '*You* kept up hatred; *you* put things in a false light; *you* suppressed what was kindest, most calculated to soften.' Augusta was bewildered by the accusations, defenceless before so many years' accumulated poisonous jealousy on the face of her rich sister-in-law, supported as she was by a sympathetic clergyman. Augusta's very innocence failed to satisfy her inquisitor. The interview was inconclusive, Annabella's hatred broke loose and she had to leave the room, worsted for the last time by the elusive Augusta. Augusta remained calm and Lady Byron's liveried servant escorted her back to the railway station, there to catch the train back to London and the slippery cobbled courtyards of St James's Palace.

On her return, the bewildered Augusta wrote punctiliously to her sister-in-law, enraging the recipient afresh, for Annabella realized that once again she had failed in her bid for 'the moral power which might have been instrumental to another's salvation.' Augusta wrote to Annabella of her astonishment and regret at Annabella's long-nourished distrust, 'ever since those words escaped you, showing that you imagined I had "encouraged a bitterness of mind" in Lord Byron towards you,' and assuring Annabella with sincerity, 'I invariably did the contrary.' But the letter remained unread and the Rev. Robertson wrote to Augusta, 'Lady Byron considers the correspondence to have been entirely closed. . . . She will never consent to another meeting.'

Augusta was already fatally ill and although near death she had tried to make peace with the woman to whom she owed so much practical help.

When the news came to Annabella that Augusta was dying she tried too late to make amends. The only way was, of course, with money. Poor Emily, aged thirty-three and unmarried, had to do the begging for her mother now. 'The poor girl,' wrote Mrs Villiers, 'her mother has been so helped . . . the Duke of Sutherland, the Duchess of Norfolk etc . . . every friend they had has helped her mother the money-lenders[11] must have been the robbers, or how could it all go!'

Emily wrote sadly to her godmother, who was now concernedly calling and offering help, 'My poor mother . . . grieved so very much over her interview with you.' Annabella wrote finally asking Emily to whisper two consoling words to her dying sister-in-law, 'dearest Augusta,' and they comforted her last moments.

Augusta died on 12 October 1851, Emily by her side. She left a legacy of mountainous debts, pressing creditors and a penniless family — but also, in Byron's love for her, an enduring niche in the gallery of women beloved by a great poet.

[11] Twenty-six in number.

Caroline

'But quiet to quick bosoms is a hell.'

Childe Harold's Pilgrimage (Canto III, Stanza 42)

Lady Caroline Ponsonby was born in 1785, the third child and only daughter of the Earl and Countess of Bessborough. Their country home was at Roehampton but from an early age Caroline spent a great deal of time at Devonshire House in London with her mother's sister Georgiana, Duchess of Devonshire.

It was a large and casual *ménage à trois*, for Lady Elizabeth Foster directed the household and was the Duke's mistress in addition to being the Duchess's devoted friend. Her two children Caroline and Clifford were part of the family circle together with the Duchess's children, of whom the Marquess of Hartington, known as Hart, was the eldest and heir to the dukedom.[1]

Adored by her grandmother, mother, brothers and cousins, Caroline grew up in an atmosphere totally free from restraint, backed by an exceptional artistic and literary erudition. The life-style was French, the impetus Celtic, for the Ponsonbys had been prominent in Irish history for several generations. Caroline's mother was a remarkably gifted woman : a brilliant linguist and a devotee of European culture. Roehampton was filled with art treasures. The two sisters easily spoke, read and wrote French, Italian, Latin, and Greek.[2] Caroline was well-taught : at four years old she could, her grandmother said, 'do the greatest part of the map of England very perfectly.' A year later when she was five her mother remarked, 'It is quite surprising to hear how well and fluently she reads and speaks both French and Italian.'

She was small and slightly built. In 1790 when she was six her

[1] He was a contemporary of Byron at Harrow.
[2] Georgiana, Duchess of Devonshire, was literary and in 1779 published anonymously an epistolary novel, *The Sylph*, which ran to three editions.

aunt Georgiana wrote, 'Caroline is remarkably well & is just 3 feet 3 inches high . . . miserably shy.' Of her childhood Caroline wrote, 'I was much flattered and much spoiled. Everyone seemed to love me.' Her grandmother Spencer, at Holywell House, St Albans, was particularly fond of her. 'I hope you have begun cutting Caroline's hair,' she wrote to her daughter at that time; 'I long to know how she is. . . . I had rather have her when I am alone than when the other children are with me.'

In 1790 Lady Bessborough left her older sons at Harrow and, taking Caroline and William, three years her junior, travelled to the continent where they spent nearly three years. It was a formative period for the impressionable child who responded ardently to all she saw in Florence. Her mother wrote exasperatedly to her sons, 'Your sister complains bitterly of being made to lie down & go to bed in broad sunshine. . . . she is grown quite a little Italian.' She early displayed an excitable restlessness. Lady Bessborough sent sketches home of their life in Italy where Caroline was able to run tomboyishly free : 'I have drawn you the picture of her little fox which she is very fond of & hopes someday to show you.' Caroline liked wild creatures and was by nature genuinely pantheistic, writing of herself later, 'I yet delighted to follow the plough, to watch the sheep upon the hills . . . an idle, wandering unruly boy.' During the Italian sojourn there were formal occasions when they dined with the King and Queen of Naples; once, persuaded to sing for them, Caroline was overcome by the strain of performing and collapsed in tears.

Caroline's intellectual nourishment was European art and literature and, possessed of a vivid imagination, she embroidered tales of her childhood to an astonished audience. Lady Morgan recalled, 'She gave curious anecdotes of high life – children neglected by their mothers – children served on silver in the morning, carrying down their plate to the kitchen – no one to attend to them – servants all at variance – ignorance of children on all subjects – thought all people were Dukes or beggars – did not know bread or butter was made – wondered if horses fed on beef – so neglected she could not write at ten years old.' All nonsense of her own invention.

Her pen was as facile as her tongue. When she was at Devonshire House she and her cousins would run and play in Green Park; indoors she wrote and sketched, imitating brilliantly not only Lady

Jersey's handwriting but her affected manner of speech, acting on paper, 'oo know *dearest love* that I '*ave* so *little* time for '*ose* things '*at* it is impossible for me to '*ite*.' She imitated Lady Jersey's signature to the letter, her cousin Hary-o adding laconically, 'Cari is journalist.'

Her mother and her governess Miss Trimmer made her study. Hary-o wrote in her diary of 'my *hopeful* cousin yawning over a column of spelling. . . . My aunt . . . read us . . . Voltaire's *enfant prodigue*,' and it would have been read to the twelve-year-old girls in French. In 1802, Caroline was taken by Lady Bessborough to Paris, where the latter delighted in the company of the cultured Gallic salons and offended the British colony by her marked preference for French conversation.

When Caroline was fourteen, she and Hary-o and the other Caroline, St Jules, Lady Elizabeth Foster's daughter by the Duke of Devonshire, were confirmed together in Westminster Abbey. The following year her half-sister Harriet Stewart was born to her mother, for it was an era when extra-marital liaisons were common and, provided certain social rules were observed, perfectly acceptable.

Miss Trimmer, whatever her other merits, neglected punctuation and Caroline never learned to spell very well. Her letters ran breathlessly on from subject to subject, devoid of commas or paragraphs. She and Hary-o were inseparable and easily bored. 'Caroline and I have composed a language with our *features*,' wrote Hary-o of their childish addiction to pulling faces; '*Poor little sings*, we were so moped in the coach.'

Staying at her grandmother's in St Albans, Hary-o wrote of balls and dances, the more formal events in the lives of high-born young ladies and Caroline wielded her agile pen in imitation of her cousin : 'Hary-o is *so so so* naughty not to write '*oo* my love. Have I not imitated her well?' asked Caroline innocently. She was later to imitate Byron's hand and forge his signature to his publisher with marked success.

When Caroline was seventeen she paid her first visit to the house which was later to become her cherished home : Brocket Hall in Hertfordshire. Not a stately mansion in the grandiose manner, but a square, solid, red-brick hall set in natural woodland through which ran the river Lea, it was described by a contemporary artist as 'a very handsome villa'. Hary-o wrote of the noisy Lamb family whose country home it was that 'if she had staid a day longer, she would have certainly returned *sourde ou muette.*' The Devonshire House circle spoke softly in affected coos interlarded with French and Italian phrases.

'William Lamb and Caro Ponsonby', reported Hary-o, 'seem . . . mutually captivated. When the rest were at games etc., William was in a corner, reading and explaining poetry to Car., and in the morning, reading tales of wonder together on the *tither tother.*' Caroline's conquest of Lord Melbourne's second son was a source of merriment to the two girls. 'She *roared* all the way from Brocket to Roehampton,' wrote Hary-o. 'He did not captivate anybody else.' It was William's interest in poetry and literature which first drew her to him, and the relationship later developed into a serious attachment. Later the same year Hary-o wrote, 'The Melbournes . . . have been quite living with us.'

Miss Trimmer did not approve of the close friendship so assiduously cultivated between the three families by Lady Melbourne. 'Miss Trimmer', wrote Hary-o, 'hates Lady Melbourne.' There are no persons more caste conscious than those who serve. 'Here come the Lambs,' maliciously remarked one of the family in French as they approached, 'dripping gold.' The Lambs' fortune had come from moneylending and the riches were relatively new.

The three families were at Ramsgate in October, from where Hary-o wrote, 'Caro Ponsonby behaves very well . . . we go on bathing though it requires some courage as the sea feels like ice.' From the sea to society : the following year Caroline swam effortlessly into the best fashionable society, to which she was born. A Miss Berry wrote of a ball she attended : 'Some of the young ladies just come forth, proved themselves excellent dancers,' a diversion Caroline adored for she was gay, high-spirited and nimble footed. When Caroline was nearly twenty Lady Elizabeth Foster wrote, '*felice si quella ragazza,*' for Caroline had become engaged to William Lamb, now Lord Melbourne's heir. Lady Melbourne was gratified when, at the same time, William's sister Emily became engaged to the wealthy Lord Cowper, who owned the neighbouring estate of Panshanger in Hertfordshire.

Caroline's cousin Hart, whose temperament was as volatile as her own, was very distressed by her engagement. He was a sensitive fifteen-year-old who stammered, and he was inconsolably miserable. 'The Ponsonbys are always making sensations,' wrote a caustic observer of the Irish branch of the family, but the future Duke of Devonshire was completely sincere in his devotion to Caroline and never subsequently married. 'He looked upon her as his wife,' wrote his sister Hary-o, '[and] had always been in hopes his papa would let him marry her when he was eighteen.' The boy was so ill that the family physician had to be summoned.

In 1805 Lady Elizabeth Foster wrote, 'Caroline Ponsonby is to be married tomorrow; she looks prettier than I ever saw her. Sometimes she is very nervous. . . . Wm Lamb seems quite devoted to her. They supped here last night and they received her presents.' These were, as Lady Elizabeth listed, 'a beautiful acqua marina clasp . . . a little pearl cross with a small diamond in the middle . . . a hair bracelet with amethyst clasp. . . . Lord Melbourne gave her a beautiful set of amethysts, and Lady M a diamond wreath . . . Harriet gives a beautiful burnt topaz cross.'

The marriage was welcomed by Lady Melbourne since Caroline's family, though not so wealthy, was ancient and aristocratic, while the Lambs' openly displayed riches and recent Irish peerage rendered them not always welcome in certain circles.

William and Caroline appeared devoted to one another. Caroline, in spite of the promiscuous society in which she moved, was completely innocent, idealistic and exalted by the high romance of her adoring new husband. He was large and comforting, with a rock-like stolidity and ponderousness of manner against which she could attractively display herself. William's vanity was gratified by his capture of an equally adoring pupil-wife, an enchantingly fey sprite who regarded him as a hero rather than a husband. Yet he had a coarse streak, and his previous sexual experience shocked her. His rationality insidiously undermined Caroline's instinctive religious convictions.

That summer Augustus Foster wrote to his mother from Washington, 'I cannot imagine Lady Caroline married. I cannot be glad of it. How changed she must be – the delicate little Fairy Queen become a wife. . . . I had just finished a letter to her as Lady Caroline Ponsonby yesterday in answer to her pretty one of March . . . it is not a love letter . . . I don't answer . . . I never can to her now she is under the laws of a man.' The perceptive Augustus continued, 'It is the first death of a woman – they must die twice . . . they change character so completely.'

In September, however, Lady Elizabeth reported to her son, 'She is the same wild, delicate, odd delightful person . . . witness her dating to Lady Maria Lane her first letter of congratulation on her marriage with her brother "Brocket Hall, heaven knows what day." ' It was an impulsively informal gesture to the girl about to become her sister-in-law and part of the family, from a Caroline to whom all days were happy and lively. Maria was won over by her warmhearted informality. 'Caro and W. Lamb . . . flirt all day,' recorded Lady Elizabeth.

'Caroline *Lamb* arrived in Town last night . . . as gentle and *posée* as if she had been a matron in the country for twenty years instead of days,' wrote Lady Elizabeth Foster later. But Caroline soon tired of the role and her docility was short lived. 'Caroline was . . . in the beau milieu of a violent quarrell. . . . They had disagreed in the morning . . . she came and dined with us,' recounted Lady Elizabeth, 'covered herself with all my aunt's trinkets; rouged herself up to the eyes, sent home her wedding ring and went with us to the play.'

In the autumn of the year of the marriage Caroline was already pregnant and Lady Elizabeth wrote, 'I went over to Brocket Hall on Saturday. . . . Caroline Lamb looked very pale and ill . . . but pretty. . . . Her situation . . . I should not have guessed excepting from her . . . walking, which she does with caution as if one quick step would be fatal.' But she was not careful enough, suffered a miscarriage at a neighbouring country-house and took some time to recover.

That Christmas William Lamb was to take part in some theatricals at the Priory, Stanmore, where his brother George's play *Who's the Dupe?* was to be performed, but Lady Elizabeth wrote, 'Caroline Lamb is . . . not yet able to leave her couch . . . must not be moved for six weeks, therefore she is to remain there till after the play at Christmas.'

Caroline was soon pregnant again. 'Lady Maria . . . adores her,' related Lady Elizabeth, 'says it is impossible she should have a child, that it will be a little thing with wings that will fly away as soon as it is born and nobody will be able to catch it.' Caroline's love of fantasy and ideals of beauty led her to become fond of this image, and she covered pages with quick sketches of little winged cherubs, *putti* dancing and flying around a pastoral setting. In spite of her ethereal appearance, Caroline had recovered better from the miscarriage than seemed likely, and her son was born the following year. She consulted her grandmother as to a suitable name. 'I have said, as eldest son, whatever will gratify Lord Melbourne,' wrote Lady Spencer; 'The Prince's being godfather will remove all difficulty . . . & Augustus is, I think, a pretty name.'

The child's baptism was celebrated together with that of her sister-in-law Lady Emily Cowper's first-born, whom the Prince also sponsored. Both events were sumptuously celebrated. 'The Prince', wrote Caroline's mother, 'came at five, and did not go till two. . . . Time hung heavy,' and the guests were entertained by playing verse-writing games in which the compositions were read out to the assembled company.

Caroline was a devoted mother. In January 1810 her grandmother wrote to Lady Bessborough, 'I long to know that dear little Augustus goes on to your heart's content. Caroline writes word that she does nothing but nurse him. I fear . . . by the tone of her letter that she does not feel easy about him,' and a few days later, 'I . . . rather wonder dear Caroline had spirits to go to the Masquerade,' for Caroline, although anxious, did not relinquish the highly social life to which she was accustomed. She had lived all her life in the public glare. One symptom of Augustus's illness was difficulty in breathing, but it was not the childish ailment croup. Lady Spencer wrote to her daughter that she had seen more of Augustus; a doctor had been summoned to make a thorough examination of the boy and she related his opinion : 'He has no defect that he can perceive in mind or body. . . . These screams are nothing but temper.' For her granddaughter she had nothing but praise : 'Nothing can be quieter or more amiable than Caroline.' Caroline, with only the nurse and a maid for company, sat by the child's bedside in the darkened nursery and wrote a long letter to her cousin Hart. She expressed her relief at Augustus's apparent recovery in verse, beginning, 'Friend of my heart, accept this letter, the child thank God is rather better.' A little later she wrote to her eldest brother, 'I am in much better health but have hardly been out at all in the gay world. . . . Since my two young men are gone I have no desire. . . . I am not to write too much. . . . My boy is better but was really very ill.' Caroline was suffering from severe overstrain and wrote to her mother, 'I have a little pain in my chest, they think from . . . carrying the dear heavy boy.'

Caroline found herself alone at Brocket, for it was thought best that Augustus should be cared for elsewhere. Her husband occupied, herself tired and unwell from nursing Augustus, Caroline's time hung heavy on her hands. Away from London there was no stimulating company. 'I live too idle a life for happiness,' she wrote; 'when one feels quite useless the pleasure of idleness is lost.'

William Lamb was a complex character. On the surface steady to the point of impassivity, underneath he was unsure of himself. He suffered the agonizing insecurity of not knowing who his father really was nor to what social strata he properly belonged. On the death of his brother Peniston, Lord Melbourne had pointedly refused to allow William, now heir to the title, the generous allowance his brother had received. It was only with difficulty and through a third party that Lady Melbourne was able to persuade her husband to give him an allowance at all.

Caroline, zestful by nature, tried to please her husband. They had fallen into a pupil-master relationship in which William played the role, soothing to an uncertain man's ego, of the plain man educating, guiding and controlling the frivolously aristocratic young wife. Caroline was child-like and played her part with consummate ease. But the difference between them was fundamentally ethnic and irreconcilable : William lived by reason, Caroline by instinct.

Not yet aware of this basic incompatibility, she applied herself and wrote to her grandmother for a volume of history to pursue a course of study proposed by William. She learned Greek, translating, peppering her letters with Greek phrases and verses, and spending a painstaking week writing a whole letter in the language. Always a voracious reader, she wrote to her mother in the spring of 1808, 'I have really been so occupied with the sorrows of Mary Queen of Scots . . . one always feels so very interested in her. . . . I have also read the Modern Philosophers . . . the Siege de la Rochelle.' She discussed her reading at length with Lady Bessborough, whose passion for learning was such that she wished to start a school of her own, dissuaded only by Lady Spencer. In the same letter Caroline wrote, 'I am convinced nothing is worse . . . than finding fault, unless it is for things one can help,' an indication of the growing rift between herself and her critical husband.

In 1809 Lady Elizabeth Foster married the Duke of Devonshire, now a widower. Acceptable as his mistress, she was an affront to the family as his wife. The same year her daughter Caroline St Jules was married to George Lamb. The two Caros were under their mother-in-law's roof at Melbourne House in Whitehall – Caro William and Caro George as they became known. Caroline noted that her husband's waning interest contrasted unfavourably with his brother's ardour towards the other Caro, and she resorted to absurd antics designed to recapture William's straying attention.

Caroline had become pregnant for the third time the previous year, but in January her mother wrote sadly to her son-in-law, 'I have been up all night from Caroline been taken ill at ten and brought to bed at one of a nice little girl who however, only lived the night through & died on my lap this morning. Caro really bears it with the greatest resignation.' Her three successive pregnancies, all with tragic results, seriously affected Caroline's health and nerves which were never very strong. On recovering, however, she hurled herself with fresh energy into various activities again.

One summer was spent on the Isle of Wight, with which Caroline was delighted. She was still, under William's guidance, pursuing her studies. 'I should take it as a great favour if you would just write me the principal dates & events, wars, risings, &c from Romulus till the time of Constantine the Great,' she asked her mother; 'It makes me remember the history which Wm is now reading to me.' Her thought for others and her sense of the ridiculous were evident in the description of a noisy, over-elaborate dinner-party : 'I could not help regretting the expence those poor people put themselves to. . . . I was then set down to Loo . . . they all turned to me & asked if I had ever played at loo before. "Yes," I replied, "and what sort of loo was that?" they said eagerly, "a very different one . . . a much quieter one." ' Thus Caroline, the grand lady, entertained the Isle of Wight provincials.

Her ability to entertain William seemed the only way to gain his approval. 'His indolence rendered him insensible to everything,' Caroline wrote. 'When I ride, play and amuse him he loves me.' But he jeered lazily at her serious love of beauty. The nervous energy she expended in acting the entertaining little doll took its toll of the slight girl, exhausted by pregnancies and by the mental distress caused by the ill-health of her only son.

Caroline tried to rouse William from his apathy by the age-old method of flirting outrageously with another man, and Sir Godfrey Webster responded, indiscreetly showering her with sentimental presents, a lap-dog and jewellery. Caroline received a severe letter from her mother-in-law : 'Your behaviour last night was so disgraceful in its appearance and so disgusting from its motives that it is quite impossible it should ever be effaced from my mind,' reprimanded Lady Melbourne. Caroline had not been serious in her flirtation, but Sir Godfrey, an experienced rake, was. William, however, appeared unconcerned, Caroline did not achieve her object, and the lap-dog snapped at Augustus, convincing her that it was a judgement upon her faithlessness.

William wrote in his commonplace book, 'Before I was married, whenever I saw the children and the dogs allowed . . . to be troublesome . . . I used to lay it all to the fault of the master. . . . Since I have married I find that this was a very rash and premature judgement.' William persisted in treating Caroline as a wayward four-year-old or a tiresome puppy, both of which are more easily governed than an intelligent and sensitive woman with a developing mind and an ardently artistic temperament. Indeed it was in his interest to suppress her urge to creativity. While he did not understand it, he recognized the unquenchably vital spark of talent she possessed and, sensing it as a threat to his masculine security, unconsciously endeavoured to crush it by encouraging her to channel it in academic directions. His attitude also reflected caste jealousy, for William's mother, despite all her power, was disliked and unaccepted in circles where Caroline and her mother were welcomed.

Neither were aware of the destructive element in William's attitude. Caroline, knowing only that she wished to please him and could not, was possessed of a doleful and bewildered certainty that she was in the wrong. 'My Dearest William,' she wrote to him, 'I only want my Augustus & Man to be perfectly happy.' Nurtured on praise and encouragement in an atmosphere where she could bloom artistically, she feared his smothering severity, drew him in her sketch-book labelled 'That black William', and added to her letter, 'Dearest Mannie when you come – pray arrive *rayonnant* with good humour.' She had been wandering through the wild parts at Brocket which she loved : 'Rover ran away from me . . . found him Parading about the top of the Park with some stray poultry. . . . I have just been stung. . . . God bless you my Dearest sweetest man. I will study to be as pleasant a friend to you. . . . I think lately . . . we have been very troublesome to each other which I take wholesale to my own account & mean to correct. . . . condemn me not . . . call me your friend-girl Darling . . . & all such pretty names as shew great love.' Conscious that she often behaved with impetuous and disturbing vivacity which did not measure up to his exacting standards, she was contrite. 'I will be silent of a morning,' she promised, 'docile, fearless as a Heroine in the last Vol. of her troubles.' She realized he wished her to *'raisonnez mieux et répliquez moins'* but it was simply not in her nature to be as rational as William. 'When man . . . struggles to overcome his passions, and to treat the woman whom he loves as if she were a rational being, she is sure to disappoint his expectation,' wrote a sadly wise Caroline. The wild Celtic imagination, the burning ambition, was to him a tedious, embarrassing bore. Eager but apologetic, Caroline knew it.

William was baffled and unable to understand the intensity of her feelings. Politically a moderate orator whose speeches never caught fire, he was normally somewhat inarticulate and only spoke when necessary. He never betrayed emotion and abhorred any verbal extravagance, pursuing a policy of determined and irritating understatement which could alienate those whose strong feelings he invariably under-rated.

Caroline found solace in a companionable correspondence with her cousin Hart, now living too far away for closer contact. Always fond of him, she now addressed him a letter of high-spirited nonsense. 'My most sanitive elixir of Julep, my most precious cordial confection, my most dilutable sal polychrist & marsh mallow paste, truly comfortable spirit of hartshorn, tincture of rhubarb & pergative senna tea! It is impossible', she told him, 'my most exquisite medicine chest, for me to describe the delightful effect of the potion you sent me this morning. . . . Prescribe such powders to all . . . who die for love of your Lordship's tricoloured eyes, & remember, cousin of my heart & heart of my cousin, that your faithful gallipot was only waiting for a line to dose you with letters every day. . . . God preserve you my dearest Tartar emetic your own Syrop of elderob.'

Later in 1810 he was her 'most delectable . . . most sneezable, yr
very giddy cousin, William Rufus-Rex.' She signed herself to him
Molly Peacock and the following month Molly Bradby. 'Here I am
safe but not over well; however,' she told him, admitting to her
dawning notoriety, 'I neither had my neck broke or got into the
newspapers.'

Her grandmother in St Albans was concerned at her riotous
behaviour, already a source of gossip. 'How is dear Caroline?' she
asked Lady Bessborough; 'A letter I had from her . . . rather vexed
me, by telling me she had jumped over a couch at some assembly.'
Caroline admitted to Hart of another occasion, 'I behaved a little
wild, riding over the Downs . . . with all the Officers at my heels.'
Her grandmother wrote again to her daughter, 'I hope she recollects
the positive promise I had from her, of her never riding without her
husband.' But William did not care for wild, exhilarating gallops,
preferring a sedate walking pace. He was in the habit of tramping,
in sunshine or in snow, home to Brocket Park from St Albans. It was
an outward sign of his essentially pedestrian nature, uncommitted,
his chosen path the middle of the road.

Caroline's attitude to the war in Spain was serious and com-
passionate. In a letter to William she showed she had read widely on
the subject and had drawn perceptive and accurate conclusions
about Spain and the psychology of its people, quoting Sir John
Moore : ' "the safety of Spain depends on the *union* of its inhabit-
ants." ' Sharply observant of the local scene, she drew an amusing
picture of a visiting evangelist. 'I went yesterday to church & heard
the same man preach you heard last Sunday – he takes rapid
advances in the Methodistical style, the last time . . . we were only
my Brethren this time we were oh my dear Brethren & Christian
warriors, and hardy veterans, with a great deal about love & souls
in torment, he so entirely lost himself at the conclusion in the
military simily . . . that he adrest three old women in a voice of
thunder which stir'd them up amazingly calling them to fight &
strive & obtain the Kingdom of Heaven by blood & loudly addressing them by the appellation of ye veteran Christian Warriors.'

Unpatronizingly she visited her servants and near neighbours, and
her vivid pen brought the scene to life. 'After dinner we went to see
the kitchen garden . . . the old gardener . . . was seventy-eight years
old he shewed . . . his walls, flushing with peaches, nectarines,

plumbs and appricots with patriarchal pride.' After a duty call in the
village she wrote, 'Before church . . . I went to call on Dr & Mrs
Hooly who live in a pretty looking cottage . . . the Doctor passing
ugly in the meek scientific way . . . nothing frank & agreeable . . . I
call it a sly polished manner, the babes bellowed incessantly.' Without
a comma or a dash her pen ran on to William, 'I have been playing
all day with that pretty little Augustus of yours, he is the dearest
child I ever saw. . . . God bless you love Your own faithful Wiffins.'

In 1812 when Augustus was six years old, Caroline drew him in
her sketch-book, a charming little boy dressed in long trousers and
a frilled shirt. In spite of what seem to have been asthmatic attacks
and screaming fits, he did not then appear abnormal. It was the
year Byron's 'Childe Harold's Pilgrimage' was published.

Caroline's devotion to literature was passionate and she identified
closely with the people in the books she read. Words moved her and
her appreciation did not exclude a critical sense. She was later to
write of the superficiality of the fashionable world's approach to the
arts, still apt 150 years after it was written, 'The reading of reviews
is to the public, what eating of many different dishes is to a child.
The organs of digestion are weakened in the one, and the mind
over-informed. . . . Sciences are skimmed over, conclusions are discovered . . . and learning runs through a brainless head, as water
through a pipe or channel, leaving it as empty as it found it. . . . It
tends to extinguish natural taste . . . instead of feeling with
enthusiasm the beauties of a play or a poem, pretend to judge by
rule and discover the defects.'

Caroline had read Mary Wollstonecraft's *Vindication of the
Rights of Women* which made an indelible impression upon her, and
an ungovernable urge for freedom grew within her. It was this urge
which found expression in her addiction to boy's clothes, which had
always suited her slim, childish figure. Only thus garbed, freed from
the niceties and refinements of inhibiting muslin, her hair cropped
into a fair aureole of curls, could she share the liberty enjoyed by
men. This licence extended to her behaviour and speech. She was
able cunningly to deceive many, and was especially fond of dressing
up as a page : she looked like a fourteen-year-old boy, costumed in
a scarlet, elaborately embroidered hussar jacket and trousers fastened
with silver buttons and carrying a little feathered cap. It may well
have been this garb that attracted Byron to her, for he had had a

number of love affairs with boys and Caroline dressed as a page was an entrancing sight, known to several of her friends as Cherubina.

'Childe Harold' created a sensation, yet Byron's instant fame was not the magnet which drew Caroline to him but the gale force of his poetry. She was not young when she met him but approaching thirty and several years older than he was. Already she was tired of life with William, which seemed to offer so little to a woman who felt the stirrings of creativity within her but was denied the prospect of further children. 'If he is as ugly as Aesop I must meet him,' she said and she meant it. Her interest was not in his reputed handsomeness nor his appeal to women but in his power with words and in his stance as a champion of liberty. When she met him the shock of his physical beauty was such that she turned away and wrote in her diary, 'That beautiful pale face will be my fate.' For the real Caroline was supremely feminine although her sexuality had lain dormant, unaroused by William's prosaic aproach or by the casual affairs she had indulged in out of boredom.

Early in May the new Duchess of Devonshire wrote to her son, 'I have sent you a very beautiful poem by Lord Byron, who continues to be made the greatest fuss with. . . . Your little friend Caro William . . . is doing all sorts of imprudent things for him and with him. . . . The ladies . . . spoil him, and the gentlemen are jealous of him. He is going back to Noxor, and then the husbands may sleep in peace.' But Byron did not leave the country yet.

From childhood Caroline had exhibited signs of manic-depression. She wrote of herself, 'I had been troubled at times by certain agitations of mind, during which my spirits were exceedingly depressed.' Now, the advent of Byron, and his intoxicating preoccupation with her following William's disheartening apathy, exhilarated her to a manic pitch. Caroline was already disillusioned with and critical of the superficiality of the society to which she belonged, and for a lady of her rank there was none other. She was later to write of such a life-style as a war on boredom : 'The light artillery of wit, sighs, smiles . . . the happy art of saying everything, with presence of mind, delicacy, tact; the lively conquest, which leaves behind it neither pain nor asperity, – so high the polish of weapons, so complete the skill of the combatants. All tediousness was avoided by the rapid change of topics which, like the scenery of a pantomime, must be shifted every instant.' To any sort of creative artist, such superficiality must be growingly intolerable and Byron gave her the impetus to action.

'But how,' asked Caroline, 'to appear tranquil when the still, small voice of conscience calls from within?' Byron's poetry, his company and his political ideals sounded to Caroline a clarion call of truth that she was eager to follow with all the ardour of the true romantic. But her suppressed and wandering feelings, so suddenly and shatteringly focussed on one individual, were too extreme. Sexually she was inexperienced; she was too thin, too intense and she did not please Byron. Moreover she was not prepared for the vagaries of a genius who also epitomized the polygamous male. Byron rarely confined himself to one woman for long.

'Love,' wrote Caroline, 'is what an angel may feel for suffering man . . . but my feelings were the overbearing violence of passion.' Her sexual awakening was the inevitable accompaniment to the spiritual union with Byron of which she was convinced. She who had been frigid, though carelessly amoral, became tragically carnal.

'Lord Byron is still upon a pedestal,' reported her cousin Hary-o, 'and Caroline William doing homage,' while Caroline later admitted, 'The tumult, the ardour, the romance, which bewildered my reason . . . clouded my understanding.' She was at his side all the time and everywhere, transported, soaring, to a stratosphere of intellectual and physical adoration she could neither control nor hide.

But by September Byron was longing to be rid of her and Caroline knew it. 'My aunt looks stout and well,' wrote Hary-o, 'but poor Caroline most terribly the contrary. She is worn to the bone, as pale as death and her eyes starting out of her head. She seems in a sad way; alternately in tearing spirits and in tears.' She was wound up to breaking point; crisis and catastrophe were inevitable. Though it was mostly over with Byron, Caroline clung on blindly, incapable of believing it, on the verge of lunacy at the shattering of her dream, prey to series of public exhibitions of her derangement which degraded her into an object of contempt.

William Lamb was persuaded by his family to take her to Ireland where she behaved with hysterical gaiety. Wherever she went she bombarded Byron with letters. Unable to resist writing the love letters which came naturally to him, he further inflamed her, giving her false hope. 'My dearest Caroline,' he wrote, 'through the *whole* of this most *nervous* affair . . . I never knew till *that moment* the madness of my dearest and most beloved friend. . . . I was and am yours freely and most entirely, to obey, to honour, to love – and fly with you when, where, and how yourself *might* and may determine.' It was too much to bear to be in receipt of such a misleading letter. Later Caroline wrote sadly of 'that dear, that angel, that misguided and misguiding Byron, whom I adore, although he left that dreadful legacy on me, my memory.'

William's apparent indifference taunted her : he 'cared nothing for my morals,' wrote Caroline; 'I might flirt and go about with whom I pleased. He was privy to my affair with Lord Byron and laughed at it.' Augustus Foster wrote to the Duchess of Devonshire, 'Poor Lady Caroline Lamb . . . it's really painful to see so delightful a person as she once was . . . so entirely unmanageable. I must say I think her husband is a great deal to blame.'

If only Caroline had contented herself with writing her novel, *Glenarvon*, and had refrained from publishing it, she might not have damned herself entirely. But she had worked herself up to a frenzy of idealistic ambition. Her delusion was not caused solely by a romantic fixation on a handsome poet; her novel was intended to be a serious indictment of a false society peopled by transparently identifiable luminaries, with Byron and herself the central figures. With it she would revenge herself on her uncaring husband, her tawdry mother-in-law and a hypocritical society which valued neither art, truth nor Caroline.

Written in a crusading spirit and at breakneck speed, it was published, mostly unrevised, a fortnight after Byron left England, by a Caroline still buoyant on the crest of a defiant wave. Therapeutic to write, it was impossible to read, written as it was in a mood of sustained daemonic frenzy. Augustus Foster wrote, 'I had not patience to get through it, it is so disordered. . . . The uncommon impudence that runs through it is to me astonishing. . . . I sadly fear a bad end for her.' But it was a certain best-seller, running to several editions, with French and German translations. The publishers were delighted and people read it avidly, identifying themselves, some with horror and others with glee. A *succès de scandale* of unedifying proportions, it ruined Caroline.

'There is nothing worse than being calumniated without the possibility of justification,' wrote Caroline, 'no situation so cruel as that of entire solitude when feverish hopes, fears and eager irritation torture the mind. From scenes . . . where events had crowded upon each other with such rapidity, the change to loneliness was insupportable.' Caroline was ostracized by an outraged society.

Caroline's only merit in Lady Melbourne's eyes was the accidental quality of her aristocratic birth, which could help to advance her husband William. Caroline's outrageous honesty was now imperilling his political career. The situation exacerbated a relationship notoriously delicate and in the Lambs' case geographically too close. Caroline's openly displayed passion for Byron and subsequent maniacal behaviour united the Lamb family in putting pressure upon William to separate legally from her. Caroline pleaded support from Lord Granville, her mother's former lover, now married to her cousin Hary-o. 'You should see my husband, who knows everything . . . and who says that he could not in honour give me up.' There had been a dreadfully unpleasant scene at Melbourne House, Caroline reminded him. 'Recollect . . . I was ordered out of the House in no gentle language : my mother was spoke to with the most barbarous roughness in my presence . . . I was *proved* mad. Mr Moore assured me I was so. . . . I appealed to a few, but my letters were not even answered. I went to Roehampton, Lady Jersey to the extreme annoyance of my father, turned her back upon me. . . . Lord Holland . . . coldly passed me by . . . I could not stand it. . . . Wm returned, a dreadful scene passed between Lord M and Mama. That night I sent the novel.'

Had Caroline been treated with greater sensitvity, the novel might never have appeared. The Lambs probably impressed upon Caroline her financial dependence upon them. Resenting this bitterly and gambling her talent alone against the forces of society, she lost her reputation, her position and, in time, her confidence.

The solitude at Brocket to which she was banished was not total. Augustus was there some of the time to remind her of her dead children who might have been bright and well. He was neither. The difficulty in breathing from which he suffered as a child had given way to periodic fits, probably the minor form of epilepsy known as *petit mal*. But the boy was cheerful and affectionate, learned to read and write and had many devoted friends. Among the various people who had charge of him, the most important was the faithful, intelligent and loving Moome.

'I met with the word "Moome"', she wrote to Augustus, 'in a book I was reading. "Moome is an appellation in the Gaelic . . . it means a person who feels the affection and performs the duties of a Mother to children not her own." I think *I* may claim it!'

Augustus was often in her care, staying at 'Rose Cottage'. 'You will have your favourite green room which is well-aired,' she wrote when he was expected once. In London and abroad Moome was often included in a theatre or opera party. She was as devoted to Caroline as to her son. 'I went with your Mama and Dr Walker to the Coburg Theatre last night,' Moome told Augustus; 'They did not stay a minute, but left me with an old Gentleman whom your Mamma had invited to be of the party. . . . I wish you had been with us, there was a dog . . . who performed admirably.' Moome's enjoyment of the theatre was matched by an intelligent interest in painting, politics and poetry, and she filled her letters to the boy who was always 'My Dearest Augustus' with news of polls and royal occasions and amusing anecdotes. She never failed to inquire tenderly about his health, for he rarely replied. 'I can imagine the beauty of Brocket Park just now,' she wrote to him; 'Have you got your little open carriage to drive about in?'

Augustus was fond of reading and Moome sent him books and puzzles. She sent him *The Hundred Wonders of the World* when he was seventeen, telling him, 'It will suit a rational young man like yourself who prefers reality to fiction.' He was especially fond of Cowper's poetry. Writing was always a difficulty and his father urged him on to academic efforts of which the boy was incapable. Caroline worried incessantly if she did not hear from him and Moome wrote to Augustus after a dinner party at Melbourne House: 'She begged me to tell you that she is greatly surprised you do not write oftener & Lord Bessborough says he can only suppose that you have *gout in your hand*, do not fail to write to both.'

Moome netted purses for Augustus and cooked especially for him. He was forgetful and once left his greatcoat in the coach at Barnet during cold winter weather; Moome sent someone after it, fearful that her boy would catch a chill and finally ran round herself to Melbourne House with the coat and a request that it be sent on to Brocket without delay.

The Earl of Bessborough was a very fond grandfather to the boy and a kindly and regular correspondent, writing to him about cricket, which Augustus loved, and sending him drawings and coins for his collection. 'Many thanks for your letter,' wrote Lord Bessborough to Augustus when he was sixteen; 'According to your desire I answer by Return of Post. . . . Give my love to your Mama & tell Susan[3] I have got her doll – I have also found your Coin of Gold – I suppose with this Rain Brocket must be in great beauty & you must almost see the leaves come out.'

'I have got you a relic of our favourite Cowper,' Moome wrote to Augustus; 'It is a bit of the hair of his favourite dog Bean. . . . Shall you like to have it?' In the midst of Moome's highly social life, Augustus was always in her thoughts. 'I had the Duke of Gloucester's box at Drury Lane last night,' she told him, 'I heard Braham sing "Scots wha hae" . . . your favourite song,' and on another occasion, 'I send my little Lamb two new eggs.' She recalled to him fondly a young person's ball he had attended : 'Your dress was a light blue velvet jacket with point lace collar falling over white silk waistcoat and trowsers – white silk stockings, black kid shoes & diamond buckles, it was a beautiful dress & became the wearer very well, you were much admired in the Ballroom, you led off the Ball and danced remarkably well.'

Although Augustus was sent for a time to a tutor, Caroline's devotion to him was constant and he was often with her while she read and sketched, when visiting her grandmother in St Albans. 'Caroline dined here today and brought Augustus,' wrote Lady Spencer; 'Caroline certainly better & happier . . . but Augustus short-breathed,' while Caroline wrote to her mother her opinion of the latest novel : 'I delight in de Stael's book . . . a vast fund of erudition . . . full of point, wit & ability.' Sometimes Augustus wrote for his mother to Lord Bessborough : 'My dearest Grandpapa, Mama . . . has been so busy drawing, she employs me to write this. . . . She has done with Dryden. . . . Tomorrow you will receive two drawings.' Augustus continued, asking for his grandfather's help on Caroline's behalf, 'Mama will be very much obliged if you will put the *sea* in for her & the *sky* . . . put a *mountain* & *convent* . . . & one of *holy places* with a little *saint* or the *virgin,* to which the girl is coming to confess. All this you will do so much better than Mama . . . she thinks she has rather overdone herself with drawing.'

---

[3] Lady Brandon's illegitimate daughter, probably by William Lamb.

In the summer of 1815 Caroline was in the Isle of Wight when news came that her brother Frederick had been severely wounded at Waterloo and she immediately wished to go to him. Her eldest brother wrote to their mother, 'I am glad . . . Caroline went, as I think she may have been a comfort to Frdk, altho' for some days I prevented her journey, I really was afraid to let her go till we heard better accounts of him.' From Brussels Caroline wrote to Lord Duncannon, 'How happy I feel at having come. Poor Fred . . . seems very weak. . . . I scarce can write, I feel so very nervous but happy. . . . He asked after you all . . . & particularly wished me to have brought Augustus.' Frederick's wounds had been severe : 'the lance pierced the lungs . . . he has been terribly trampled on & hurt,' and Brussels was a distressing place to be in at that time. 'The crowd of wounded in churches & around is very melancholy,' wrote Caroline but reported movingly, 'The English name stands so high from Ostend here that it makes one feel proud. The moment they see you every one pulls off their hats & caps, – & if they ask yr. country & you say "English" they answer "that is passport enough." '

For her wounded brother in 1815 Caroline begged for what has ever proved a solace and a diversion to the expatriate Englishman : 'We are in great want of English papers &c for Fred he wants them very much.' War and wounds did not put a stop to social life : 'The great amusement at Bruxelles, indeed the only one except visiting the sick is to make large parties & go to the field of Battle – & pick up a skull or a grape shot or an old shoe or a letter, & bring it home . . . There is a great affectation here of making lint & bandages . . . it is rather a love making moment, the half-wounded Officers reclining with pretty ladies visiting them. . . . I also observe a great coxcombability in the dress of the sick which prognosticates a speedy recovery. It is rather heart-breaking to be here, however, & one goes blubbering about – seeing such fine people without their legs & arms, some in agony, & some getting better. . . . Lady Mountmoress . . . stuck her parasol yesterday into a skull at Waterloo. . . . The Duchess of Richmond's fatal Ball has been much censured . . . so fine & so sad – all the young men who appeared there shot dead a few hours after.' Under the gay exterior she assumed for the tea-parties, she worried about her son. 'Caroline is very low,' wrote William, 'never hearing about Augustus.'

From Brussels Caroline went on to Paris. 'Nothing is *agissant* but

Caroline in a purple riding habit,' reported Hary-o, 'ready primed for an attack upon the Duke of Wellington . . . she will to a certain extent succeed, as no dose of flattery is too strong for him to swallow.'

'And this,' observed Hary-o indignantly disbelieving, 'is the broken-hearted Calantha,' the name Caroline had chosen lightly to disguise her self-portrait in *Glenarvon.* 'With respect to going out,' Caroline defended herself to Hary-o's husband, 'hear me. . . . William having once decidedly said "I will stand by you or fall with you" it was my duty. . . . You cannot know the shabbiness of many. . . . Some, very friendly advised me to come out . . . Lady Salisbury who has ever been most good natured to me . . . no mean dirty view of getting in or out of society actuates me. . . . If I did not see how anxious William is about it, for myself I should not care if I retired for ever. . . . I am not wordly enough to take measures for what can be purchased any time by a few balls and dinners.'

'I went to Whitehall,' wrote Hary-o, 'was received with rapturous joy, embraces and tremendous spirits,' but Caroline was putting on an act and her brave public defiance hid her real feelings. 'I'm sick of fame – I'm gorged with it,' was the opening line of a long, wittily prophetic poem she published in 1819. (See Appendix, p. 212.)

Caroline's former association with Byron and present notoriety were now so well known that an aspiring young writer who was a Hertfordshire neighbour wrote her a sycophantic letter enclosing some of his verses. The boy was a Cambridge undergraduate, his poem pompously dedicated : 'To Lady Caroline L – who at the last Hoo races set a noble & glorious example of her feeling & humanity when a poor man being much hurt she had him conveyed to her own carriage & interested herself most charitably in his recovery.' The would-be poet was Edward Bulwer Lytton.

Caroline was kind to the young man, who persisted in sending her his novels and verses, which Caroline returned with pages of carefully thought-out, detailed, constructive criticism. 'Lady Caroline Lamb presents her compliments to Mr Bulwer Lytton and begs to thank him for his poems which she acknowledges surprised her. . . . If she may offer one word of advice to a person who seems so little to need it . . . new writers instead of expressing their own sentiments are seeking in old authors . . . the sublimities that have stood the test of ages. . . . To obtain his celebrity now, if Mr Lytton with his surprising facility . . . would for some years read much . . . she takes the liberty of suggesting it will form his taste . . . give his work originality.' Delivering a broadside she told him, 'One bright thought and five or six lines' would not excuse 'rheams of trash', and pointed out that in Byron's poetry 'There was truth in every line.'

Caroline was often ill, distracting herself with wine and unsavoury company, dulling her senses with laudanum. She confined herself to the solitary pursuit of writing, to try again for the success she craved. In her second novel, *Graham Hamilton*, which she delayed publishing for two years, she made heroic efforts to discipline herself into writing well and constructing with care. Written in a mood of elegiac despair, it describes the hallucinatory effects of the drug laudanum, freely available at that time and often casually taken for an aching tooth or a slight headache. 'It was as if my imagination was struck . . . as if material objects vanished, and the perceptions of the mind became too bright and vivid for the understanding to bear. I was as if endowed for a few instants with a new sense; memory appeared to cease and futurity to open.' She suffered nightmare visions : It was as if a mist had enveloped me. I saw no more . . . a singing in my ears – a sickness and violent beating of the heart oppressed me. . . . I put my hand to my head – I had not power to speak . . . a vision wholly different seemed to fill the scene; everyone appeared clad in black . . . then all was terror, uproar, noise.'

But the novel, containing neither the sensational gossip of *Glenarvon*, nor a Byronic hero, failed, and Caroline suffered the discouragement of rejection in the one art she deeply cared for and in which she had laboured alone, hoping for recognition of the ability she knew she possessed. Her spark of talent, ignited by Byron and fanned by her own ambition into a consuming conflagration, wavered fatally but did not quite go out.

In 1821 Caroline wrote to her mother in Florence, 'Dearest of own Heart's blood, dearest I would you were in England. There is a strange wild story called Ada Reis, written they say by an American.' Caroline had somehow summoned up the energy and had confined herself to the solitude she detested and feared, to try again with a third novel, also published anonymously and also a failure. Her hopes of repeating the financial success achieved by *Glenarvon* were not fulfilled.

In Florence later that year, Lady Bessborough, exhausted and ill from nursing a dying grandson, herself died. Frederick wrote of their dying mother to Caroline, 'She sent you her kindest love, she begged me to take to you her pink diamond ring which belonged to her Grandmother.' On her death-bed Lady Bessborough's last thoughts were for that other poor grandson Augustus; hope had come to her with the knowledge that the physician attending her had suffered the same disability and she begged Frederick to re-assure Caroline that 'Dr Downe . . . suffered most terribly till four-teen or fifteen from epileptic fits & since that period has had no return.' Lord Bessborough added a similar message, adding 'Kiss Augustus for me.'

But the boy was steadily deteriorating mentally. His aunt Lady Emily Cowper callously wrote, 'I went to the play last night to see *Frankenstein* and the huge creature without any sense put us in mind of Augustus.' Lord Bessborough, Moome and Caroline con-stantly wrote to him, the Lamb side of the family scarcely, if at all. 'Dearest boy,' wrote his mother in 1821, 'yr Papa sends you a pheasant as you wish it so much and have so little amusement in this life. . . . Pray let them call for a hackney coach & send you here immediately where a nice fire & your own Mum await you.' From Hastings, where Caroline stayed for a time, she wrote to her son, 'Do write and tell me what you are doing how you are & everything about you. . . . It is beautiful I wish you were here but if you are at Brocket Hall it is still better how is Bell how my little kitten How the peacocks tell Sarah to send my flannel petticoats . . . I cannot say it is very warm here but I am on top of a Hill almost a mountain.'

In spite of his love of cricket and exuberant activities there seemed to be something wrong with Augustus's bones, unexplained by epilepsy or mental retardation. Though he could read well, he had difficulty holding a pen and writing more than a little tired him, although he wrote a well-formed hand. Moome constantly worried about his posture and his inability to hold himself upright as he had once done. *Syphilis hereditaria tarda* manifests itself after birth, and one of its symptoms is abnormal softness of the bone.

Caroline took refuge from her disappointment and disillusion in frenetic activity, galloping wildly about Hertfordshire. Always a fearless horsewoman, she rode dangerously and was on one occasion thrown by her beautiful black mare, lying injured and ill for some time afterwards. Edward Bulwer Lytton described her at this time as 'a slight rounded figure and a childlike mode of wearing her hair which was of a pale golden colour in fine curls.' Caroline was forty, but she had not learned to conform to the dignified life-style required of a staid parochial matron, although her London life was now over.

During her frequent illnesses a younger woman, also a writer with an Irish background, became her close friend. Rosina Doyle Wheeler, who later married Edward Bulwer Lytton, often wrote Caroline's letters for her when she was unwell and they shared a deep love of literature. In 1827 Rosina agreed, after numerous refusals, to marry her persistent admirer, Edward Bulwer Lytton, whom she had met at Brocket. 'I recollect, at Brocket,' wrote Rosina in later life, 'poor Lady Caroline Lamb, with the tears streaming down her cheek, said, "Whatever you do, don't marry Edward Lytton Bulwer." ' Rosina did and lived to regret it.

William Godwin was another of Caroline's literary friends whose philosophy 'To do my part to free the human mind from slavery' strongly appealed to Caroline. To him she wrote, 'Life, after all that has been said of its brevity, is very very long.' She found the company of the sympathetic and erudite man a solace and he was invited to Brocket. 'Your room shall be always ready,' she told him and when he was in financial difficulties she helped him in practical ways, enlisting John Murray's aid. She confided to him her most moving self-analysis : 'It is all very well if one died at the end of a tragic scene, after playing a desperate part : but if one lives, and instead of growing wiser, one remains the same victim of every folly and passion, without the excuse of youth and inexperience, what then ?'

In 1825 the Lamb family, who had been unsuccessful in their first efforts to persuade William to abandon Caroline, tried again. They were all convinced of Caroline's insanity, although the family physician had told William Lamb that she would respond to kind treatment. 'I feel violently,' implored Caroline of her cousin Hart, 'Is that madness?' But William agreed to a legal separation, and the Lambs and the Milbankes formidably united against Caroline who felt she had been unfairly treated financially. She wrote despairingly to her cousin Hart, 'After you left me I remained at Melbourne

House for the Deed . . . and when at length it came it differed materially from your agreement with Lord Cowper. . . . I did not sign it . . . bid adieu to my few remaining friends and my boy, and went off to Calais.' A jubilant Emily wrote, 'Conceive what luck! She marched out without beat of drum last Friday morning at eight o'clock by the steamboat to Calais. . . . She will I trust, have been so sick as to feel little anxiety to cross the water again directly . . . she behaved remarkably well . . . she was very quiet and said nothing.'

From Calais Caroline wrote to her husband, although she was at once homesick for the country life and the horses she loved, 'I do not know that I shall ever return.' The unhappy exile stayed several months in France, where she lived in a rented room without a maid, pathetically clinging to one of the Brocket pet dogs she had taken with her: 'I shall send poor little Bijou back for I fear she is with puppies. . . . I want Gupp or Bell – instead – but you like Bell, therefore the puppy would do. . . . remember me to my own sweet kind boy – no one wrote to me on his birthday – write to me pray do.'

William Lamb was moved by her letters and relented; Caroline thankfully returned to Brocket and Augustus. William had always expected too much of the boy: whenever he had written to him it was to exhort him to impossible tasks such as the study of Euclid, bidding him write at least three letters a week. Caroline had urged differently and at last William saw the wisdom of gentler treatment. Caroline told him, 'Thank you for keeping the boy so much with you I always told you it would be better for him.' But when he again wrote critically to his son, Caroline told him sadly, 'Your letter caused him such violent grief that it gave him three fits.' Still she was content to be back home with her horses, delighting in a fine new filly.

The creative impulse which from childhood had poured out in innumerable sketches and poems, crushed by lack of encouragement, now deserted her. Feverishly restless, she lacked outlets. 'Action was the light of life,' she wrote; 'I cannot labour. . . . were I to publish what I write, I should only make enemies.' She was suffering the agonizing bitterness of the rejected artist. 'Shall I throw myself upon those who no longer want me?' she asked Lady Morgan, 'shall I live a good sort of a half-kind of life in some cheap street . . . or upon

1   Augusta Leigh. *Drawing by Sir George Hayter.*

2 Self-portrait of Caroline Lamb with her son, Augustus, aged two.
From her sketch-book.

3 Brocket Hall, Lemsford, Lady Melbourne's Hertfordshire house, where
Caroline Lamb spent her later years.

the top of a shop – or shall I give lectures to little children and keep a seminary, and thus earn my bread? Or shall I write a kind of quiet everyday novel . . . attempt to be poetical, and failing, beg my friends for a guinea a piece . . . and sell my work upon the best foolscap paper; or shall I fret, fret, fret and die?'

In her last years Caroline worried increasingly about Augustus. To Hart, after the second separation from William, she wrote, 'I feel too much to live long.' Broken in spirit and in health she was aware that death was not very distant. She wrote to Augustus, 'My dearest Boy, you ask me what I wish you to learn. . . . I am very anxious that you should have some knowledge of the History of England – what is daily going on and particularly that you should attend to yr writing and get to write a decent small hand or running hand – as if it please God you live you will have business of this sort to transact & I should like you to know enough of affairs in general to prevent you being in the power of Ragamuffins . . . no more . . . for you should not overload yr memory nor strain yr understanding. God bless you & take charge of you here & hereafter your most affectionate Mother Caroline Lamb.' She mourned his absence on his birthday when the loyal local villagers celebrated with a cricket match and much jollification that she knew he would have enjoyed.

In 1827 William Lamb who, in spite of Caroline's behaviour, had now a brilliant political future ahead of him, was appointed Chief Secretary for Ireland, and left England taking Augustus with him. Caroline's subjugation and defeat had signalled William's triumph and rise. It was ironic that he, who epitomized the Anglo-Saxon, should be sent to govern Ireland, the island from whence Caroline's artistic spirit had sprung. Freed from his obligation to Caroline, he now resumed his liaison with Lady Brandon. In October Dr Goddard wrote to him from Hertfordshire, 'Lady Caroline has just desired me to let you know how she is – some time ago I had wished to do so, but her Ladyship prevented me, as she by no means would unnecessarily frighten or distress you. . . . It has been with feelings of deepest regret . . . I have apprehensions of the greatest danger. . . . she appears convinced she cannot ultimately recover but with feelings of perfect resignation says she does not mind to die.'

Emily Lady Cowper and Frederick Lamb had the grace to visit her. 'He does not look at all well,' Caroline told her husband, 'wears very long curly hair . . . but it is not,' she added sadly, 'as ours is, turning gray.'

To his mistress William Lamb wrote in January, 'You do not know the melancholy here . . . she is dying. . . . the only bitter feelings which affect her are those which I knew she would suffer . . . repentance of the course she has run.' Absent from her dying moments, a few days later he was immersed in politics.

Some months afterwards, early in March 1828, a bewildered Moome wrote to Augustus from Paris, 'I write this to condole with you My dear Augustus on the late melancholy event in your family. I was very much shocked when I received a letter from Mr Ponsonby announcing the death of Lady Caroline . . . had anyone informed me of the dangerous state she was in, and her desire to see me, I should have returned to England to see her, and hear what she appears to have been so anxious to communicate. It was no doubt you my Dear Boy who she would have spoken to me about.' Caroline had managed to send word, but Moome continued, 'It is alas too late now to answer her letter – nor to comply with her wish. . . . tell me how you are and if you were with your Mother at her death . . . I understand her sufferings were great.' No one in the family had relayed to Moome Caroline's dying wish to see her.

Caroline had written to her beloved Hart a few years before her death, 'I loved you when an infant, adored you when a boy; for one or two years my heart wandered from you, but every early recollection, every early thought or wish is with you.' In his handbook to Chatsworth written after Caroline's death, the Duke of Devonshire spoke of the honesty which devastated and destroyed her but singled her out as a beacon of courageous womanhood: 'She had a candour.' In her own poem 'A New Canto', she wryly prophesied that her name would be kept 'in capitals, like Kean'.

Annabella

'A great opinion of her own good qualities.'

Don Juan (Canto I, Stanza 20)

Anne Isabella Milbanke was born, 1792, in a village near Stockton-on-Tees in Durham. Her parents were gentry and their lives revolved round the traditional country pursuits of landed provincials: the families entertained each other, the women busied themselves with good works and the men hunted, shot or were politically active.

The daughter's advent had been long awaited and when she finally arrived her parents were no longer young. She was an only daughter and an only child and her parents doted on her. Her late birth was an unpopular event in the rest of the family, for it displaced her cousin John Milbanke, his aunt Lady Melbourne's favourite nephew, who had confidently expected to inherit in due course a title and considerable property.[1] Her father became Sir Ralph when the child was two years old.

Anne Isabella was soon contracted to 'Annabella', and she entered a childhood cocooned with care. In addition to her immediate family she had a nurse, the spinsterish Mrs Clermont, one of that breed of women who adopt the family they serve as their own, and for whom its members become an obsessive interest. Mrs Clermont came to the Milbanke household when Annabella was under two; all her frustrated sexual and maternal instincts were centred on the child and, later, the woman. She was a difficult employee and could not get on with the other servants, yet by some power of personality she subjugated Mrs Milbanke, who dared not dismiss her.

Her own account of her beginnings, 'I was born in the house of my father, a respectable tradesman,' suggests a plain woman of fairly prosperous lower middle-class; she and her brother inherited

---

[1] It was entailed on Lady Milbanke's only child.

67

both money and property from their mother. The image could not be more solid. Yet according to Annabella her origins were more mysterious: 'Mrs Clermont was the daughter of a French emigré.' She was no ordinary nursemaid. She was intelligent and wished to learn, and Lady Milbanke taught her. Ingratiating herself with the family, she became indispensable so that when Annabella was still under two and she threatened to leave, it was deemed such a crisis that she was persuaded to remain.

Later, when she inherited her family property, she relinquished it to the impecunious Sir Ralph, who purchased Mrs Clermont an annuity. Her emotional hold upon the family was therefore strengthened by a financial one.

Everything the adored Annabella did was remarked upon and written about; paeons of praise about her ankles, her dancing and her character at six years old were written. She was an unending source of admiration and interest to those about her. Justly so, for she was a remarkable girl. Highly intelligent, serious and mistress of an astonishing self-discipline, she had strong feelings which she taught herself to hide and control with an impenetrable reserve. In a crisis she tended to break down and she had no sense of humour. As a child she did not care for dolls, yet years later she displayed a resolute maternity in her active concern for the unprotected young.

Annabella's parents were zealous in their public duties. Lady Milbanke cared for the poor in her district while Sir Ralph and his nephew busied themselves with public affairs, for theirs was a political family. Neither had brilliant brains – Sir Ralph was known as 'Old twaddle Ralph' for his loquacity – but Annabella was precocious; she soon learned to beat her elders at chess and astonished her circle by becoming an embryonic mathematician.

Sir Ralph's sister, Annabella's aunt, was Lady Melbourne, one of the most powerful and scintillating hostesses at that time regnant in London society and the very reverse of provincial. Sir Ralph and his sister shared a love of words and with her he could indulge his mild hobby for writing verses which, when Annabella was older, he shared with her. Annabella believed her father's correspondence brilliant.

The girl grew up earnestly desiring to become a writer, painstakingly thorough to the point of pedantry, awe-inspiringly well-read and humourless. Like many over-serious persons she had a

penchant for coarse humour. The slippers she wore were soft kid
leather made by her own hands, but her chief occupation was
the single-minded cultivation of her very considerable intellectual
powers and she early began to translate Horace.

When the gaieties of her first London season in 1812 beckoned
she temporarily put away her studies, but the round of balls and
calls bored her and she was uninterested in such feminine frivolities
as clothes. She felt herself to be of superior intellect and arrogantly
conscious of more important matters. In addition she was obsessed
by a prim morality against which she measured all whom she met,
and which was to rule and wreck her life.

She was more relaxed during her second season and enjoyed herself dancing, even unbending sufficiently to flirt a little. The erudite
young lady's appearance belied her brains. She liked a good dinner
and her figure reflected her hearty appetite. Her plump face with
its apple-red cheeks, together with her connections and expected
fortune, attracted a flock of suitors to her side. She was cautious
with her favours : 'One of my smiles would encourage him,' she
wrote warily of a discouraged admirer, 'but I am niggardly of my
glances.'

In spite of her success she was aloofly critical of her new and
fashionable acquaintances. 'Lady Caroline baa-a-a-a's till she makes
me sick,' Annabella wrote after a house party at the Melbournes'
Brocket Park where Lady Caroline Lamb, who had married Annabella's cousin William, was the aristocratically lisping hostess.

This was Byron's season and everybody seized, read and exclaimed
upon his every word. Annabella declined to join in the raging,
waited for a week, then read 'Childe Harold' carefully and pronounced it too mannered. The day following her patronizing comment in her diary, Annabella met Byron at Caroline Lamb's waltz-
ing morning party. Byron's lame foot precluded his joining in the
dancing but he was surrounded by a swarm of females and Annabella watched from a distance, unwilling to gush with the others.
But he did not fail to make a powerful impression and she grudgingly conceded that his features were well-formed. She declined,
however, to be captivated. It was highly satisfying to Annabella to
refrain from the lionizing of the notorious Lord Byron, poet and
profligate, who was at the height of his affair with Caroline Lamb.
It would be a different matter actually to resist his attentions when

once the full force of them should be concentrated upon herself. Like other women who might have thought themselves impervious, Annabella was ultimately powerless. She struggled longer than any of the others, and Byron found the straight-backed Annabella, whose principles were guided by reason rather than emotion, an unexpected challenge. 'She really is an icicle,' wrote the Duchess of Devonshire.

By mid-April 1812, however, she was as good as lost. 'Lord Byron', she wrote of his performance at a party, 'shone with his customary glory.' Soon she was writing, 'Lord Byron and I had some very pleasing conversation,' and admitted, 'he is very handsome!' He interested her further by talking about himself to other people in her hearing, and with such remarks as 'I have not a friend in the world' arousing her compassion, an infallibly successful gambit with aloof young ladies resistant to conquest, especially so when the words were uttered by a beautiful lame young poet of wild reputation. She decided to become the friend he needed. It is the virtuous woman's common failing to be filled with crusading zeal for a rake's reformation.

She was unaware of her peril. 'He is not a dangerous person to me,' she told her anxious parents, innocently and firmly adding that it was her 'Christian duty not to deny him my acquaintance.'

Annabella sent Byron some of her verses, eliciting his amazed comment, 'She certainly is an extraordinary girl . . . so much strength . . . under that placid countenance.' But he was not yet ready to be tamed; 'I should like her more if she were less perfect.'

By the autumn of 1812 he had cast off the hysterical Caroline Lamb and was writing, 'I was, am and shall be, I fear attached to another.' He meant the universally esteemed Miss Milbanke and he proposed to her through his confidante, Annabella's dazzling aunt, Lady Melbourne.

Annabella struggled with herself and turned him down. Accurately prophetic, she thought Byron would not 'make me happy in domestic life'. Later she equally accurately forecast: 'his *theoretical* idea of my perfection . . . must end in his disappointment.' But she could not so easily dismiss him from her mind. 'The effects upon my feelings were serious,' she confessed; 'My state was that of high excitement,' and she regretted her rejection of him.

Byron appeared unaffected by her decision and declared that he had never really been seriously interested in her : Annabella was too mathematically exact for him. Yet his rejection by the girl he called the Princess of Parallelograms sourly rankled.

The next spring Byron and Annabella met again and Annabella admitted to extreme agitation at the sight of him, reporting on his pallor as a sign that he was equally moved – which may have been romantic fancy, since he was normally pale. Annabella refused invitations, fearful of meeting him, but by late summer, hearing of his imminent escape abroad, she took the initiative and capitulated, asking her all-knowing aunt to pass Byron a message. He acknowledged it and the correspondence between them began. The long pedantic letter she wrote to him was unlikely to arouse his passionate feelings but his immediate reply was of a vividness to overthrow the most secludedly genteel young lady : 'I doubt whether I could help loving you.' So the correspondence proceeded despite Byron's additional involvement with Lady Oxford, while a distraught Caroline Lamb still clung on, relations with Augusta were probably resumed, and Lady Frances Webster hovered on his horizon. Lady Melbourne was also on hand as *deus ex machina* at this turbulent period in his life.

Annabella demanded secrecy for their correspondence, a request Byron ignored and sent her letters off to an amused Lady Melbourne, but the letters were so dull and prosy and full of solemn preachings that the correspondence languished. Annabella tried to convince a friend it was not the poet she longed for, she wished to rescue his immortal soul, but privately she confessed to a bursting heart and soon, fearful of losing him, she unguardedly poured out to him that she preferred poetry to mathematics. Hastily assuring him she would not argue about religion, she hoped to meet him the following spring. He had written of the advent of a seven-year-old cousin, Eliza Byron, 'the prettiest little black-eyed girl of Paradise,' and Annabella invited the child to stay. Young ladies, even those as erudite as Annabella, know well how much more attractive they may seem to the man of their choice in company with a child. But Eliza did not come to stay and Annabella languished, although she reasoned to a friend, 'My mother may prefer my health to a son-in-law.' Still, she wrote anxiously to Byron again, since there was news he was about to leave the country.

In desperate flight from his many troubles Byron turned to Annabella for peace and relief from his persecutors. Now his letters were serious; he was more reflective and respectful, carefully adding courteous postscripts to her parents. He had decided on Annabella for a wife and the courtship had begun in earnest. She was twenty-four years old and eager to respond, emboldened by his now apparently very serious intentions. Still conscious of his Godlessness she continued to mention religion to him, and on receipt of one of her didactic diatribes, he could not resist an impatient outburst : 'Why I came here, I know not; where I shall go, it is useless to enquire.' Annabella timidly invited him to visit the family home, but her hopes of his early advent were dashed when he told her, 'Italy is my magnet,' and said that he would go there for an indefinite period. This stirred Annabella into an impulsive declaration, fearful that she had cooled him off.

In early August Byron's decision was hardening and he committed himself : 'I did – do – and always shall love you.' Still he could not make up his mind to go to her and told her it would be impossible that year. Annabella hid her dismay and sought distraction from romance by undertaking a daunting task, reading the whole of Gibbon. Here at least she and Byron shared common ground. Both knew their historians and there was an easy comradeship in their writings on this subject, for Byron respected Annabella's fine mind, although he instructed her what to read and what to think about it.

Both had tentatively advanced and as regularly retreated, but it was not long now before Byron penned a direct proposal to Annabella, showed it to an approving Augusta and posted it. Overcome, Annabella was his and the formal engagement was announced two years after their first meeting.

He promised to go to her but he did not hasten to be with the girl to whom he had penned such a passionate proposal. Though expected hourly, he lingered with his sister at her home at Six Mile Bottom. When he finally arrived the couple had not met for a year. 'I was sitting in my own room reading when I heard the carriage,' recalled Annabella; 'He was in the drawing room, standing by the side of the chimney piece.' Annabella entered but he did not move towards her as an eager lover should. Insufficiently overcome by emotion at the sight of her, he probably remembered his lame foot and stayed by the fire, while she went to him and extended a hand to touch the being who was unbelievably with her and had declared himself to be hers. He kissed her hand. Annabella 'felt overpowered and made the excuse of calling my parents to leave the room.'

The next morning he again was oddly reluctant to meet the girl he had asked to become his wife. It was midday before he appeared and then his manner was offhand. He appeared indifferent but she remained calm, although his frequent references to his sister caused her a jealous pang which she hid well.

Indeed she was too silent altogether, too lacking in vivacity. Annabella cast a chill on Byron who was only warmed by her physical response. She was more ardent than he thought, he told Lady Melbourne, and Byron the sensualist remained more attracted than he had expected to be. The strain of the lengthy correspondence, the long year's absence, the sudden feverish effect of his presence on her, which must be controlled, was too great for Annabella. She was frequently unwell and he could not understand why. It was quite impossible to relax with her unless she was being made love to. She was tense and worried and Byron, fatigued by the stress of her analytical mind, had recourse to more eloquent action. A few days later he was gone, on his way to Augusta.

Annabella's alarmed letters followed him, fearful she had disappointed him, analysing their every word, sure she had been too tedious. She could at times, she told him, be light-hearted. Byron wrote lovingly, reassuringly, 'Don't scold yourself any more,' and signed himself winningly 'thine, B'. Annabella gained in confidence and was soon writing her heart out : 'I wish for you, want you, Byron mine, more every hour.' Anxious to put her new-found boldness to the test, she pressed for his early return to her. But he was in London preoccupied with other matters, an election at Cambridge, a debate in the House of Lords, and Annabella occupied herself with matters at home and preparations for her married life. She engaged a cook, bored Byron with tales of a misbehaving servant and told him excitedly about the wedding cake already in the making. They were to be married at Seaham by special licence and Sir Ralph was busy composing an 'Epithalamium' to be sung at the ceremony. Still she impatiently awaited him. 'I shall be making a visit to the Albany some day if you stay there much longer,' she threatened him in December, and Byron wrote wryly, 'The Cake! I must try and be ready before it is baked.'

Annabella wrote to him smugly, 'I believe you are the only man who ever really loved one that had not flattered him.' She should not have been so self-satisfied. It was a serious mistake. It is impossible to flatter a man too much. The winter wore on with Annabella in the north and Byron in London carousing with old friends, often insensibly drunk, when sober harassed by debts and marriage settlements. Annabella assured him that her tastes were modest and she would be content with 'only one carriage and one house'. Forgetting his love of bibulous company she held out to him the happy prospect of retirement and of only seeing 'that quiet kind of society which I think we both prefer.' The wedding date was fixed but he wavered wearily, suggesting postponement.

Her parents' pride was piqued on her behalf and Annabella tartly signed herself in her reply, 'wife or not – always thine'. This brought Byron to take the matter a little more seriously and he applied to the Archbishop of Canterbury for a special licence enabling them to marry within a week. 'On obtaining his Grace's fiat,' Byron told Annabella, they could be married 'any morning or evening in your drawing room.' Annabella welcomed the action but warned him, 'Don't let me marry you against your will,' a stricture Byron ignored and simply got on with the arrangements. But Annabella was dubious and asked, 'Are you less confident than you were in the happiness of our marriage?' He rounded on her crisply. 'It would be presumptuous . . . to feel too certain of uninterrupted felicity.' The following Saturday was decided upon and he was on his way, stopping of course en route to spend a family Christmas with Augusta and her children at Six Mile Bottom. Uncertain still but accompanied by his best man, John Cam Hobhouse, Byron arrived on the evening of the 30 December 1814. The family's chilly reception matched the wintry weather but they thawed, and the couple were married in the drawing room on New Year's morning 1815, Annabella wearing plain white muslin trimmed with lace and attended by the faithful, watchful Mrs Clermont.

It was January and snowing. In the carriage on their journey to a Yorkshire honeymoon, Byron and Annabella found themselves alone and apprehensive. They had not spent longer than a fortnight together during the two years since their first meeting and had then usually been in the company of guests or relatives. They had exhaustively corresponded but whereas Annabella had been at pains

to bare her true self to him, Byron could scarcely be as candid.
Though Annabella was aware of his reputation she was blissfully
ignorant of the extent and range of his amatory exploits during
their long engagement.

Immediately he resented his capture and began to chafe at the
bonds he had himself sought. He behaved insultingly on the long
drive and later, after their arrival at their honeymoon home,
Halnaby Hall in the North Riding, in a black ungovernable rage he
railed at his young bride. Aghast at his torrents of vituperation,
alternating with boorish silence, her natural nervousness and hyper-
sensitivity enabled her to respond with paralysed calm. The insults
continued unabated and the morning after the wedding night 'the
deadliest chill fell on my heart,' Annabella wrote, meeting his
behaviour with a saintly goodness which only served to foment his
hatred.

He stopped at nothing to increase her misery. That very first
morning he began taunting her with his love for his sister, for
already Augusta had written lovingly and he could torture Annabella with jealousy by reading out the letter to her. The day after
their marriage he had found an ideal weapon with which to destroy
the clever young lady who had had the audacity to refuse his earliest
advances and who had believed she could withstand his demon
charm. Like all the others, she had succumbed, but he had had to
pay the heaviest price – marriage.

During the three weeks they spent in Yorkshire it snowed heavily
and the cold January weather meant they were much confined.
Togetherness with Annabella was anathema and Byron showed it.
His few efforts at grace gave moments of cherished tenderness which
Annabella gratefully seized and clung to, drowning in the unfathom-
able ocean of misery into which she had been deliberately tossed. In
moments of playfulness he called her 'pippin' on account of her
round, pink-cheeked apple face, so at odds with her immaculate
reserve but indicative of her inner warmth; she called him 'Duck'
in return.

These lighter moments heightened the black horror of the shock-
ing revelations he insistently hinted at, till Annabella could restrain
her pent-up feelings no longer. 'I am sure there has been something
dreadful between him and his sister!' she burst out to her maid,
Mrs Minns. For Annabella, to whom stoicism was a rigid religion,

to have revealed her suspicions to a servant appalled her. Byron threatened her with a dagger; the outward calm of which she was mistress saved her but goaded him to still further insults. 'I will live with you if I can, until I have got an heir, then I shall leave you,' he told her. He was unable to stay the constancy of her affection no matter what he said or did. She knelt to him by the fire, her arms about his neck and tried to comfort him. Another night she found him wandering about armed. She persuaded him to bed and soothed him into an anguished cry, 'You should have a softer pillow than my heart.' 'Which will break first, yours or mine?' she wondered aloud to him, and the answer was neither. Annabella's indomitable spirit saved her heart from breaking. The cracks she seldom permitted to show. Byron's self-torment expressed itself compulsively in a desire to torture, and Annabella's sweet pliancy made her the ideal victim. It was natural to her to be so, and she was not experienced in the strategies necessary for some human relationships. She could play her part no other way than straight. Resolving to face her fate and her adversary, she invited Augusta to stay with them, but with insincere expressions of affection Augusta declined to join the pair.

The newly married couple returned to Annabella's family home where, distracted by the diversions of mixed company, family meals and games, Byron was shamed into behaving tolerably well. He employed his wife to copy 'Parisina' while her father played the violin. Annabella's hopes rose. She steadfastly ministered to him again when his tortured calvinistic conscience rose. 'I have tried everything,' he said, exhausted with raving, 'I will try virtue I think.' At these moments Annabella was his 'good-natured Pip – the best wife in the world.' His perplexing behaviour was compounded of wild protestations of his guilt and a touching, child-like dependence – enough to test the most devoted wife. Annabella responded to the bewildering alternations of his moods with consoling patience, and Sir Ralph and Lady Milbanke knew nothing then of the heroic private struggle with the apparently half-demented genius their daughter had married.

Family life inevitably began to pall. 'I must go to tea,' Byron wrote. 'Damn tea; I wish it were Kinnaird's brandy.' Byron and Annabella stayed with Sir Ralph and Lady Milbanke till March, six long weeks, then, troubled, departed for Six Mile Bottom.

Augusta's home was relaxed and easy, full of romping children, Augusta's husband absent as usual. The gentilities of the Milbanke family were left behind and a warm, untidy, cheerfully sinning aristocratic household awaited him.

Annabella had been married for eight weeks and she had patiently borne the undreamed-of behaviour of her husband. Byron's few kinds words to her were singly counted, blessed and weighed against his unkindnesses, giving her but a wan hope of happiness. On the way to Six Mile Bottom he assured her she did make him happy and 'tears of joy . . . rose from my heart,' she recalled.

Annabella arrived for her only visit to Six Mile Bottom and her sister-in-law, a moment instinct with unspoken drama which must have given Byron sardonic pleasure. Annabella greeted Augusta with a sisterly kiss, a fond gesture Augusta could not bring herself to return. They stayed for three weeks, both women subject to Byron's continued tauntings : Augusta that she had been her brother's lover, Annabella that her husband could only love his sister. 'No-one could make him happy but Augusta,' Annabella wrote later and this was his refrain. His behaviour at this time was no less than obscene. He wished, he declared, 'to work them both well'. Augusta would not let him touch her and Annabella was stricken. 'A sense of desolation came upon me,' she wrote, weeping alone in her room.

The consciousness of Medora, nearly a year old, often with the trio and remarkably resembling Byron in looks, was inescapable. The excitement Byron felt at being the centre of such a charged drama galvanized him. He openly displayed such fondness for the child that Annabella's heart was touched by the tenderness of his expression. She told the other two she wished for a portrait of Byron painted whilst contemplating the infant, and thus elicited Byron's startled comment, 'You know that is my child.'

Annabella, stunned at her situation, summed up her stay at Six Mile Bottom as 'indescribable'. When they left for London she was pregnant.

But a week later Augusta was to join them again, as if the fascination she held for Annabella must be plumbed whatever the cost. Annabella's unshaken determination to face and vanquish their passion with her virtue showed her ardent ignorance of human nature. Under-estimating the strength of her own violent feelings and goaded beyond her usual control, at one moment she nearly lost it. 'I turned round to use a deadly weapon lying by – not against him, but against one whose treachery seemed at that instant revealed.' She meant Augusta, who never noticed the gesture.

Annabella's pregnancy wore on, accompanied by Augusta's abrasive presence. After the latter's return to Six Mile Bottom there came a peaceful interlude, with Byron often out alone at the play. Annabella was preoccupied with her diet; always fond of food, she ate heartily and soon felt she would be 'needing a writing table cut like a shaving dish'. At this time, the sinister Mrs Clermont formed the third side of the triangle. Byron found the house intolerable and left to stay with Augusta.

Annabella followed him in spirit with affectionate, wifely letters addressed to her 'Darling Duck.' She wrote of the expected child's quickening and the maid's ferocious cleaning, and made her letters short for fear of boring him. Meanwhile, with Augusta and her children at his elbow, Byron signed his letter to her 'always most conjugally'.

On his return Annabella tried to be self-effacing but Byron countered with ferocity, and Annabella again begged Augusta to return to Piccadilly. The trials of being Lady Byron continued and increased; she could only be grateful when he was less than cruelly vindictive, reporting with astonishment Byron's romantic fancy of fathering a 'winged child'.

Annabella's consciousness of her undeviating virtue amongst the moral laxity of London society at that time amused her and was a distraction from the distresses of life with Byron. She wrote neatly of the 'varnish of vice' at Holland House and of her hostess 'treating her as fearfully as a hedgehog', so unaccustomed was Lady Holland to the uncommon virtue of a Lady Byron. Annabella kept aloof from the society she despised and sardonically noted its vanities, among which was the continued adulation of her husband, invariably surrounded by gushing ladies of all ages.

But these were lighter moments in an existence almost continually tormented. Byron sought relief from the boredom of domesticity in his usual way. 'He sat drinking with Kinnaird's party till half-past four in the morning,' Annabella reported and her despair deepened. Often she only saw him briefly during the day, and when he was present he was usually disagreeable, no matter how hard she tried to please him.

At this time Byron was much in the company of George Colman the younger, a poet and dramatist and the supposed author of the poems, 'Don Leon' and 'Don Leon to Annabella', which appeared some years later. These may have been based on information given to him by Byron in a drunken moment. Byron may at some time have indulged in *coitus per anum* with Annabella, whose conscience may have been tormented by the knowledge that she had instinctively responded to what she considered an 'unnatural vice'.[2]

Annabella wrote, 'I have waited until the last in the hope of some change,' but finally she decided that she must leave Byron, just as Byron's cousin, also of the household, had predicted she would.

Annabella's room was next of that of Mrs Clermont who believed that her mistress was in danger of serious injury from her husband. 'I might die,' wrote Annabella, when she was contemplating leaving the house before the birth, 'and be spared.' During the rest of her confinement, Mrs Clermont protected Annabella, and Augusta kept Byron company.

Their daughter was born on 10 December 1815. Her parents, inescapably fascinated by their extraordinary situation, named the child Augusta Ada and invited Augusta, whom Byron said the child resembled, to be godmother.

In January Byron wrote Annabella a curt note : 'When you are disposed to leave London it would be convenient that a day should be fixed. . . . the child will of course accompany you.' Annabella swiftly returned, 'I shall obey your wishes.' The day before she left they met briefly, their infant Ada between them, parted, and early the following morning Annabella and Ada left London. On passing Byron's door Annabella paused, observed his dog reclining on the mat outside, and was tempted similarly to prostrate herself to her husband whom she dearly loved. She had been as doggedly loyal as that animal and more provoked. Byron had treated his wife with the pathological mental cruelty Englishmen reserve more for their women than their dogs. 'I passed on,' wrote Annabella, and the carriage which had borne her to her honeymoon carried her back to her parents.

They never met again.

---

[2] Annabella was, as the psychiatrists say, a man. Harriet Beecher-Stowe said that she 'had the soul . . . of a strong reasoning man.'

When a woman leaves her husband, it is not for one single reason but many, which combine to make him impossible (for her) to live with. A young, conventionally-reared virgin, Annabella had suffered a cataclysmically shattering year. Her adored husband had confessed to homosexuality and to incest of which he declared a child was the result. He was nearly bankrupt and his behaviour so erratic that she seriously thought he might be insane. According to one of her letters written at the time, Byron's mind was full of an extraordinary 'Paris Scheme', which encouraged her belief that he was deranged. Her loved uncle had died and her father was about to be put into a debtor's prison. For nine months of that year she had had the added burden of her pregnancy.

All these things contributed to her decision temporarily to leave Piccadilly. If ever a woman needed a respite, Annabella did.

The depth of the breach was only slowly realized. At first Annabella wrote to her 'Dearest Duck' soothingly as she had been advised to do, sent him Ada's love and admonished him not to waste his time writing poetry, since it was 'an abominable trade', nor to imbibe too much brandy. Annabella's opinion of her husband's genius was not then very high. She wrote daily to Augusta, left in London to care for her brother, but Mrs Clermont was also in Piccadilly, sending bulletins about Byron back to Annabella. 'It does not appear he has any desire that you should return . . . constantly declares his dislike to being a married man,' she told her mistress. Her morbidly jealous letters hardened Annabella's resolve. Mrs Clermont raked over their past : 'He first sought you out because you took no notice of him . . . and pride urged him to continue.' Skilfully she played her Iago-like role. 'His real wish is that a separation should take place, at the same time he would choose that you should remain attached to him.' She flattered the wretched Annabella, whom she so familiarly addressed, already regretting her departure : 'Great powers have been given to you by God and you will be criminal in allowing them to be destroyed. . . . had you continued with him they would have been.'

Meanwhile Annabella breast-fed her child. 'Oh dear! She pinches me,' she complained, while in receipt of the scarcely comforting news from Mrs Clermont that 'Lord Byron has his dinner and goes to the play as usual.' On hearing that Byron had written to his wife the maid was afraid Annabella's resolve would weaken.

Gradually Annabella's parents, overjoyed at their daughter's renewed presence in the house with their grandchild, learned something, but not all, of the ordeal their adored daughter had suffered at Byron's hands. 'I must never see him again,' wrote Annabella; 'Let me be preserved from it by every means.' This her parents were resolved to do in spite of Annabella's conflicting private feelings : 'Oh that I were in London, if in the coal hold !' It was too late. Her mother had taken control of the situation and she was in no mood to relinquish Annabella and Ada to Byron a second time. 'Old birds are not caught by sweet chaff,' she assured Annabella; 'The first thing to be attended to . . . is the state of *your own mind.*' Lady Milbanke's indignation was eloquent : 'Who could see that suffering angel sinking under such unmanly and despicable treatment and not feel?'

Sir Ralph proposed a legal agreement to separate, in support of which Annabella wrote coldly to Byron, 'Lord Byron . . . has too painfully convinced me that all attempts to contribute to his happiness were wholly useless.' Her two lawyers were Sir Samuel Romilly and Dr Stephen Lushington, both of whom had seats in the House of Commons, as had Annabella's father. Sir Samuel had abandoned Byron and incurred his hatred by taking part in a secret plan to make Ada a Ward in Chancery. Unfortunately, Dr Lushington, while sympathetic to what Annabella had suffered, could not then advise a separation. Two weeks later, however, on receipt of additional information, he 'considered a reconciliation impossible' and absolutely refused to take part in attempting to effect one. Whatever Annabella confided to him, whatever had passed during the previous two weeks, had a decisive effect in securing Ada to her mother.

Caroline Lamb wrote to Annabella, 'I will tell you that which if you merely menace him with the knowledge shall make him tremble.' Annabella, who despised her cousin-in-law, was yet unable to resist her invitation to hear what this dreadful secret was. Annabella was most probably regaled with a whole string of vices – incest, sodomy and dangerous political ideas. For Caroline was not without serious political opinions of her own on the issues of the day : she was a radical, and a bold one, as she described herself.[3]

[3] In 'A New Canto', a long poem which appears to anticipate revolution (see Appendix, p. 212).

She was a friend of the politically active Lady Oxford, who had supplanted her as Byron's mistress.[4]

Byron was amazed at the gravity of his position. He did not wish to relinquish his daughter, for he liked children and still sought the family life he had never enjoyed during an often lonely childhood. He now begged Augusta to intercede for him and she wrote on her brother's behalf, asking if Sir Ralph had acted with Annabella's concurrence. Annabella answered with two words, 'He has.' Apparently inflexible, privately she lost physical control and was found shrieking on the floor of her room.

Probably, the chief factor activating the Milbanke's determination to make the separation permanent was a political one. The men in Annabella's family were all prominent politically and her aunt, Lady Melbourne, was a potent influence behind the scenes of the twin London political theatres, the House of Commons and the House of Lords. Annabella's cousin, William Lamb, was a future Prime Minister and another cousin, the daughter of Admiral John Milbanke, had married the prominent Member of Parliament William Huskisson, who served in the Duke of Wellington's administration. Both her lawyers were MPs. Byron's ideas were revolutionary. The two speeches he had made in the Lords in favour of Catholic Emancipation and in sympathy with the frame-breakers of Nottingham had been duly noted. He greatly admired Napoleon,[5] considered the Duke of Wellington[6] the Frenchman's intellectual inferior, despised both the French and English monarchies. Byron's marital behaviour was a convenient weapon which may have been seized upon by the Establishment of the day to propel him out of the country. The young poet was seen as a socially, politically and morally disturbing influence whose ideas, if carried to their logical conclusion, would result in the total disintegration of society – a society in which a sexual misdemeanour was less heinous than caste treachery.

[4] Lady Oxford's lover was Arthur O'Connor, a high-born Irishman who defected to Napoleon.
[5] He was delighted when later he was enabled by his mother-in-law's death to add 'Noel' to Byron and sign himself with Napoleon's initials, NB.
[6] In 1818 there was an attempted assassination of the Duke of Wellington who escaped, warned by Lord Kinnaird who, however, refused to name the informant. At the subsequent Paris trial, the accused stated that the plot had long been planned by 'persons of consideration'.

'The general impression,' Mrs Villiers told Annabella, 'is so perfectly *now* what it should be – a very judicious letter of yours which I have seen circulated respecting Ld B's systematic cruelty has done much good.' While Annabella was at pains to conceal the 'unnatural vices' which Byron had confessed to her since their marriage, she made no attempt to stop the rumours of incest which were circulating, as these could only support her case against Byron. When Byron, tardily repentant, approached her on the subject of a reconciliation, she told him with withering disdain, 'It is unhappily your disposition to consider what you have as worthless – what you have *lost* as invaluable.'

Rumours of incest, instigated and broadcast by Caroline Lamb, were now flying about London and Augusta begged for a meeting with Annabella. However, Lady Byron replied: 'I cannot refuse without the greatest pain. . . . We might both be called upon to answer for words uttered in the *most private* conversation.' The Deed of Separation was signed at negotiations for which Mrs Clermont was promoted to a secretarial capacity, assisting Annabella's father, now Sir Ralph Noel.

It was springtime in London and a despondent Byron, his affairs inextricably chaotic, prepared to leave the country.

When Ada was six months old, Annabella took her to a small house she had taken at Lowestoft in East Anglia. Mother and child were stared and pointed at as objects of curiosity on the way. It was Annabella's first serious attempt at housekeeping; she was alone but for a few servants, for the possessive Mrs Clermont had been left behind, declining to take any interest in Byron's daughter, her new rival in Annabella's life. Annabella probably never forgave whatever part Mrs Clermont may have played in the plot to expel Byron from his wife, child and country, for Mrs Clermont wrote complaining of her 'coldness'.

Annabella now turned to a serious interest in organized religion, and became a Methodist. She wrote, 'I am not very likely to turn saint just now,' but she was tireless in her efforts to be as near one as possible. She had many useful years ahead of her and determined to fill them with worthwhile schemes. With difficulty she had secured her child's guardianship and, this anxiety allayed, she could turn to good works with earnest dedication.

Below the calm exterior, however, ran the turbulent current of her preoccupation with her marriage and Augusta, from whom she could never really break free. The love letters Byron was sending from Italy to Augusta, all of which were sent on to the rejected wife, continually disturbed her; the triangle was still very much in existence. Augusta, puzzled and flustered, was coerced into a series of macabre meetings, witnessed by Mrs Villiers, the object of which was to force Augusta to confess her incest to Annabella. Any satisfaction the latter may have obtained from this subtle revenge was undermined by Byron's letters to Augusta, full of affection for the sister, reviling the wife – his 'Mathematical Medea'. Annabella may have felt some sort of expiation had been achieved by the confessions, but Byron's subsequent attempt at reconciliation was repulsed. She wrote, 'My determination ought not to be changed.'

The role of Virtue triumphant was at times hard to sustain. It needed, she admitted to a friend in 1816, more energy than she could command. The self-styled angel saw herself as not only a guardian but a martyr. In order to strengthen her resolve she composed a set of self-imposed commandments which should dictate her attitude to the two sinners, Byron and Augusta. She set herself the task of trying not to injure Byron by attracting public sympathy towards herself, yet, perhaps unconsciously, this was exactly what she tried to do.

Annabella's struggle with her natural jealousy of Augusta was considerable. Her relationship with Augusta had always been an ambivalent one for, while she resented her deeply as the cause of her broken marriage, she had always been cordially treated by Byron's sister, who seemed to possess a kind of fascination for Annabella. The relationship was almost a masochistic one. Annabella never learned that love cannot be bought. Rejected again and again, she preferred to keep what she called her 'flinty character' and as she hardened she suffered. Sexual frustration took its toll. She punished herself physically by starving herself : her once plump features and portly frame shrank. If she could not be loved she would be pitied.

A public storm was created by Sir Walter Scott's criticism of her, but she remained calm and proceeded to cross verbal swords with him, earning his respect and an invitation to Scotland. The author found her extraordinarily interesting, but Annabella thought him somewhat pretentious. 'I shall become a shrew after I have engaged a few more reviewers,' she commented.

Her pen became more incisive. Travelling restlessly in an effort to escape the agony of her failed marriage, she visited the cathedral at St Albans, a few miles away across the green Hertfordshire pastures from Brocket Hall, where Caroline Lamb was scandalously frenetic still. 'My ambition is to go to the tower,' she wrote, 'and I hope to look down on Brocket Hall.'

When Byron's 'Manfred' was published, public consternation broke out again. A horrified Annabella accused Augusta, 'He . . . practically gives you away, and implies you were guilty *after* marriage.'[7] To a friend she wondered, 'What does the Queen think?'

In the face of the inevitable publicity, Annabella straightened her back and adopted an attitude of lofty detachment. The strain of maintaining this public front was considerable, and she would often succumb privately to periods of depression and lethargy. Ada, though, was a comfort, and soon another child claimed her attention – Augusta's daughter Emily, whose godmother Annabella had agreed to become. Moved by the strength and beauty of a new 'Childe Harold' canto, she patiently averred her wish to forget the past, but 'How is it possible,' she despairingly wrote, 'when Lord Byron continually revives that discussion . . . through a medium much more powerful than I can command?' Later she conceded, 'He is a monarch of words.'

In May 1817 she visited Newstead Abbey and was enraptured by its loveliness in the early summer sunshine. All she saw and touched – Byron's swords, the flags he handed out on his birthday, the skulls that amused him – recalled the man. 'He might have walked in,' she wrote. 'The parapets and steps where he sat, the leads where he walked. His room – where I was rooted.' The housekeeper did not recognize her visitor and gossiped about Augusta to her, unknowingly turning an old knife in an ever-present wound. Lord Byron, she told Annabella, was 'very fond of Mrs Leigh, very loving to her indeed.' A depression descended on Annabella after this traumatic visit. 'Sorrow had come down upon us with the ice, as well as the weight of the avalanche,' she wrote and declined to be in London

---

[7] Byron wrote, 'In rhyme I can keep more away from fact, but the thought always runs through – through.'

while Augusta was there, fearful of exposing Ada to her supposed evil influence. 'I have an insurmountable repugnance to Ada's being in her company,' she wrote.

Annabella, who had been so loved herself as a child, had lost confidence in her ability to inspire affection in her daughter. 'I had a strange prepossession that she would never be fond of me,' she wrote and the child's love for her mother surprised her. Though consoling, it could not adequately compensate for Byron's loss. Surrounded by women friends, she was often lonely.

News that Byron was writing his memoirs filtered through to Annabella but when offered them she refused to read them and wrote with dismay, 'I am sick, quite sick, of taking my own part.' She prepared to ignore his expected relevations as her best defence. However, confiding that she must *save from ruin a near connection of his* (which could only mean Augusta), she wrote that if he persisted in publishing, she would 'be compelled to make a disclosure of the past in the *most authentic* form.' The question of the memoirs was postponed.

In 1822 Annabella's mother died, forgiving Byron on her deathbed. Her death increased his fortune and Annabella became Lady Noel-Byron, mistress of two country estates. Two years later, aged thirty-seven, Byron was dying, a last message to Annabella unuttered on his lips. Annabella received the news of his death with frightful and frightening distress.

Immediately she was plunged into altercations about Byron's memoirs, a decision about which lay with Augusta, Byron's chief legatee. The manuscript was likely to contain awful revelations and the frantic Augusta wrote to Annabella, 'There is quite sufficient known . . . without this unfortunate memoir having to be canvassed and squabbled over.' Plagued with sick children Augusta yet dreaded the day when, in spite of last minute protests, Annabella's representative Col. Doyle firmly put the memoirs into the fire and they were burned.

The memoirs disposed of, there remained the inheritance, which Annabella believed to be more than £100,000. 'On this subject I shall inviolably adhere to the determination of making no remarks.' Thus wrote the dignified Lady Byron, disinherited by her husband in favour of his sister and her children. Augusta herself was shocked at the reputed sum Byron had bequeathed away from the title and the new Lord Byron. Annabella offered part of the income from her marriage settlement to him, assuring Augusta bleakly, 'I have more than once said to my husband that it was his duty to provide for you and yours.'

In 1825 a new drama was about to unfold, the characters a second Byronic generation. Georgiana Leigh, eldest of Augusta's seven children, became engaged to Henry Trevannion. In spite of Byron's bequest, Augusta, short of money again, wrote to Annabella to beg for financial help to accomplish the marriage, assuring her that the young couple were steady, with modest tastes. Annabella obliged wearily, received Augusta's gushing thanks cynically and further helped the young couple by lending them her house at Canterbury.

Annabella fulfilled her promise to Byron to help Augusta, but Augusta managed to keep her at a distance socially. Annabella confided to a friend similarly treated, 'We have *served her* purpose and are to be discarded it seems.' Augusta was mistress of the gentlewoman's art of using the moneyed. She avoided offering Annabella the affection she desired. Returning to the subject of Augusta and Byron, Annabella wrote, 'I believe she was actuated by it to disunite Lord Byron and me . . . [she] may have *feigned* resistance to his wishes *before me* and permitted them in *private*,' adding contemptuously, 'She has suffered from a kind of moral idiocy since birth.'

Immersing herself seriously in philanthropic activities, Annabella initially and with enthusiasm joined the Co-operative movement but found the meetings, run by pedestrian tradesmen, very disappointing and the back-biting of small societies disillusioning. A learned woman obsessively concerned with educational reform, she opened a school in 1834 with the aim of educating together 'the class out of which the children would be taken and the class to which my family belongs'. The boys were to learn gardening, carpentry and masonry.

For years, Annabella, deeply shocked and indignant, had pondered Byron's confessed homosexuality. Revealed only after her marriage, it had probably been concealed by Augusta, who almost certainly knew of Byron's poems to 'Thyrza', the boy he had loved at Cambridge. Annabella was sure the blame lay with the British Public Schools and a classical education. 'Harrow', Byron had told her, 'had been the grave of his moral being.' Clear-sighted in practical matters and imbued with the ideals of the great Swiss educational reformers, Pestallozzi and his disciple Emmanuel de Fellenberg, whose schools she had seen in action on a continental tour, she determined to expose the British Public Schools as the 'nurseries of corruption and crime', rife with bullying, drunkenness, gambling and sodomy. 'Parents,' she wrote, 'risk the characters and happiness of their sons' by sending them to those establishments. Single-handed and single-minded, nearly a century and a half before the state comprehensive school, she put her ideals of classless learning into practice. The forty-two-year-old widow forestalled the twentieth-century educational reformers in England. Her school was a success and it flourished under her patronage for nearly thirty years. She founded schools in Leicestershire and Ealing, a reformatory for wayward girls at Bristol,[8] and became the friend of Harriet Beecher-Stowe, whose championship of coloured people in America she admired and shared, bequeathing a legacy to a dedicated young abolitionist.

On the subject of the emancipation of slaves, she wrote to that lady : 'There is always in England a floating fund of sympathy . . . and these better feelings . . . are just set free. . . . If you can lay hold of them, they may bring about a deeper abolition than any legislative one – the abolition of heart-heresy, that man's worth comes, not from God, but from man.' Never part of the London society prone to patronize the Charity Ball type of philanthropy,[9] her travels had given her a broad view of coming changes and social needs. Observing the gradual decay of the English church, she advocated unity and a missionary laity. 'Would not a *wider* love supersede the *creed-bound* charity of sects?' she asked.

In 1833 Ada was presented at Court and Lady Byron was obliged to put aside temporarily her philanthropic occupations, to which she had added prison reform, and take a half-hearted interest in dressing her daughter suitably for the Season. 'You would have been amused,' she wrote to a friend, 'had you seen me throwing my mind into ball-dresses . . . but I should be sorry,' she added repressively, 'were she to become occupied with frivolities.' Ada's expressed

[8] Possibly the result of her experience with Medora, who was reduced to the semi-prostitution known as 'protection'.
[9] According to Harriet Martineau's obituary.

fondness for dancing softened Annabella's attitude to social pleasures and though she feared that dancing could be harmful, she conceded it might have a good influence. However, she tried to provide more suitable distractions for Ada by installing a target at her country house in Hampshire, considering archery to be a worthier pastime.

Practical as ever and true to her promise to Byron, when applied to by a Canterbury clergyman, she came to the rescue of Augusta's daughter Medora. The girl was living with her sister Georgiana and her husband Henry Trevannion at Patrixbourne, just outside the cathedral city, where Annabella had lent them her cold, impersonal mansion, Bifrons. Henry Trevannion had seduced Medora, who in 1829 became pregnant. Annabella immediately assisted all three young people to go to France, where the infant died. As compulsively attractive as only a Byron could be, Medora was unable to resist the amoral Trevannion; a second child was born and died and in 1834, a third, surviving child, Marie. For two years Annabella had no contact with Medora.

In the meantime she found herself at Windsor where Queen Victoria's Prime Minister, William Lamb, Lord Melbourne, now a widower, was a frequent visitor. He exercised a paternal influence upon the young Queen as he had been unable to do with his intractable artist-wife Caroline. Since Lord Melbourne was Lady Byron's first cousin, the Queen's curiosity was aroused and Annabella was approached indirectly through him, the Queen wishing to meet Byron's widow. But Annabella had little interest in Royal personages and could not conceive of them as being other than ordinary human beings in an extraordinary position. She declined. 'I have no notion of slaying myself for what is after all of so little importance,' she wrote. 'Rank', she had once written to Lady Melbourne, who had an excessive regard for it, 'is indifferent to me.'

Two years later, discovering that Medora was destitute and desperately ill, Lady Byron went to France to rescue her, armed with zeal for the troubled young Byron who had winningly turned to her for the help only she appeared willing to provide. They travelled together, and in Paris Annabella told Medora what she believed to be the truth about her parentage. 'Her husband', Medora wrote, 'had been my father.' Annabella declared later that Medora already knew the truth but the confirmed fact exacerbated her already highly-strung condition. For the moment, however, the young mother was grateful and showed Annabella all the love for which she craved. Medora was allowed to call her benefactress by the name 'Pip', which Byron only had used to his wife. 'This is a little gleam in my life,' wrote Annabella, 'It will not last, but its memory will be sweet.' She was aware that disillusion would follow.

Annabella unjustly charged the constantly harassed Augusta with neglect of Medora. 'Your affectionate letters to her', she accused, 'must appear a cruel mockery to those who know that you left her, for so long a time, only the alternatives of vice or starvation.' Furiously protective, she adjured Medora's mother, 'Leave her in peace!'

In 1835 Ada, at Annabella's suggestion, travelled to Paris to meet her supposed half-sister Medora, and the two young women became friends. Annabella had written to Ada perhaps the most difficult letter a woman ever had to write to a daughter about her father, only to find that the intelligent Ada had already divined the truth about Byron's relationship with Augusta.

A year as Medora's guardian had convinced Annabella that the girl's wild and wayward temperament was an incurable defect. The person she had come to care for had changed : Medora's gratitude had turned to a furious hatred of her dependence upon Annabella, and her lavish endearments now alternated with petulant outbursts. Annabella had dared to hope that she might be loved by a Byron at last, but she had merely invited a further rejection. Medora sheltered for a time in Annabella's English home, but her paranoia increasingly alienated Lady Byron. Determined to leave the country and longing to dispense with Annabella's necessary bounty, the imprisoned Medora had no choice but to clutch at every penny offered her, meanwhile complaining of its insufficiency.

Worn out from the emotional thrashing she had been subjected to by the girl who yet wrote her affectionate letters from France, Annabella resignedly told a friend, 'My pounds will only follow many others into the vortex of that family,' but she steadfastly continued to support Medora, 'over whose cradle I had watched with peculiar feelings.' Although Medora returned to England once again, ceaselessly harrying Lady Byron among others, the exhausted Annabella refused any further assistance in her own name, wishing to help her anonymously. Medora returned to the south of France, where she finally achieved her dearest wish, marriage, and died in 1849.

The ghost of Augusta's elusive affection continued to torment Lady Byron, who wrote to a friend, 'I love her still! I cannot help it. I shall see her once more in this world before I die.' In 1851 she took active steps to effect a last meeting. Her motive was compounded of a strange mixture of affection and revenge for her life-long rejection by a woman whose charm for Byron and herself the rational Annabella could not fathom. A third party was to be present, a personable and magnetic young preacher who had become Annabella's confidante and adviser.

The two women, both in their sixties, met again at Reigate, thirty-five years after Annabella's separation from Byron. Annabella was intent on extracting a final confession from Augusta of fomenting Byron's continuing hate. 'I told her,' wrote Annabella, 'it was not in human nature for anyone to keep up such animosity as Lord Byron had shown towards me, unless it had been *fed*.' The sight of Augusta disarmed her. 'I saw Death in her face at once,' she wrote. 'I felt utterly hopeless.' But it did not stop her asking her dying sister-in-law her prepared questions. Unable to control her rage and frustration at Augusta's bewildered denials, she had to leave the room. Later the same year Augusta died, Annabella tardily trying to make amends with gifts of money.

The following year Ada died. She had failed to confide to her mother the catastrophic state of her affairs and, unknown to Lady Byron, had enlisted the aid of an Irish writer, another of the many recipients of Lady Byron's bounty. Annabella felt betrayed again, and was only reconciled with her daughter at her last illness. 'I have been taught to accept survivorship,' she wrote.

Her companion now was her grandson Ralph, Ada's third child whom she had made her heir and whose education and character she was determined to develop privately, without subjecting him to the depravities of a Public School. Separated from his family, he went to live with Lady Byron when he was nine years old. Intellectually he prospered under her supervision and, although often lonely and deprived of young company, he did not complain and was devotedly fond of his grandmother.

'This grandson of mine, Ralph, lately eighteen,' Annabella wrote contentedly, 'is I am thankful to say, free of vicious propensity or low habit.' Her tortured experience with Byron, Augusta and

Medora was in the past and at last her theories appeared justified
by the boy under her care, 'his tastes being pure and elevated and
his desire of knowledge almost too great.' While he had not chafed
against living with his ageing grandmother, an unquenchable thirst
for adventure stirred and Annabella, understanding him as easily
as his forbears had perplexed her, wrote, 'He wants to be left to
go . . . where his fancy may lead him,' and she thoughtfully arranged
for him to travel to Scotland alone.

Brought up free of religious convictions, she wrote, 'I hold it to
be a sin to *make* a child say "*I believe.*" . . . Lead it to utter that
belief spontaneously.' Ralph grew to be as honest a free-thinker as
she herself was.

Aged twenty, he wrote to her from Oxford, where his uncon-
ventional upbringing rendered him something of an outcast, 'I
neither have been nor wish to be confirmed. . . . What a mistake it
is to suppose that going to chapel . . . works as an exorcism on the
follies of youth like the sign of the cross to the devil.' She had
tutored him well. 'All forcing-down of religion seems to me a mixture of blasphemy and tyranny,' he wrote and reading this Annabella must have felt gratified.

Ralph supported her pioneering views on education even though
he at times felt an unhappy victim of them. 'The much-praised
classical education of the schools has a less good effect on the mind
than some freer and less exclusive system,' he felt. It was, he told
her, 'chaining the living to the dead.'

In the winter of her life, the comfort of Ralph's respect and
affection at last warmed her chilled heart. Her granddaughter wrote
on her death in 1860 at the age of sixty-eight, 'The end was in sleep,
which passed into the sleep of death – gently and calmly.' Separated
in death as in life from the man she had loved, she was buried, far
from Nottingham and Byron's tomb at Hucknall Torkard, at Kensal
Green next to the family of her lawyer.

Lady Melbourne

'Society is now one polish'd horde.'

Don Juan (Canto XIII, Stanza 9)

Elizabeth Milbanke was born in 1753, daughter of Sir Ralph Milbanke and elder sister to the Ralph Milbanke who was to become Lord Byron's father-in-law. Her family was politically prominent and established in the north of England where three generations had been Members of Parliament. She was beautiful, possessed of a ready charm and early became a skilled opportunist. Elizabeth Milbanke's gifts were too brilliant for restricted northern society and of this she was soon aware. Only in London could she properly scintillate, and when she was sixteen she cleverly chose a husband who could take her there – a woman's only passport to success in those days. She married the baronet Peniston Lamb in 1769 and thus became Lady Melbourne. She was beautiful and clever; he had wealth, and her impecunious father was glad to borrow from his son-in-law for the marriage settlement. Her husband was only twenty years old. He brought his bride to Melbourne House in Piccadilly, and Elizabeth, Lady Melbourne, set out to conquer society.

Confined though she had been to provincial England during her youth, she early acquired, through her relatives, an infallible instinct in how to manoeuvre and rise. Her aims were political and social power, and her weapons a woman's traditional ones, masking a logical mind and a ruthless heart.

Her husband was less gifted and he was also susceptible to other women. Thus, a few months after their marriage he became the devoted lover of a Drury Lane actress. Mrs Sophia Baddeley was a favourite performer of the time, in and out of the theatre, but 'an indulgent public will always make allowances for the frailties of human nature . . . in the contemplation of those striking characteristics which attract attention,' wrote Mrs Elizabeth Steele, the actress's friend and protectress. Having made her début as Cordelia in *King Lear*, Mrs Baddeley quickly acquired a court of numerous high-born lovers from the Prince of Wales downwards, of which Lord Melbourne was the most faithful and the most generous both with cash and diamonds.

'Lord Melbourne took every opportunity to come forward and prove himself,' wrote Mrs Steele. 'This gentleman was about twenty-one years of age, and had been married about ten months to a very amiable woman. . . . He applied . . . to make her . . . an offer of a share of his fortune, in exchange for the possession of her heart. . . . His passion increased . . . and his liberality kept pace with it.' Mrs Baddeley 'had a natural turn for spending money. . . . having almost the command of his Lordship's purse. . . . Lord Melbourne was the son and heir of Sir Matthew Lamb, who amassed great riches by lending out his money to the needy. . . . Had Lord Melbourne been as good a calculator as his father, and not squandered his money as he did, he would have been a much richer man than he now is. . . . His Lordship told me, that he gave a painter two thousand pounds, to paint only one ceiling at his seat at Brocket Hall,' wrote Mrs Steele. For Brocket Hall in Hertfordshire had only recently been completed, replacing a Tudor manor, and the brash bright red brick of which it was built dominated the surrounding landscape.

Mrs Baddeley was usually addressed as 'My Dearest Love' in Lord Melbourne's letters and her husband's infatuation for the notorious Mrs Baddeley was a source of embarrassment to Lady Melbourne's limitless ambition. Lady Melbourne demanded his constant attention and Mrs Steele records that Lord Melbourne 'excused himself for leaving us with so much abruptness, being in great haste he said, to attend his dear Betsy to the play.' On another occasion Mrs Steele recalled that 'Lord Melbourne was come to stay for a few hours. He told her he was going to Bath, at least, he supposed he should; for his dear Betsy had talked of it.' Glumly Lord Melbourne added that 'if he went, he should be gone three weeks.' The pleasures of Bath clearly could not compete with the joys of Mrs Baddeley's company.

Later in the course of this liaison Mrs Steele wrote, 'Mrs Baddeley found herself not well . . . in the way of a married woman; but, wished it might be kept a secret, till Lord Melbourne found it out for himself; but . . . owing to a fright, in losing a favourite cat which . . . was killed by a dog . . . she miscarried.'

Lady Melbourne was in the painful position of having publicly to acknowledge her husband's infatuation with the actress for, as a public favourite, she was unavoidable. 'There was to be a ridotto at the Opera House and the ladies were to appear in fancied dresses without masks,' wrote Mrs Steele. 'The house was crowded with persons of the first rank. . . . Lord and Lady Melbourne were there arm in arm, walked together the whole evening; but, his Lordship did not omit to give Mrs Baddeley many pleasant looks; and even Lady Melbourne bestowed a smile upon her. . . . We staid,' added Mrs Steele, 'till five in the morning.'

While Lord Melbourne, full of compliments, told Mrs Baddeley 'his dear Betsy admired her dress at the Ridotto, and said many civil things of her,' the young Lady Melbourne, still under eighteen was far too astute to express any distaste for her husband's choice of mistress. 'Lord Melbourne could have kissed her dear feet for it,' recalled Mrs Steele; he 'often declared he scarce knew which he loved the best, his wife or Mrs Baddeley,' and Lady Melbourne smilingly hid her contempt. 'My love,' Lord Melbourne wrote to Mrs Baddeley, 'I fear I cannot see you tonight. I am just come to Town to attend Lady Melbourne. . . . I will be with you tomorrow if I can, before you are up.'

Mrs Steele wrote of him, 'Lord Melbourne was not the brightest man of his age . . . acquainted neither with good grammar nor orthography.' Neither was he beloved by the very romantic Mrs Baddeley who, despite her penchant for luxury, succumbed to a grand passion and died in penury. 'Mrs Baddeley was never truly happy in his company, though he had done all in his power to make her so,' wrote Mrs Steele and finally she recorded, 'Lord Melbourne's expence about his house in Piccadilly had occasioned his not being as bountiful as he had been.' Mrs Baddeley became less compliant and his Lordship declared, 'I now see the impropriety of my conduct with Mrs Baddeley, and I have done with her.' The liaison was over.

Elizabeth Lady Melbourne's first son, Peniston, was born in 1770, when she was seventeen. Lord Melbourne's infatuation with Mrs Baddeley left the field open for her to find a lover more to her intelligent taste than her foolish husband. His behaviour quickly instilled in the young wife a completely cynical attitude to the world and its ways. She established herself as one of the leaders of London society and after a time cultivated an intimacy with the less clever but deliciously romantic Duchess of Devonshire, her junior by seven years, whom she chaperoned and instructed in her worldly philosophy. Georgiana, the beautiful young Duchess, had married into a more august line than the Lambs. Lady Melbourne made herself useful in innumerable ways, lending her a maid, recommending a currently modish *frizeur* and introducing her to the sophisticated pleasures of the gaming tables. She also advised her on how to conduct discreet but inevitable love-affairs. Gay husbands, the Duchess was told, have tastes which must be fed with variety.

The Duchess of Devonshire and her sister, Lady Bessborough, lived emotional lives of the utmost complexity. Lady Melbourne appeared to be their friend; that is to say, Lady Melbourne used them as a means to climb the social ladder. They confided in her, but Lady Melbourne confided in no one, a very rare quality in a woman : her romantic secrets remained inviolate, subject only to rumour. Beautiful, intelligent and ambitious, desiring power and success for her children, she sought lovers to further her ambition. She chose carefully and with discretion. Though gossip about her lovers abounded, she was careful not to commit herself to paper nor to a confidante. Lady Melbourne never experienced the reckless courage of a woman in love; she was never anyone's mistress but her own.

William Lamb, her second son, was born nine years after Peniston, by which time Lady Melbourne had taken, learned from and discarded various lovers, and was now established nearer the heart of her universe, Whitehall. The Prince of Wales, later the Prince Regent, had encouraged an exchange of houses between the Duke of York and Lady Melbourne. The former had taken a fancy to the house in Piccadilly upon which Lady Melbourne had lavished large sums in redecoration. But she had no objection to living nearer to Westminster in the house designed by the man who had also designed Brocket Hall. She would also be obliging the Prince of Wales, who had given her his portrait; it now hung at Brocket Hall opposite her own, painted by Reynolds, with Peniston in her arms and entitled 'Maternal Affection'.

Developing a passion for politics not rare in a woman of that time, but in her case all-consuming, she was a frequent visitor to both

4   Elizabeth, Viscountess Melbourne. *Painting by Hoppner.*

5   Melbourne House, Whitehall.

6   Anne Isabella, Lady Byron. *After the painting by J. Newton.*

Houses of Parliament, following every word in an acrimonious debate and glorying in a statesman's brilliant speech. Statesmen were both attracted by her looks and happy to avail themselves of her abundant hospitality, which she was able to offer them conveniently adjacent to the Palace of Westminster. Her astute political sense made her a brilliant conversationalist, well able to influence the most able minds in power. She was not an *eminence grise* but an *eminence rose*, strategically feminine when necessary, ruthlessly masculine when public affairs were under discussion.

Lord Egremont, generally supposed to be William Lamb's father, was a very unusual man. Politically unambitious and a great art patron, he disdained the Englishman's tendency to acquire old masters, but had the taste, foresight and sense of adventure to value and encourage the artists of his own day. He discovered and patronized Turner, to whom he gave the freedom of Petworth Place, later to be immortalized in paint; he also invited the artist to his London dinner table.

Brocket Hall had been as lavishly decorated under Lord Egremont's advice as the house in Piccadilly. The ceiling in the great drawing room, of which Lord Melbourne had so proudly boasted to his Mrs Baddeley, displayed representations of the twelve signs of the zodiac and the four seasons, and was greatly admired. Lord Egremont was consulted about landscapers for the grounds, for Brocket Hall at Lemsford was situated in the heart of lush Hertfordshire, where several noble and ancient families had resided for generations. Set in the valley of the river Lea, it was a pocket of feudalism, and the Lambs, newly arrived from the north, were not always graciously received. Lord Melbourne's peerage, which was Irish and considered inferior, did not carry a seat in the House of Lords. It had been brave of the moneyed northerners to settle in the midst of the inhospitably historic enclave; it required remarkable tenacity and a thick skin to remain. Lady Melbourne had both. However, despite the perfection to which she brought Brocket, she preferred London, the true seat of power, where her resilience and beauty could overcome any snubs occasioned by the display of her husband's affluence.

Lord Egremont was wealthy and leisured enough not to care what the great world thought of him and his mistress. His dislike of ceremony and his warm hospitality made his home seem 'like a great inn' and his motto was 'live and let live'. His generosity to his people in Sussex was limitless. The handsome eccentric, who cared little for the ways of the fashionable world that Lady Melbourne had taken such care to conquer, presented something of an enigma to her. She lived in great style but characteristically avoided feckless extravagance; her establishments were efficiently run with all the business acumen of the Yorkshire woman she had once been. She instantly dropped anyone not likely to prove useful socially. Her younger brother Ralph Milbanke married some years after his glittering sister and his wife Judith was plainly jealous, aware of her deficiencies in the *haut monde* in which Lady Melbourne was secure, sought after and celebrated.

The provincially prudish Lady Milbanke had herself instigated the coolness between herself and Lady Melbourne, of which she later complained, as a result of her sister-in-law's liaison with George Prince of Wales who was probably the father of Lady Melbourne's fourth son, also named George. Since then, Sir Ralph and his Lady had not been seen at Brocket Hall. While Lady Milbanke indignantly drew aside from her promiscuous sister-in-law, Sir Ralph regretted the breach, since, as the leading political hostess of the day, whose home in Westminster was open house to the Prime Minister and other statesmen, Lady Melbourne's influence on his career could be important. He was often at Brocket on his way to and from the north and, unused to lavish dinners and much wine, was prone to fall asleep at his sister's dinner table. 'I am determined not to dispute or quarrel with either of you about anything that has past,' wrote Lady Melbourne to her brother; 'There has been no Coldness on my part. . . . I am just good friends with both of you . . . and if you are not the same it is not my fault.'

Lady Milbanke wrote to her that 'On my return from Brighthelmstone Milbanke showed me some letters which had passed between you and him during my absence. . . . I have with difficulty continued silent.' Feeling unjustly neglected she continued, 'Ever since I married it has been my sincere wish to conciliate the good opinion of Mr Milbanke's family,' but 'I have every reason to believe these endeavours have not met with the success permit me to say they meritted.' Lady Milbanke was hyper-sensitive to the smallest slight, real or imagined, on the part of her powerful sister-in-law, and felt that Lady Melbourne had been two-faced in her

relations with her. There had been, wrote Judith Milbanke, 'in-
sinuations . . . dropped to *others* . . . whilst to my face you observed
the appearance of civility.' Her exclusion from every consultation
between the brother and sister was another sore point, for Judith
Milbanke was not *au fait* with politics as were Lady Melbourne,
Sir Ralph and their brother John. However, Lady Milbanke had the
gratification of seeing their efforts to advance their nephew John,
also a Member of Parliament, come to grief. 'Mr John Milbanke's
schemes have fail'd,' wrote a triumphant Mrs Milbanke; 'He exposed himself greatly, came down to Durham with his Wife & Child
& no Gentleman or Lady took the smallest notice of him.' Clearly
the Milbanke men were not their sister's political equal.

Social jealousy also made things worse between the two sisters-
in-law. 'Visiting is the business of the Mil's life,' wrote a relative
about them. But visiting in the county of Durham could hardly
compete with the splendours of Melbourne House in Whitehall, the
delightfully accessible Brocket only twenty miles or so from London,
and Melbourne in Derbyshire, not to mention Windsor Castle
and Petworth Place to which Lady Melbourne had obtained the
entrée.

The Duchess of Devonshire wrote to her mother of a provincial
festivity she attended with Lady Melbourne in 1779, 'We went to
the ball, it is the most extraordinary sight you ever saw, the odd
dresses and looks of the women, and the number of officers make a
curious medley.' The world Lady Melbourne had escaped from was
one of ill-dressed women and ugly men. The lovely Duchess wrote
that her friend 'Lady Melbourne and I did not intend dancing at
this occasion,' so far below their customary style, unlike another
which the Duchess missed : 'I could not go. . . . My gown was
beautiful, a pale blue, with the drapery etc. of an embroider'd gauze
in *paillons.* I am a little comforted for not going by two messages I
have received by Ly Melbourne and the Duke from the Prince of
Wales to express his disappointment at having missed dancing with
me.'

Lady Melbourne's son Frederick was born in 1782 and George
Lamb two years later. The Prince of Wales was then twenty-two
years old and Lady Melbourne thirty-one. The previous year he had
discovered 'Brighthelmstone', where he was later to rebel against the
severities of classical architecture and build that sumptuously happy

expression of oriental opulence by the English seaside, Prinny's fun palace, the Royal Pavilion at Brighton.

Lady Melbourne's liaison with George Prince of Wales was probably at its height in 1782 when she wrote to the Duchess of Devonshire, 'If you want news, my dt Dss, I must send you a list of all the people that are sick, for that is the only news in town, and unless you have the same disorder going about at Bath, I advise you and the Duke to remain there till this vile nastey influenza ceases. . . . Ld M is at present quite ill . . . I have a cold in my head which I am told is a beginning, but I don't intend to have it any worse, tho' it might perhaps be an advantage to me as it would shake off some of my fat. . . . The De of Richmond has been here and told me you and I were two rival queens, and I believe, if there had not been some people in the room, who might have thought it odd, that I should have slap'd his face . . . and he wished me joy of having the P to myself.' Coolly as she handled most situations, Lady Melbourne commented, 'How odious people are, upon my life, I have no patience with them.' The Prince was often at Brocket and Lady Melbourne at Windsor; she was a channel through which statesmen could influence him. But she used her own judgement. When approached to influence the Prince Regent in favour of Catholic Emancipation in Ireland, she refrained. The Prince remained implacably opposed and Lady Melbourne ever distrusted liberal ideas.

Having conquered her pinnacles of personal achievement in acquiring the future George the Fourth and bearing a fourth son, her object in life became to consolidate her position and advance her children's and her husband's careers. By 1781 her husband had become Viscount Melbourne and was made a Gentleman of the Bedchamber to the Prince of Wales, an appointment which, in addition to his peerages, according to the *Complete Peerage*, Volume VIII, 'can safely be attributed to his wife's charm and skill.'[1]

Lady Melbourne was yet to bear two daughters, Emily in 1787 and Harriet in 1792, retaining always her triumphant position as London's political hostess regnant. She was wise, tactful and tough. Lady Granville wrote of life at Melbourne House, which revolved around the political activities of the time, 'They wander about all

[1] He did not become an English Peer until 1815.

day and sleep about all the evening; no meal is at a given hour, but drops upon them as an unexpected pleasure.'

She promoted her children's advancement tirelessly. It was hard work and required all Lady Melbourne's vitality. She admitted to Lady Holland that 'Bringing them to what is called polish [is] . . . a very arduous undertaking.' In flight from his mother's rigorous grooming, her eldest son found refuge in the more socially relaxed continental life. Frustrated in his determination to continue living there by the French Revolution, he dissipated the last years of his life and died from tuberculosis at the early age of thirty-four. After his death, the Prince Regent thoughtfully lent Lady Melbourne his Royal Pavilion at Brighton in which to recover from her grief.

Two years earlier, the thirteen-year-old Harriet had died from the same disease, greatly mourned by her brother William who wrote that she had 'quickness of perception . . . and promised much.' A spell in a milder climate on the continent had been advised, since the frequent fogs in that part of Hertfordshire were thought to be endangering the child's recovery, but Lady Melbourne did not care for 'abroad' and disregarded the advice.

In 1800 Lady Melbourne, now aged forty-seven, began a correspondence with her near neighbour at Panshanger, the young, handsome, rich and rakish Earl Cowper, aged twenty-two. He appeared to be a most desirable match for her daughter. In addition to Panshanger there was a residence in Hanover Square. Lord Cowper's steadier friend Henry Luttrell wrote to him enviously, 'The spell which binds you to London has I perceive lost none of its force. . . . It is . . . too daring a flight of imagination ever to *suppose* you at Panshanger. The Morning Post corrected me yesterday . . . and ascertained that you were the other night no nearer the great oak than Lady Melbourne's supper room.'

'Death is not a greater leveller than the country,' wrote a miserably confined Luttrell, a hundred miles away from London, 'We must both put up with . . . the shallow stream of rural topics, in place of the full flow of London talk. . . . When you see Lady Melbourne which I suppose will often happen, when she is settled at Brocket, keep me alive in her recollection. I like her, as we are told we should love God, with all my heart, mind and strength.' Lady Melbourne wrote to Lord Cowper numerous, closely-written letters filled with detailed reportage of the parliamentary activity of the day. While the spendthrift young earl was abroad in 1802, Lady Melbourne told him that she had been to the House of Commons to hear his brother speak. 'I must tell you how very well Mr Cowper spoke in the House of Commons. . . . They say his manner was uncommonly pleasing and gentlemanly, & the matter very sensible & well express'd. . . . The situation of parties remains much the same as it was, when I wrote you a very long letter, which I doubt your yet having had the perseverance to read.' Undeterred by her youthful correspondent's probable indifference, Lady Melbourne continued 'Sheridan made a most brilliant speech . . . it is impossible to say too much of the Wit and ability display'd. . . . Of course if you should have ye English newspapers you will see a great deal about it.' This was the year in which all fashionable London went to Paris to pay court to Napoleon. Among the pilgrims were Lady Oxford and her Irish rebel lover, Arthur O'Connor, who had defected to the Napoleonic forces. Lady Melbourne, however, declined to join in the general lionizing, distrusting any alliance with Europe and its ideas, prophetic in her sense of the future gradual erosion of the forces then in power.

In 1803 Lady Melbourne wrote in answer to a disappointed Lord Cowper, 'I was yesterday reminded by a letter from Mr Luttrell, in which he mentioned your having written to me, that I had not answered that of yrs. . . . So great a favour required, it must be confess'd, an earlier acknowledgement, & considering all the difficulties with which you had to struggle, such as bad materials, candlelight & weary eyes deserved warm expressions of gratitude.' Lady Melbourne was aware that her obsession with politics might have bored the young rake. 'I . . . have been unwilling to return it by sending you an uninteresting letter, & only hope that after reading this you will not say, that I had better have waited a little longer. . . . I have not yet forgot yr turn for criticism. . . . My great regard for you & my friendship . . . must give way . . .', and Lady Melbourne returned to her passion for public affairs.

Two years later, a newly-engaged Emily Lamb, eighteen, wrote to her fiancé Lord Cowper, 'That I should be writing to you today, appears so very surprising so very extraordinary that I can hardly bring myself to believe that it is not all a dream. – And yet I should be very sorry to doubt the reality – I can tell you no news except . . . that I have been riding with Caro up the park and saw Lady

Harrington at her window who for a wonder smiled upon me . . . I enclose the sketches of two rural Bridges which you may perhaps think pretty Goodbye dear Lord C I don't know how to make a *proper* ending so I will break off at once & hope you like short endings as much as I do short speeches.'

Lady Melbourne wrote gracefully to Lord Cowper about his engagement to the charming Emily, 'If you should not have any particular engagement you will perhaps meet us at Brocket Hall. . . . my mind has of late been so harassed between grief & Joy that this additional happiness has nearly overcome me – I had hardly suffered myself to form a wish upon the subject of her marriage as I was so decided that it ought to depend entirely upon her own choice but no other would have made me so completely happy & I assure you that ye delight I feel at giving her to you, has entirely replaced ye regrets I expected to feel at parting with her.' But ever astutely practical she added, 'I must say one word upon business – We were told . . . that it was always the *proper form* for the Lady's attorney to go to ye Gentleman. . . . whenever ye chuse this should be done let me know to whom you would have him go – after this I hope I shall not have to bore you any more about all these forms.' Lady Melbourne's morals might be questioned but she did not err when it came to 'proper form'.

In 1805 William Lamb, now heir to the title, became engaged to Caroline Ponsonby, daughter of Lady Melbourne's close friend Lady Bessborough and niece of the Duchess of Devonshire. The match was welcomed although 'there was no fortune to speak of on the Bessborough side,' wrote Lord Granville Leveson-Gower. The Bessboroughs were an ancient family whereas the Lamb title was, as they say in the servants' hall, bought. Lady Bessborough wrote, 'Yesterday, after various unpleasant *cuts*, she told me she hoped the Daughter would turn out better than the Mother. . . . I felt hurt . . . and only said I hoped and believed she would prove much better – "especially (I added) with the help of your advice" (I would not say example).' Lady Melbourne was jealous of Lady Bessborough's charm which had first captivated her son before he fell in love with her daughter. She was also anxious about William's income, for Lord Melbourne, foolish though he was, realized that his heir was probably not his son and declined to allow him the munificent £5,000 a year that Peniston had enjoyed.

Cuts, delivered by her sharp tongue, earned Lady Melbourne the name of 'The Thorn', bestowed on her by the softly gentle Lady Bessborough. The verbal sparring she excelled at made mincemeat of the two aristocratic sisters' sensibilities.

William Lamb gently reproved his mother about this waspish trait : 'Everybody has foibles from which no quarantine can purify them. No resource remains but to make up your mind to put up with them.' He was critical of the intolerantly cruel fun she made : 'As to . . . laughing people out of them,' he told her, 'which by the way you are . . . inclined . . . it only confirms them – makes the person ridiculed hate you into the bargain.'

William was Lady Melbourne's most able son whose ability she recognized and for whom she was most ambitious; to see him enamoured of lisping, boyish Caroline, with her convention-flouting ways, was anathema to Lady Melbourne although her concealed jealousy of her daughter-in-law was only properly revealed later.

1805, the year of Peniston Lamb's death, saw George Lamb's début as a dramatist. George loved the theatre and the company of actors and Lady Elizabeth Foster wrote to her son of a visit 'with Lord and Lady Abercorn at the Priory, Stanmore, where rehearsing was going on for an opera by George Lamb called "Whistle for it" in which William Lamb was to play.' It was 'more like bedlam than a house in the country. The snow was falling so fast and was so deep Georgiana decided not to wait for the performances but to go to Chiswick as fast as she could to avoid being stranded.' The opera the Duchess of Devonshire missed was a moderate success when it was later produced at the Drury Lane theatre as were several farces George Lamb wrote.

During this momentous year Lady Elizabeth Foster wrote 'Of private news . . . Caroline Ponsonby is to be married to William Lamb, now an elder brother. It is to be next week, and Lord Cowper's marriage is declared with Emily Lamb, and they are all to be here tonight. These are certainly two as pretty marriages as possible. The Melbournes, as the Queen goodnaturedly said, wanted this consolation after their trying misfortunes.'

Lady Melbourne's misfortunes, after some years of uninterrupted triumph, had just begun. For her to manipulate politicians, princes and Prime Ministers was easy. To handle Caroline Lamb was less feasible. In 1807 Lady Melbourne's first grandson was born, a moment when a woman sees the dynasty she has founded spread out before her into the unseen future. Given his parentage and prospects he should have been a brilliant boy. When it became clear that he was not, Lady Melbourne dismissed him from her mind.

Emily Lady Cowper was settled near her mother at Panshanger. Here, Lord Cowper exercised the greatest self-indulgence, advised by his friend Henry Luttrell to take 'an hour or more brisk exercise either on foot or horse back, *before breakfast* . . . But above all, my dear Lord Cowper, *less wine* . . . much *less wine*.' A guest at Panshanger wrote, 'I have discovered a tendency to inflammation in the back of my great toe. . . . In consequence of an uncontrolled indulgence in the pleasures of the table for the last three days, which a turtle of the justest proportions, made it impossible to resist . . . the great work is expected to be finally settled this present evening . . . the spoon is to be in yr mouth at six o'clock precisely. Should his Lordship go up to Parliament . . . and offer the Vicar a place in his post-chaise, he would do very wrong to let . . . an opportunity escape of tasting one quart of Lord Cowper's best claret.'

Such a licentious age had its penalties. Members of the Royal College of Surgeons advertised openly in the *Morning Post* that they 'May be consulted in every stage of the VENEREAL DISEASE, with that delicacy and honorable secresy . . . Cases of a slight nature they are enabled to eradicate in three days. . . . their efforts in the case of syphilis . . . a success . . . greatly evinced by the number of private testimonials. . . . Country Patients corresponded with until recovered.'

Meanwhile the free-loving and -living aristocracy had favours to be sought. A cringing curate waiting to step into another's shoes wrote supplicatingly to Lord Cowper of 'Lucton School in Herefordshire where I had the felicity of being flogged occasionally for nine or ten years . . . It is very probable that the Perpetual Curacy of Orlton in Herefordshire in the disposal of the Governors of Lucton School will soon be vacant, for the incumbent has been ill for the last three years and [I] shall be much obliged to you to say anything you can for me . . . I wrote more than two years ago on this subject, but he declined giving any promise till the Curacy was vacant.'

In London, the Peninsular War was the dominant topic of conversation. In 1808 Lady Elizabeth Foster wrote to her son, 'Nothing but Spain hardly is talked or thought of. . . . Besides the

great interest which everybody feels about the Spaniards, the having
an English army now actually joined . . . and ready to co-operate
with them, brings the war home to everybody's feelings. . . . .
From Galicia you will see accounts are every day expected of action.'
Eighteen months later Lady Elizabeth wrote, 'The Tower guns have
announced today the glorious victory gained by our favourite Sir
Arthur Wellesley . . . Twenty pieces of cannon, four eagles, and
10,000 slain of the French army. . . . If they imitate their countrymen at Zaragossa and Gerona they will do so. . . . I and Lady Granville had been fighting with Mr Vernon, and he was saying that he
wished Sir Arthur back again . . . that he could not advance from
want of shoes and money. . . . To Lady Melbourne he said he hoped
she was not John Bull enough to believe we could fight the French
with such inferiority of numbers.' To this, Lady Melbourne cut-
tingly replied that 'She longed to see him again to triumph over
him.'

Frederick Lamb was Lady Melbourne's third and most devoted
son. Unable to find her equal, he did not marry until long after her
death. During her lifetime he was often abroad but in spite of suffering 'all the full horrors of sea-sickness', Frederick wrote to his
mother frequently with a steady hand. In his letters a fond domestic
note is struck, at odds with Lady Melbourne's public image of a
scheming beauty. Frederick had sent his sister Emily some attar of
rose and offered to send his mother some, 'for it is not dear,' he
added frugally. 'I send you six shawls,' he wrote in 1818, 'one red
for yourself because you're supposed to like it best, a yellow one for
Ly Holland with my love . . . four others out of which you, Emily
and the two Caros are to choose.' From Germany he wrote, 'With
this you will receive a parcel of sable fur which I ordered from
Russia. . . . I think it may save you many colds for many winters
coming out of the opera house . . . Only don't be stingy of it but
have a good pelisse lined with it as they do here.'

For her part Lady Melbourne, the affectionate mother, sent him
the home comforts he asked for. 'Let Brogan ferret or Titmus stoat
a dozen or two of rabbits,' he requested, 'and do you order House
to make me as much more palatable soup as she did before – it has
been my breakfast all this hot weather . . . only half a bladder full
left.' She sent him venison and a riding whip, but Frederick was
firm about her efforts to advance his career – 'None o' your swigging

my dear mother,' he told her; 'power restrained is more honourable than power employed.' Lady Melbourne wrote to the Prince Regent on Frederick's behalf, 'Many thanks dear Lady Melbourne for your kind note respecting Fred,' he replied, 'If you have nothing particularly to do this evening & will allow me to call upon you at eleven o'clock, I will then talk the whole matter over with you. . . . I think it an age since I have had the pleasure of seeing you. . . . ever your sincere Friend & humble servant George.'

George Lamb's proposed marriage with the other Caroline was considered disastrous by Lady Melbourne. Aged twenty-two, he was in love with Caroline St Jules, illegitimate daughter of Lady Elizabeth Foster, later to become the second Duchess of Devonshire. 'Zooks,' wrote Frederick to his mother, 'hang these marrying fellows. . . . I am most sincerely sorry for . . . his having fallen among such a set of ladies . . . that poor G had a sort of marrying genius I always knew.' Frederick suspected his sister-in-law's meddling : 'I remember something as if our Caro had had no small hand in it.' For a time Frederick was stationed in a troubled Ireland, 'fifteen regiments coming from England in the middle of a stormy winter and a hundred dragoons patrolling Dublin every night without the least apparent reason.' But George Lamb's marriage turned out better than the family feared, although childless. William wrote in later years praising Caro George, as she was known, for her kindness and stability. The two Caros and their husbands were quartered under Lady Melbourne's shrewd eye at Melbourne House as was the custom of the day.

On one occasion Frederick wrote to his mother indignantly, 'What, is it possible you can have as much demeaned yourself as to go to the Priory after the contempt and neglect with which they have treated you?' Aware that Lady Melbourne's reputation was not untarnished, his devotion to her was loyally constant. 'I don't like to burn your letters,' he wrote whilst at sea, 'and have nowhere to put them, and no pocket . . . would hold another so tomorrow some must be torn . . . believe how much more I regret you than I have ever said.'

In 1812 Byron, then aged twenty-four, made his maiden speech in the House of Lords. The following year, despair and distress at her daughter-in-law's Byronic exhibitionism, added to the private unhappiness of her ablest son, whose burgeoning political career was being jeopardized by Caroline, pointed the way for Lady Melbourne to use her greatest arts. Aged sixty-two and decidedly plump, her good looks were by no means gone. She still had fine eyes, a sharp intelligence and years of successfully practised female charm behind her. Men had always found it easy to confide in her since she was discreet and unshockable; by September the correspondence between Byron and Lady Melbourne had begun. 'If she had been a few years younger, what a fool she would have made of me,' wrote Byron. Writing as candidly as he would have to a man, 'One must make love mechanically, as one swims,' he told her, 'but now as I never swim, unless I tumble into the water, I don't make love till almost obliged.'

Lady Melbourne had launched her children on their various courses and needed a new outlet for her abundant energies. Her family and Caroline's were outraged by the latter's antics and Byron was desperate to be free of her : all looked to the dominating Lady Melbourne for a solution. Byron agreed he needed managing. 'So far from being ashamed of being governed,' he wrote to Lady Melbourne, 'I am always but too happy to find one to regulate me or misregulate me. . . . Will you undertake me?' She would. Byron wrote, returning a letter Lady Melbourne had sent on from Lady Bessborough, 'The end of Lady B's letter shall be the beginning of mine. "For Heaven's sake do not lose your hold on him." Pray don't, *I* repeat, and assure you it is a very firm one.'

Lady Melbourne's letters were as fascinating as her presence. 'Will you honour me with a line at your leisure?' asked Byron, 'On the most *indifferent* subjects you please.'

Lady Melbourne in her late middle age was still not without the power to arouse Byron's romantic feelings. Doubtless if he had been encouraged to do so he might have made love to her, and his letters throughout their correspondence were full of a blind admiration which flattered the older woman with their constant references to her beauty and power over him. He was, however, aware of her duplicity. 'If I were looking in your face, "entre les deux yeux" ', wrote Byron, 'I do not know whether I should find "frankness or truth" but . . . I would not have it changed for any other expression; as it has defied time, no wonder it should perplex me.' He maintained a barrage of overwhelming gallantry, and it says much for her control and discretion that she was able to retain her cool influence over him. '*You* would be obeyed even in absence,' he told her.

Early in their correspondence Lady Melbourne's niece Annabella was mentioned, since Byron admitted, 'My dear Lady M., I am completely in your power. . . . If through your means . . . I can be free, or at least change my fetters . . . The woman I mean is Miss Milbanke . . . and I am told that her father is ruined.' He was not quite ruined but, should he be, Miss Milbanke was heiress to the Wentworth estates.

Lady Melbourne knew of her brother's financial problems, incurred through unsuccessful electioneering, and here seemed a splendid opportunity of killing three troublesome birds with one brilliant stone. If she could arrange Annabella's marriage to Byron, he would be 'governed', for her niece was known to be a strong character. Her brother's money problems might be eased and, once Byron was safely married, Caroline's volcanic imprudences would subside. 'Poor Annabella,' wrote Lady Melbourne mockingly to Byron. Her prudish niece's disapproval of her glittering wordly aunt was voiced early on her introduction to the supposed pleasures of opera-going, used by the fashionable world merely as a transparent excuse for coquetry. Annabella scornfully commented, 'It was a considerable fatigue to me who do not take pleasure in flirting.' Lady Melbourne had no such repressive instincts and wrote to Byron that her niece's 'innocent eyes will improve if she should be in love with you. Eyes require that sort of inspiration.' But she cautioned him, 'Do you think you can manage both her and C? Impossible!'

'I should like it of all things, were it only for the pleasure of calling you *aunt*!' Byron told Lady Melbourne. 'When I do see a woman superior not only to all her own [sex] but to most of ours, I worship her . . . And when I know that men of the first judgement and the most distinguished abilities have entertained . . . an opinion which my own humble observation, without any great effort of discernment, has enabled me to confirm . . . you will not blame me for following the example of my elders and betters, and admiring you certainly as much as you were ever admired.'

Lady Melbourne was not squeamish in her methods of disentangling Byron from Caroline, who had been sent to Ireland. 'A Letter of mine to you (before the voyage) was found by her . . . but *who* was careless? *Ma tante* . . . if you left it in ye way on purpose, it had a blessed effect. . . . How could you, Lady M., how could you "wear a pocket with a hole in it ! !" ' he disbelievingly mocked. He reassured Lady Melbourne, 'Whatever step you take to break off this affair has my full concurrence.' But he remonstrated at the callousness of a suggestion of hers, *'What* you wished me to write, would be a little too indifferent; and that would be an insult, and I am much unwilling to hurt her feelings.'

Lady Melbourne was flamboyantly addressed by Byron as *'mia carissima Zia! !'* but she did not care for the name. 'Not Zia; what then shall it be? Choose your own name,' he invited.

In October of that year Byron proposed to Annabella Milbanke through her aunt Lady Melbourne and was refused, Byron thought because of another attachment. 'I should have very much liked to be *your relation,*' he wrote; 'Tell A that I am more proud of her *rejection* than I can ever be of *another's acceptance* . . . with one of your wicked laughs.'

Though in reality this rejection rankled, Byron was enjoying the correspondence with Lady Melbourne too much to dwell on it. 'What famous letters *your own* are,' he told her, 'I never saw such traits of discernment, observation of character, knowledge of your *own sex* and sly concealment of your *knowledge* of the *foibles* of *ours.*' Lady Melbourne had not given up hope of securing Annabella for Byron and Annabella's interest had been sufficiently aroused for her to send her aunt an analysis of his character, which she promptly sent on to the poet. Byron told Lady Melbourne, 'Say what you please for, or of me,' to Annabella, but he agreed with her sage counsel : 'Not a word to C !' and assured her, 'I who do not write at all, am in no danger of betraying our conspiracies.'

Now enjoying an affair with the experienced Lady Oxford, Byron wrote still to Lady Melbourne, 'I would not give up your friendship . . . for five thousand Carolines . . . I mean (*entre nous,* my dear Machiavel) to play off Ldy O against her,' adding an ironic postscript, 'My *love* to Ld M.' Byron had not yet come to know Lord Melbourne, so compartmented a life did Lady Melbourne lead.

Between the letters they met, and her ascendancy over him was confirmed. 'I thank my good genius that I have still two good eyes left to admire you with,' wrote Byron, 'and a head (uncracked) which will derive great benefits from anything which may spring from your own . . . *everywhere* I remember you . . . I certainly am very much enchanted, but *your spells* will always retain their full force. Try them,' he challenged.

The subject of Annabella was kept alive by Lady Melbourne. Byron told her, 'My principal inducement was the tie to yourself, which I confess would have delighted me,' but admitted, 'I congratulate A and myself on our mutual escape. That would have been but a cold *collation*, and I prefer hot dinners.'

Caroline was a continuing disturbance. Byron wrote, 'My hope now rests with you and your influence over her, which I know to be great over *all* who *know* you . . . she at most can only *guess* at what has passed of our correspondence. Upon your advice much will depend . . . You will tell me if Ldy B and I are to be on terms, and *how*, and *why*, and *wherefore*, and *when,* and *but*, and *if*, &c., down to the very "*pourquoi* of the *pourquoi*".'

In November the Prince Regent opened Parliament and Byron wrote to Lady Melbourne, 'I never laughed at P (by the bye, this is an initial which might puzzle posterity when our correspondence bursts forth in the 20th century).' The future George IV had become a butt for the satirists of the day and Byron wrote to Lady Melbourne ridiculing the 'romantic melodrama' of 'the regency début'. Disillusioned with his own country, he planned to leave. 'All I like now is gone,' he told Lady Melbourne, 'and all I abhor remains, viz. the R(egent), his government; and most of his subjects.' The Prince's circle Byron held in scorn : 'I missed you last night,' he told Lady Melbourne; 'Our party had all the refuse of the Regent . . . I never saw anything like it but a print from a scene in Dante's Inferno.'[2]

At some time they had exchanged rings, indicating a closer relationship than a friendship between a young man and an older woman. You have long ago forgotten a certain ring,' Byron told Lady Melbourne, 'and I hope you will not reject the only thing I ever dared to present you, nor violate ye conditions on which I accepted your own !' The ageing viscountess's senses may have been

---

[2] Byron's disgust with the obese Regent and his entourage, shared by many, had no doubt been aroused partly by the Prince's treatment of his wife, Caroline. Caroline of Brunswick, the Prince Regent's cousin and estranged wife, whom he married after Mrs Fitzherbert, enjoyed great public affection and popularity. Markedly egalitarian, she preferred the company of commoners and shared Byron's fervent admiration for Napoleon. Although she lived in Kensington Palace for a time, records have suppressed her connection, and she was excluded from her husband's coronation, dying seventeen days later.

more stirred than Byron realized. They were together on a number
of occasions at Middleton and at Eywood and a puzzled Byron
wrote, 'I don't understand you,' to Lady Melbourne when she confessed to him, 'What I found fault with at M[iddleton] I should have
wished at E[ywood],' to which Byron answered, 'Your Ladyship is
enigmatical – a perfect Sphinx – and I am not Oedipus . . . you
don't say whether you will patronize me any further.'

At this time Byron was flashing between Lady Oxford, Lady
Frances Webster and Augusta Leigh. Lady Melbourne wrote from
Cheltenham Spa, 'You cannot expect me, with my head full of these
Waters . . . to understand and unravel the confusion tht. exists
amongst all the different ladies you allude to.' 'If you knew but *ten*
of the *twenty* scrapes I am in at this moment,' he confided to Lady
Melbourne, who neatly impaled him with the sharpest thorn in her
armoury, her niece Annabella. 'As a friend I say flirt as much as you
please but do not get into a serious scrape before you are safe from
the *present* one . . . the best thing you can do is to marry, & that in
fact you can get out of this scrape by no other means.' For a woman
renowned for her sagacity this advice was extraordinarily ill-judged.
Why did she do it? For an ageing, beautiful star who has wielded
power in the highest sphere, there is no more disagreeable prospect
than a withering old age of fading influence. By pinning Byron, as
she thought, to her side through Annabella, she vainly attempted to
ensure the continuity of her reign.

In February of the following year Lady Melbourne proposed a
meeting with Annabella. Byron wrote, 'I shall be very happy to
encounter A,' in the same letter showing that he was sensitive about
having appeared unattractive before Lady Melbourne. 'I saw you
last night,' he wrote, 'but I was literally jammed in between a cursed
card-table and an elbow-chair, so that I could not rise but in the
most ungainly of all possible postures, and you are the last person
before whom I would appear more awkward in my devoirs than I
naturally am.' On the 22nd of the same month he wrote, 'Today I
am twenty-five years of age, and yours for as many centuries, dear
Ldy M.'

In March in answer to Lady Melbourne's request for a lock of
his hair, Byron wrote, 'I send you . . . the precious addition, though
I already gave you enough for a peruque,' and in May Lady Melbourne had persuaded her husband to ask him to dinner. 'Your

invitation is tempting in various ways :– firstly, I never yet dined at M House – there is *novelty*; secondly, I never expected that Lord M at all events would be my inviter – there is *surprise*; thirdly, the pleasure of meeting you . . . something better than both.'

During that spring Lady Melbourne suggested a rendezvous with Byron to view the portrait Reynolds had painted of her with the infant Peniston. 'I MUST see you at Sir Joshua's,' wrote Byron, 'though I don't much like venturing on the sight of *seventeen*; it is bad enough *now*,' he added mockingly, 'and must have been *worse then*.' Lady Melbourne considered that Reynolds had depicted her looking older than the seventeen she then was. 'The painter was not so much to blame as you seem to imagine by adding a few years,' Byron told her with irresistible gallantry; 'He foresaw you would lose nothing by them.'

Her conversation, he told her, was 'really *champagne*' to his spirits and demanded, 'Ld M . . . how many years has he been your proprietor? . . . Why won't *you* go off with me?' Teasingly he added, 'I am sure our elopement would . . . cause a "greater sensation" . . . since Eve ran away with the apple.'

Lady Melbourne complained to Byron about Caroline's behaviour and he answered, 'I don't wonder at your dislike to C. . . . I do think you have already done at least tenfold more than anyone on earth would have done.' Heroic efforts to persuade William Lamb to arrange a legal separation from his wife were being made, his mother being the prime mover. Lady Melbourne, impatient at her son's surrender to Caroline, exploded to Byron that she was surrounded by fools and felt that she had lost control over the situation and was no longer in Byron's confidence. He retorted, 'I don't tell you anything ! . . . everybody rates me about my confidences with you.' Augusta had written and warned him ' "This must not go to Ly M" ', he told her, 'and, to punish you, it *shan't*.'

Augusta was aware of Lady Melbourne's propensity for manipulating people; she had herself been a victim seven years earlier. Byron wrote to Lady Melbourne, 'My sister . . . I wish she were not married . . . Poor soul ! . . . thanking you for your abetment of her abominable marriage !' Though how Lady Melbourne promoted Augusta's match to her feckless cousin is unknown.[3]

[3] They were distantly related by marriage.

Aware that incest had been practised in Ancient Rome, Byron was blindingly honest about his feelings for his sister. Addressing Lady Melbourne as '*ma mère*', he demanded 'why I should not marry X.'⁴ But Lady Melbourne respected only the laws of the universe as represented by English society and accused him of 'depriving of all future peace . . . a woman who has hitherto . . . maintained a good reputation.' The heart's laws signified nothing in her sphere.

At Annabella's request her aunt was not to know of the renewed correspondence between the heiress and Byron, and he respected her wish. It must have been something of a surprise to Lady Melbourne, therefore, when she received a brief sentence from Byron, 'Miss Milbanke has accepted me . . . May I hope for your consent, too? Without it,' he told her, 'I should be unhappy.' Lady Melbourne had slyly praised Annabella to Byron by pointing out the niece's resemblance to her aunt. 'So her "eyes are like yours" ', he answered; 'a little less mischievous I hope; though I believe you see without them, at least you observe things that escape all other optics.'

Emily wrote, as mischievous if less openly designing than her mother, to Lord Cowper, 'I must tell you of a marriage which I think will amuse you and as it is a great secret I shall put it in cypher for security and as good practice if you have curiosity enough to unravel it . . . jmsc axsmp to bppbadjjb.' Unwilling to strain her husband's brain too much Emily made her code transparently simple : Lord Byron to Annabella. 'It will make a certain devil go mad if it takes place,' she prophesied, meaning of course Caroline. Her pen running on without dash or comma she added, 'The P has been staying three days at Hampton Court . . . sitting up all night and getting very drunk. . . . write me some long letters as I do this filled with trifles . . . I shall not have courage to gather mushrooms by myself.'

Later, Emily, who had suffered a fall and was recovering with her mother, wrote to her husband again, 'Caroline has got the House full of people, Bessboroughs innumerable, so that Mama says she is very glad to go with me and to avoid them. . . . Lord Byron's

⁴ Byron's sign for Augusta was 'X'. Caligula married his sister Agrippina AD 37-47. Incest did not enter the criminal law calendar until 1908, but the Incest Act of 1567 made incest a crime under Scottish law. The frisson of horror the word incest aroused was based on a religious taboo, not founded on biological fact.

marriage is publicly announced in all the Papers. I should like to see George with his Physiognomic machine . . . the weather continues delightfully warm and fine tho' now and then a little easterly wind.' Lady Melbourne added a note to her daughter's letter, 'I hope the perfect quiet of this place will restore her strength. . . . Emily has I believe told you everything like news that this place affords.' The chill breeze from the east was a portent.

Lady Melbourne wrote urgently to Byron from Brocket a few days later, 'I find that we shall certainly be in Town on Monday. . . . Pray let me see you on Tuesday morning, at any time. . . . If it should so happen that you are setting out on Tuesday you might call upon me Monday evening. *Les entrées sont libre pour un Neveu a toute heure* . . . yours ever, E.M.'

George Leigh, Augusta's husband, was not enthusiastic about the forthcoming marriage of his brother-in-law, 'He knows that I have made X my heiress,' Byron told Lady Melbourne '. . . I can see he don't like . . . my wife's being in his way . . . he advised me not to be in a hurry, and I know but one motive.' Lady Melbourne, an able administrator, took a hand in the arrangements for the marriage settlement, advising Lord Byron and considering the family solicitor Hanson tiresomely slow.

In November Byron had taken a house in Hampshire for his bride. 'I think it will suit us very well,' he told Lady Melbourne, but this idea did not suit Lady Melbourne. Hampshire was very out of the way and on her suggestion Byron instead took the large and expensive house in Piccadilly Terrace belonging to the Duchess of Devonshire, which was to add very considerably to his financial troubles.

'My dearest Aunt,' he wrote to Lady Melbourne on 3 January, 'We were married yesterday . . . so there's an end of that matter, and the beginning of many others.' A few days later he reminded his new aunt, 'Recollect *we* are to keep our secrets and correspondence as heretofore, mind that.' Towards the end of the month Byron wrote ironically, 'I cannot sufficiently admire your cautious style since I became chicken-pecked, but I love thee, *ma tante* . . . your doubts (implied but not expressed) . . . will last till the next scrape I get into; and then we shall wax confidential again. . . . I look upon you as my good genius.'

On the last day of January Lady Melbourne was unwell and

wrote at length to Byron, 'I have been longing to write to you these
three or four days, but have been incapable – a complaint . . . laid
me upon my couch in a state of stupefaction. . . . It is a sort of
nervous headache which affects your sight, and sometimes you see
half a face, and sometimes two faces . . . when it goes off it
terminates in a violent headache, and leaves you quite unhinged.'
The powerful Lady Melbourne's reign was drawing to a close, for
her health was failing. She teased him, 'What a suspicious person
you are ! . . . I willingly accept the office in which you have installed
me, and hope always to be your *corbeau blanc*.' There followed
gossip about a Duke, upon whom Lady Melbourne commented,
'When a fool shows such a want of steadiness and principle I only
laugh at him.' More entertaining tittle-tattle followed but in between
a serious note was sounded : 'Write to me, *mon cher Neveu, et
choississez votre temps* . . . keep faith with me, and say nothing . . .
although you have no *Corbeau noir*, you may have one flying about,
with many black feathers in her plumage.'

In February, ignorant of Byron's terrifying behaviour towards his
wife, she wrote again in reply to a letter from Byron in which he
gave no hint of being anything other than a contented bridegroom.
'The future depends upon yourself,' Lady Melbourne told him,
adding intimately, 'When I write to you it is as I talk to you, *à
coeur ouvert*, when you are sitting on ye couch opposite to me – and
we soon laugh away an hour . . . Does the end make up for the
beginning?' She reminded him, 'You know you gave me *liberté
entière*,' and, unaware of impending catastrophe, added a postscript,
'You seem altogether comfortable, which delights me.'

Byron's erupting personal problems caused their intimacy to cease
somewhat abruptly. Possibly Byron realized too late how ill his
divine goddess had served him, that she had indeed been his dark
omen, his 'black raven'. He was seriously in debt, and disastrously
ill-matched with Annabella.

In April Byron wrote a strangely stilted note to Lady Melbourne.
It reads in complete contrast to his former frankness. He had
glimpsed her, half-hidden behind the curtains of a theatre box, and
he now informed her of Annabella's pregnancy.

In 1813 Byron had made his second speech in the House of Lords
on the subject of Catholic Emancipation in Ireland. It was an
emotional speech, full of drama and psychological truth and, together

with his previous year's speech in support of the frame-breakers of Nottingham, must have aroused considerable hostility. Byron was neither mad nor bad, as Caroline had written, but he was politically dangerous to know. It was during this summer that he confided to Annabella his plans for a 'Paris Scheme'. Annabella had written to her sister-in-law that her mother had 'relieved my mind about the foreign scheme by a mode of prevention.'[5]

Early the following year, Annabella and the infant Ada departed from Piccadilly and a puzzled, ailing Lady Melbourne wrote to Byron, 'There is a report about you . . . I think you should be informed of it. They say you and Annabella are parted. . . . I think you ought to desire her to come to Town, or go to her yourself.' She herself was unwell again, she told him; 'I am still confined to the house. . . . I should like to see you . . . and tell you several things which I do not like to write.' Byron went to see her and, although she attempted to mediate between them, his charm and sincerity convinced her that the breach was Annabella's fault. It was not difficult. Lady Melbourne had always disliked her prudish and disapproving niece.

Caroline, unwilling to be excluded from the developing drama, induced Annabella to pay her a visit, reported to her that her mother-in-law was completely infatuated with Byron and blamed the failure of the marriage on Annabella's cold and rigid nature. Caroline also alleged that Lady Melbourne had at one time persuaded Byron to make love to her and that, although repelled by her ageing person, he had reluctantly obliged. While it is impossible to give credence to this, Lady Melbourne had certainly not remained unaffected by Byron's constant flattery. Although older than he, and reputedly so sagacious, she too had fallen prey to his magnetism and had become yet another of his victims. She whose heart had seemed impregnable for nearly fifty years, had made the one great personal mistake of her career. She had allied herself to a losing party : Byron's.

Lady Melbourne's day was over. Ill, disappointed and distressed by the public furore, she wrote to her brother, 'I am miserable to think what A must have suffered before she would have resolved to

---

[5] The truth about the 'Paris Scheme', whatever it may have been, has yet to emerge.

bring such an appeal before the World. . . . Ld Byron . . . came to me the day before this report . . . and for an hour talk'd only of her many amiable qualities and how much he lov'd her. . . . I must feel extremely sorry for both at the same time that I respect your motives for concealment . . . you speak of the necessity of the measures you have taken. . . .' Certain forces of the reigning Establishment had quietly concerted to oust the poet and his dangerous ideas from a country where he could be a potent influence for republicanism. During the separation crisis, an august personage had called on Byron, suggesting that he should change his political opinions. Byron had refused.

Byron had been too devotedly her admirer to criticize Lady Melbourne; soon he was in exile and she was dying. William sent daily bulletins to the family and Frederick was summoned from abroad. Lord Egremont did not stay for her death, but wrote to William Lamb, 'I never met with her equal for strong understanding . . . in another sex.' This to the man who was probably his son and Queen Victoria's Prime Minister.

The brilliantly gifted Lady Melbourne was born 200 years too early. In the twentieth century she need not have used 'her *own canal*', as Henry Luttrell coarsely put it, in order to influence events through her lovers and children,[6] but could have become a powerful stateswoman in her own right, with the highest office in the land her goal.

[6] Her daughter Emily became the wife of Lord Palmerston, another of Queen Victoria's Prime Ministers.

Claire

'And thus the heart will break, yet brokenly live on.'

Childe Harold's Pilgrimage
(Canto III, Stanza 32)

Clara Mary Jane Clairmont was born in 1798 of mysterious parentage. Her mother, Mrs Clairmont, supposedly a widow who had lived in Switzerland and Spain, came with Claire and her brother Charles to live next door to the widowed philosopher and social reformer, William Godwin, brazenly attracted his attention and later became his second wife.

William Godwin's first wife had been Mary Wollstonecraft, the author of *The Vindication of the Rights of Women*, who had died in a woman's then inescapable labour, childbirth. Their daughter Mary was of the household[1] and the same age as Claire, and the two girls became inseparable companions in an intellectually rigorous environment. The hard-working Mrs Godwin had a facility for languages and had translated a number of children's books from the French. Claire inherited her mother's linguistic ability.

Known then as Jane, Claire was neither pretty nor particularly clever. Her skin was sallow and her black hair lank. The occasional vivacity which stirred her heavy features was not displayed within her family, for she was outshone there, being intellectually inferior to her step-sister, whom she slavishly emulated in the hope of developing similar talents, and rejected her mother's feeble attempts to guide her daughter into more practical interests. The girl remained firmly addicted to romantic poetry and her favourite poem was Byron's 'The Corsair'.

A frequent visitor to the household when Claire was sixteen years old was Percy Bysshe Shelley. Unhappily married, he was, like

[1] Fanny Imlay, Mary Wollstonecraft's illegitimate daughter, was also there.

William Godwin, an advocate of free love and sexual equality. He
first came to the Godwin house at a time when Mary Godwin was
away, and Mrs Godwin wrote of his relationship with Claire that
'Shelley took much to her like a brother to his younger sister. He
took her everywhere with him, for it was a mood of his never to go
out alone if he could help it.' He was attracted to the impressionable
young girl, and they at some time became lovers.

On Mary's return from Scotland some months later, however,
Shelley was drawn irresistibly to her by her powerful intellect; they
became lovers and Claire was supplanted. But the trio went for
walks together, Claire trailing behind the others – mostly at
Mary's selfish insistence. Mary explained that they wished to explore
philosophy, callously telling the unwanted Claire that she was too
ignorant to join in their discussions. Humbly Claire remained at a
distance, adoring her impatient and clever step-sister.

Mary in time confided to Claire that Shelley wished her to elope
with him. Shelley, who was married with two children, threatened
suicide if Mary would not go with him and they decided to leave
for the continent in 1814. Claire was sixteen and already she was
discontented with the drab limitations of life over Mrs Godwin's
book-shop. Claire was expected to help in the kitchen, for the household was impecunious and all money had to be earned the hard
way. Shelley, considering that Claire's command of French might
make her a useful companion abroad, decided to take her with
them. 'Our family is consumptive,' she wrote later; 'Our readiness
to oblige, our energy gives an appearance of strength we do not
possess.'

The trio left, Claire armed with an old notebook of Shelley's to
use as a journal. It was precious to Claire for Shelley had used the
note-book in which to write some poems and to her he was always
to be a mystic being. 'His whole existence [was] . . . visionary . . . his
thought lofty supreme and powerful. . . . his actions dropped balm
and peace everywhere like the wings of an angel. . . . Through that
gay air of careless loveliness . . . there peeped slight traces of
melancholy and dejection, as if unconsciously he was longing for a
brighter home than Earth. . . . His undying spirit . . . the calm
majesty of a constant communion with high thoughts . . . win me·
to think him immortal. . . . There was a spell . . . in his presence,
which opened a new world of nobleness and wisdom to one's gaze.'

Yet she admitted that he was not physically impressive: 'a certain grace of imperfection in his outward nature assured me he was human.' The poet stooped, and spoke in a strange, high voice.

Mrs Godwin followed her daughter to Dover, where the lovers were spending a night, prior to crossing the Channel. There she tried to reclaim Claire and persuade her back to Skinner Street, but the obstinate girl was adamant. Her future, she felt, lay with Mary and Shelley.

The three travelled to Paris where Shelley bought a donkey and they began to walk to Switzerland. With no experience of life outside the shabby London book-shop, and travelling with only the lovers for company, Claire's romantic nature responded to the variety and beauty of all she saw. The hardships of the journey did not deter her. They slept when and where they fancied. It was summer and though the conditions were often primitive and unclean, to Claire the journey was an idyll never to be repeated. They stayed in Neuchâtel for two days and then returned by steamer up the river Rhine, Claire's delight in her surroundings being somewhat impaired by the vulgarity of the bourgeois passengers. Shelley did not care for meat and they had subsisted on a vegetarian diet. They arrived back in London in mid-September, penniless, light-headed and hungry.

Shelley's comfort was Claire's daily concern. 'Love and be silent,' she wrote after reading *King Lear* and identifying with Cordelia, for under Shelley's tutelage she was studying Shakespeare. Emulating the minds about her, she outlined a pretentious scheme for a book. But the material she produced was unable, even with Shelley's assistance, to find a publisher. As an acolyte of Shelley she was for the moment content, but the relationship between him and Mary was of a profundity Claire was never to experience. Jealous, spiteful and quarrelsome, she had fits of sulking and admitted that her ill-temper was the result of bitter disappointment. Mary was now pregnant and was occasionally jealous of Claire. Shelley, teased by their friends about his two 'wives', tried to keep the peace between the two girls and the couple tried to persuade Claire to become a governess. But Claire still clung to them. Her envy was personal and intellectual: she was an impatient nonentity. She wrote after the death of her step-sister's week old child, 'I am seventeen now. When will something happen to me? . . . Mary has Shelley while I have no-one.' Under Shelley's guidance, she pursued her studies, reading *Political Justice*, which bored her, and lamenting meanwhile that she was 'merely vegetating not living'. They were short of money and Shelley's microscope had to be sold to pay for their lodgings.

In spring 1816, she and the Shelleys were in London again. Tired of waiting for the romantic destiny she was sure must be hers, Claire, who had been known as Mary Jane, changed her name. She now deliberately concocted a ridiculous letter which she sent to Byron at Drury Lane Theatre, in a desperate desire to obtain the attention she craved. Her ambitious effrontery was aimed at the greatest romantic figure of his own, if not of all time. Celebrated as he was by all London, what was it in Claire's letter which caught and held Byron's attention? Claire wrote to him from an address in Mary le Bonne and told him of her 'unstained reputation', placed her 'happiness in yr hands . . . with a beating heart' and 'confessed her love'. That could not have been what aroused Byron's curiosity, for he was besieged by romantic young ladies. She 'trembled at the fate of this letter', but perhaps the vivid phrase which aroused his interest was, 'It is for the piercing eye of genius to discover her disguise,' for she signed herself enigmatically, 'E.Trefusis', after a Cornish connection of her father's.

Fate should never be jogged; the results are invariably disastrous. Byron replied to her second letter and an assignation was made for Claire to visit him at seven o'clock one evening. Once there, she told him she had written a play and entreated his help to realize her ambition to become an actress. They quickly became lovers and he must often have cursed his weakness for what was to prove a tragic entanglement for them both.

Soon she was perpetually writing him lengthy, breathless letters. Uneasy and awkward with such a prize for a lover, physically his intimate yet writing with a craven idolatry any man would despise, she told him, 'I feel you are superior.' 'A man is a man,' wrote Byron to a friend, 'and if a girl of eighteen comes prancing to you at all hours, there is but one way.' She wished to crouch on a stool at his feet and promised him, 'Time will show you that I love gently and with affection, that I am incapable of revenge.' Her blend of humility and tenacity displayed the essential arrogance of her nature which invited rejection and yet resented it. He already treated 'that odd-headed girl', as he called her, with contempt but, devoid of pride, she meekly allowed herself to be kept hanging about in his hall while she waited for a chance to see him.

Having acquired the most famous literary lion of the day as her lover, Claire longed to display her conquest for, as Byron's mistress, she had more than equalled her step-sister Mary who was unaware of the liaison. In due course, Mary was introduced to Byron. Shelley and Mary were planning to escape the confines of English society and go to Switzerland and they agreed to meet in Geneva.

Claire's pathetic efforts to retain her hold on Byron never ceased but they only increased his indifference. Her letters to him were ignored and she prepared to leave with Shelley and Mary, telling Byron that she would never forget 'the wild originality of your countenance'. Still incredulous of her experience, she set out for the continent again, only now she was pregnant. From the very beginning Byron had barely tolerated her presence; she aroused his interest only when she sang, for Claire had a passion for music which was never fully developed, and she was an agreeable addition at London social occasions, where her singing was admired. Disliking England and her family, she yearned for the freedom of the continent; the airy mountain landscapes of Switzerland had an especial appeal, associated as they were with her earlier journey and its summer liberty. Her father had been Swiss and Geneva, she said, was to her 'the most beautiful and endearing of words'.

'I shall die if you don't write,' Claire wrote to Byron. The latter, having decided to visit Switzerland, agreed to stay at the same hotel where Claire, Shelley, Mary and their child were staying. Claire told Byron coyly that she expected him to fall in love with her handsome, brilliant step-sister, cravenly assuring him that she would sacrifice herself to them both. 'I will redouble my attentions to please her,' she wrote. On arrival in Switzerland, she called herself Mrs Clairville, for Byron had expressed disliked of the second half of the name Clairmont. 'I chuse to be married because I am so and Madames have their full liberty abroad.'

Claire was in the flattering position of being able to introduce the two poets to each other. She had waited impatiently for her lover's arrival. When he arrived, exhausted after a long journey in his defiantly extravagant Napoleonic carriage, he signed his age in the visitors' book as 100 years old. Claire chided him for his slowness but, with an ardent disregard for his obvious indifference to her, she happily anticipated a renewal of the relationship.

Byron rented the Villa Diodati, beside Lake Geneva, and Claire and the Shelleys stayed at a smaller villa set among the vineyards below. Byron regaled them one evening at the lakeside with a wild song he had learned in Albania and the primitive music enraptured his companions. They began to call him Albé. Shelley, Mary and Byron found much to talk and write about and it was during this period that Mary Shelley began to write her novel, *Frankenstein*. Claire was employed merely as a copyist and once again excluded from the serious creative work the other three were engaged upon.

'I could not exactly play the stoic with a woman who had scrambled eight hundred miles to unphilosophize me,' wrote Byron after he and Claire briefly became lovers again. She plagued him with notes which he ignored. While Byron was enjoying Shelley's and Mary's stimulating company, writing and drinking, Claire was an unhappy outsider. Her clear and careful handwriting was her only valuable attribute, and Byron made good use of it. She went up to the Villa Diodati frequently but though she hoped for Byron's more intimate attention, he avoided her.

'A foolish girl', wrote Byron, 'would come after me and I have had all the plague possible to persuade her to go back again.' Claire was finally persuaded to leave for England again to await the birth of her child. Shelley and Mary were to go with her. 'Farewell then my dearest Lord Byron, I shall love you to the end of my life and nobody else,' she wrote. At eighteen Claire's life was already set on a tragically unhappy path. She and Byron were never to be together again.

Claire reluctantly returned to England in the late summer, her current copying of the 'Prisoner of Chillon' unfinished, and hid with Mary and Shelley in Bath, for Claire's parents were unaware of her pregnancy. She helped to care for the Shelley's young son, with a Swiss nursemaid, Elise, for company. It was at this time that Mary and Shelley, whose first wife had drowned herself, were able to marry. Claire wrote repeatedly to Byron, not fearing her own uncertain future but still maintaining her humble begging, promising him that she would not complain if only he would 'love and take care of the child'. She hoped it would be a girl. She and the Shelleys whiled away the time reading *Glenarvon,* which William Godwin had recommended to them. 'Papa . . . says it contains a great deal of talent,' Claire observed. Grinding poverty was visible even in prosperous fashionable Bath : 'A fortnight ago Shelley and I went to take a little walk about dusk up and down our street. At one of the doors there was a woman with three children who were actually crying for hunger.' Shelley, prodigally generous, gave what he could.

As her confinement approached, Claire's optimism wavered and she was overwhelmed with depression at the contemplation of her lonely future, which she contrasted with the newly-married Shelleys' mutual devotion. Shelley and Mary did not desert her and loyally stayed with her when in January 1817 Claire's daughter was born. Shelley informed Byron of the birth of a back-haired, blue-eyed, infant, at first named Alba. Secure in the knowledge that the child was his, for he had confirmed that Claire had had no relations with Shelley at the relevant time, Byron was unable to restrain his paternal pride, reporting on the baby's beauty and her dimpled chin which was part of her Byronic inheritance. However, he was 'a little puzzled how to dispose of this new production'. He decided that he would probably 'place it in a convent to become a nun, being a character somewhat wanted in our family.' He would, he said, 'acknowledge and breed her myself, giving her the name of Biron . . . and mean to christen her Allegra which is a Venetian name.' The word means happiness, and the child developed a sweet disposition.

Admitting the unlikelihood of ever seeing much of his legitimate daughter, Ada, Byron felt that the new infant might possibly console him as he grew older, and initially he proposed that the child should be cared for by Augusta Leigh at Six Mile Bottom in what Byron described as her 'rabbit warren of a family'. Claire could not agree to this and Byron yielded, determining to rear the child himself.

In Italy, Byron sent for the child, suggesting with masculine casualness that a clerk could bring her out at the same time as some legal documents, tooth powder and the latest novels. The child was to be brought up by her father on condition that he would have no further dealings with Claire, but Byron agreed that Allegra should spend periods of time with each parent in turn.

Shelley and Mary with their two young children, and Claire with Allegra set out for Italy where Allegra was to join her father in Venice. Shelley wrote to Byron, 'You will find your little Allegra quite well. .. . . . Her attendant is . . . a Swiss . . . in whom Mrs S entirely confides . . . and whom Mary parts with solely that Claire and yourself may be assured that Allegra will be attended almost with a mother's care.' Elise the nursemaid was a young woman aged about thirty and herself the mother of a child. The British Consul's wife in Venice was also Swiss. Appalled by Byron's profligate mode of living, she took her countrywoman and Allegra into her own household, as being more suitable for the care of a young child than Byron's domain, where a vulgar Italian mistress now reigned.

Relinquishing her infant to a father who had never disguised his contempt for the mother, Claire told him she envied him. 'You will have a little darling to crawl on your knees.' Rapturously she imagined him giving Allegra 'a raisin off your own plate and a tiny drop of wine from your own glass and she will think herself a little Queen of Creation.'

Absent from both her child and her lover, Claire longed to be with them, sharing their joys. She added wonderingly, 'You may look at her and think "this is my work!"' Like many another discarded mistress, Claire made the mistake of believing that her lover's child's winsome ways might soften him into kindness towards herself. 'I have sent you my child because I love her too well to keep her,' Claire told Byron, convinced that his power and fame would benefit the child more than anything she could offer it.

But qualms soon arose about the wisdom of having parted with Allegra so readily. She had consigned the child to the care of an irresponsible poet of scandalous reputation. 'I so fear she will be unhappy . . . left perhaps to servants while you are drowning sense and reason in wine,' she told Byron; 'Who will there be to watch over her?' Deprived of her child, Claire was lonely, unhappy and bewildered. Pathetically she turned once again to study, trying to console herself with serious books in which she noted miserably that she found 'nothing but incitements to virtue and abstinence'. Mary Shelley was an ever-present reminder of what she was not : a brilliant intellect, a handsome woman, devotedly loved by a major poet. Still, with a vain hope Claire confided to her diary, 'I am twenty. At thirty I shall be better.'

The Shelleys' family contentment was a daily reminder of her own lost child and soon she was imploring Byron to remember his promise to let her see Allegra, but he callously told her that her letters were like ' bad German novels', upon which she wretchedly commented, 'they may be bad . . . they may be worse.'

Meanwhile Byron became fond of the small child, who quickly endeared herself to him, chattering in Italian, lisping her 'r's', frowning and pouting prettily. The child was not popular with the Hoppners[2] who had so readily taken her into their family. Their own son was a year younger and claimed most of their attention. The unsympathetic Mrs Hoppner was Claire's only source of news of her child. Allegra lived a shuttle-cock existence between the cold austerities of life with the Hoppners and the tempestuous irregularities of Byron's household.

Claire's constant begging for news of Allegra irritated Byron and had the reverse effect to that intended. Her Byron-worship increased his dislike to hatred. Anxious for news, Claire travelled to Venice with Shelley where, unknown to Byron, she was reunited with Allegra for a few ecstatic hours. Shelley was able to see Byron and extract the promise that Claire should spend a week with Allegra, but Byron declined to see Claire at all, when apprised of her presence, for he feared that in spite of himself he might become attracted to her again.

The solitary week Claire was to spend with her child was arranged and Byron prevailed upon the Hoppners to lend him their villa at Este for Claire and Allegra. The Shelleys were to be there too, but the week was marked by tragedy for them, for their daughter Clara became dangerously ill, and died. Mary was approaching another confinement.

'I am overjoyed to have my darling little one again. A whole week!' wrote an ecstatic Claire to Byron, but by the time Claire was permitted the precious few days, the child had been parted long enough from her mother to have forgotten her, and the desperate girl, starved of love, was rejected yet again. Seven days was scarcely long enough for Claire to regain the child's confidence before having to relinquish her again. Although Shelley pleaded with Byron on Claire's behalf for an extension of the child's stay, Byron was insistent that she be returned to him. Allegra travelled back to hot, humid Venice, and the Hoppner family. It was a cruelty from which Claire never recovered.

[2] Son of the painter.

Gradually she fell into helpless grief, partly relieved by the ever-present sympathy of Shelly who suggested travel as a distraction. For a time she stayed in various places, but peace of mind always eluded her. Still she pestered Byron with letters. 'I am very unhappy over Allegra,' she wrote to him. 'It is now a whole year since that one week I spent with her.' Claire was still with Shelley and Mary, a witness to their increasing fame. Mary's extraordinary novel *Frankenstein* had been published and she was at work on another book. Claire had nothing, no lover, no child, no talent, and a sour, poisoned note crept into her letters. 'Every word that falls from my mouth is serpents and toads to you,' she told Byron; 'It is . . . your fault that they are not pearls and diamonds. . . . Good God! If anybody could see how double I am getting with bending lowly to entreat the slightest favour of you.'

In December 1818 they were in Naples for the winter. There, a mysterious daughter was born to Shelley, registered by him and named Elena Adelaide. She was not taken into the family but cared for in a foundling hospital. The nursemaid Elise confided later to her countrywoman Mrs Hoppner at Venice that the child was Claire's. With this information Elise's Italian husband, Paolo Foggi, embarked on a blackmailing scheme, for Elise maintained that Mary Shelley was in complete ignorance of the circumstances surrounding the birth. Claire's misery was so great that Shelley may have felt constrained to offer consolation. Her envy and jealousy of Mary must have been a contributory factor : Shelley was the man whom she had first adored. Mary in her turn had come to resent Shelley's constant concern for and preoccupation with Claire's infant Allegra, and the *ménage à trois* had become very discordant. In December of that year Claire was reported to be unwell, but she wrote jauntily enough in her journal, 'Heigh ho! the Claire and the May, Find something to fight about every day.'

Shelley wrote to his wife, 'Elise says that Claire was my mistress; that is very well, and so far there is nothing new . . . people may believe or not believe. . . . She then proceeds to say that Claire was with child by me,' but what most disturbed Shelley were the allegations by Elise that the child had been abandoned. Shelley cared deeply for children. Child mortality was high and especially so in Shelley's family; the child was not expected to live. 'It will', wrote Shelley, 'leave me another memory to those which already

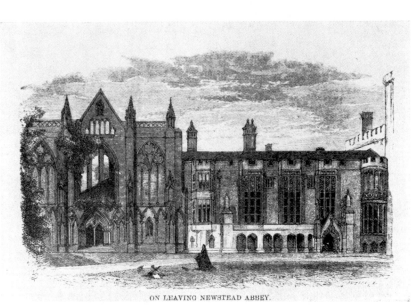

ON LEAVING NEWSTEAD ABBEY.

7   Newstead Abbey, Nottinghamshire, Byron's ancestral home.

8   St James's Palace, London, where Augusta lived while Lady of the Bed-chamber to Queen Charlotte.

9   Claire Clairmont in her later years.

10   The Villa Diodati, Switzerland, where Claire copied poems for Byron.

torture me. . . . I have taken every possible precaution for her, and hope they will succeed. She is to come to us as soon as she recovers.' The child was sickly and died six months after her birth, which remained carefully hidden and unreferred to in either Claire's or Mary's letters. If the child was Claire's, she confided her feelings to no one.

In Rome, Claire resumed her singing, again taking long lessons to fill her empty days, and touring the antiquities with Shelley, for she was an avid sight-seer. Any occupation helped smother her anxiety about Allegra. Byron's 'Don Juan' was being devoured by its London readers and Claire wrote a bitter comment upon it. 'His poem appears to me, a soliloquy upon his own ill-luck – ungraceful and selfish – like a beggar hawking his own sores about and which create disgust instead of pity.' In Italy's capital and in Florence and Pisa, however, the cosmopolitan society found Claire attractive and she blossomed occasionally into vivacity away from the Shelleys who, though kindly, only served to emphasize her failures both as a writer and as a woman unable to succeed in an emotional relationship. Among the Russian colony in Italy she made acquaintances who were later to prove useful. At Pisa she met Edward J. Trelawny but, obsessed by anxiety about Allegra, she could not respond to him though he was evidently seriously attracted to her.

When Lady Noel, Annabella's mother, died Claire wrote to Byron, 'I am extremely glad to hear that by your succession to a large fortune your affairs have become more prosperous than ever,' but still Byron's attitude to Claire did not soften. In 1820 Claire wrote to Byron about Allegra : 'Already her health has suffered. The first summer she had a dysentery, at the end of the second an ague. . . . Nothing must induce me to venture her life a third time . . . she must be guarded from the disorders of an Italian climate.' Byron now had Allegra at Ravenna, part of a large *ménage* of dogs, cats, monkeys and assorted birds. The child had had once again to adapt herself to a strange environment, lacking the ordinary routine and family affection a child needs. However, the sympathetic Teresa Guiccioli had devoted herself to Allegra's care. News reached Claire of Byron's infatuation with Teresa, whom little Allegra called 'Mammita', seemingly quite happy with her new 'mother'. This could only serve to make Claire more wretched still.

With a clear premonition of Allegra's death, Claire's dignity grew and a quiet despair pervaded her letters to Byron : 'My dear friend, I can no longer resist the internal inexplicable feeling which haunts me that I shall never see her any more. I entreat you to destroy this feeling by allowing me to see her. . . . I am sensible how little this letter is calculated to persuade . . . I know how much you are prejudiced against me. . . . Do not make the world dark to me as if my Allegra were dead?'

In 1821 Italy was in a state of ferment : Austrian troops in their thousands were pouring into Florence and Bologna. Byron had placed the four-year-old Allegra in a convent at Bagnacavallo; there she was equipped by her father with his Peer's robes and her own pieces of furniture. The convent had not taken Allegra willingly. She was considerably younger than the other children there, but some of them were Teresa's young cousins and it must have seemed a happy solution at the time, guaranteeing her a safety impossible to ensure outside in a land torn by strife. It also offered her comfort and companions. But it was not cheap and Byron was asked to pay double the usual fees.

In later years Claire was to write, 'What pangs of anguish I suffered in the winter of '21 when I saw a bright fire and people warming themselves by it, and knew my darling never saw or felt a cheerful blaze and was more starved with cold than an English pauper child !' The convent at Bagnacavallo was set in an unhealthy spot near a swamp. The nuns were of an austere Capuchin order; they practised a rigorous diet and did not eat meat. Instinct fed Claire's fears; she became distraught and desperate to rescue her child from the convent. Unable to act alone, she 'went about wildly from one to another, imploring them to help me get her out.' She was convinced that Allegra had been sent there by Teresa out of jealousy, for Byron was known to be fond of the child, and Teresa was unable to bear him one. But Claire found no one willing to commit himself : she 'received everywhere a refusal to do anything,' and was advised to be 'patient and wait for more favourable circumstances.' Inactivity in such a state of mind is impossible to tolerate.

From the seclusion of the convent where little Allegra was a great favourite with the kindly nuns, the child wrote to her father asking him to visit her and take her to the fair but Byron ignored her plea. His experience of small children was minimal and he dismissed Allegra's wishes as inspired by greed. But the loving-natured Shelley spent three hours with her at the convent, taking her sweetmeats and a gold chain. In an attempt to comfort the unhappy Claire, he wrote to her, 'Love me better than you do . . . The wind, the light, the air, the smell of a flower, affects me with violent emotions. . . . Occupy, amuse, instruct, multiply yourself and your faculties. . . . I wish to Heaven, my dear girl, that *I* could be of any avail to add to your pleasure . . . how ardently you cannot know.' Signing himself 'yours tenderly', he urged her to persist in her German studies. Claire travelled to Vienna for a time, where her brother Charles was establishing himself as a tutor and writer of textbooks.

The following spring Allegra became feverishly ill. Claire was at Pisa and was not told of the illness; when the child died in April 1822 it was some time before Claire knew of her daughter's death. The Shelleys dreaded breaking the news to her and the dead child was despatched before Claire could view the body. Byron was overcome with grief and sent Claire a miniature of the child she had seen only twice since handing her over to Byron, and a lock of hair. 'The blow', he admitted later, 'was stunning and unexpected.' Despite his grief, he yet felt, 'I do not know that I have anything to reproach in my conduct.' He arranged with Teresa's help to have the child buried in Harrow churchyard, with a marble memorial tablet inscribed 'In Memory of Allegra, daughter of G.G. Lord Byron, "I shall go to her, but she shall not return to me." ' But convention and the Church of England dictated otherwise: the Rector of Harrow objected to the tablet 'proclaiming the paternity of the little bastard'. Speaking for 'every man of refined taste not to say of sound morals', he found the proposal 'an offence against taste and propriety', and Byron's daughter was buried inside the church porch without a memorial.

After Allegra's death Claire wore a calm, resigned air, in contrast to her years of frantic misery. Violence was not in her nature and though she realized that nothing but Byron's death would have freed her child, she did not wish him harm. Goaded to the point where some women might have attacked him, she wrote, 'I was not cast in that mould.'

Later the same year Claire suffered the incalculable loss of Shelley's friendship. Unable to swim, he had set sail in the *Don Juan*, and had been pursued by two *feluccas* whose crews mistakenly believed Byron was on board with a great deal of money. The intention was to murder Byron. Shelley was drowned. While Mary went frantically in search of him, Claire looked after their son, Percy Florence.

The burning of Shelley's recovered corpse on the beach was described by Edward J. Trelawny:

> The sea, with the islands of Gorgona, Capraji, and Elba, was before us . . . not a human dwelling was in sight. . . . I felt we were no better than a herd of wolves or a pack of wild dogs, in tearing out his battered and naked body from the pure yellow sand that lay so lightly over it, to drag him back to the light of day . . . not a word was spoken, for the Italians have a touch of sentiment, and their feelings are easily excited into sympathy. Even Byron was silent and thoughtful. We were startled and drawn together by the dull hollow sound that followed the blow of a mattock, the iron had struck a skull, and the body soon uncovered . . . the corpse fell open and the heart was laid bare. . . . Although we made a tremendous fire—it burnt exceedingly slow, [continued Trelawny's recollection] and it was nearly four o'clock before the body was wholly consumed, that part nearest the heart being the last that became ashes – and the heart itself seemed proof against fire, for it was still perfect . . . although bedded in fire – would not burn – and after waiting an hour continually adding fuel – there was a bright flame round it . . . I took the heart in my hand.

The poet whom Claire had first loved and who had in his fashion loved her, remembered her in his will and bequeathed her £12,000. He had done everything he could to support Claire through her misery. Every day her devotion to his memory became more complete as her bitterness towards Byron increased. Shelley's physical beauty had, she wrote, 'that kind of beauty which Bacon says is the best, "that which a picture cannot express",' and she attempted to put into words his unique quality : 'Other men had as fair, open and commanding foreheads, and as dark and luxuriant brown hair to shade them, eyes as full of poetic fire, and lips as expressive of gentle serenity; but they wanted that nameless something which touched the heart at every glance.'

Claire journeyed alone again to Vienna and her brother Charles. She had spent five hopeless years in Italy and had lost everything that was dear to her. Tramping in the autumn rain up mountain-sides, en route, she hoped by physical exhaustion to oust from her mind the bitter memories of the past few years. It was impossible; everywhere she went Allegra's face was before her : 'I only saw my little lost darling.' She was still only twenty-four.

Later she wrote to Mary Shelley, 'My sentiments have not experienced any change with regard to Lord Byron . . . it would give me pleasure to know that he was happy, for I am not revengeful . . . not even to him.' But in her resignation she accused him. Byron, she said, 'Wantonly, wilfully, destroyed my Allegra.' 'I never loved her nor pretended to love her,' wrote Byron of Claire.

Often she longed for death. 'A happy passion like Death has Finis written . . . I am unhappily the victim of a *happy passion*. . . . Like all things perfect, it was fleeting . . . only lasted ten minutes . . . but these ten minutes have discomposed the rest of my life.'

The Trelawny who had helped cremate Shelley on the beach remained a close friend and he and Claire corresponded from time to time. 'Our friendship', he wrote many years later, 'had a violent commencement.' He proposed marriage to Claire, but she, rejected by the two poets and geniuses she had adored, could not contemplate life with a lesser being, and refused him. 'Lured by fancy or driven by fate, we wandered by different paths,' he told her.

Claire had not abandoned her aspirations as a writer and her critical sense was admired by Mary Shelley, who was occasionally able to place an article or story by Claire in London journals. Humiliatingly for Claire, one was readily published under Mary's name, for the latter had now an established reputation as a writer, whereas Claire's name excited no interest. The only way in which Claire could earn a living was by teaching. In Vienna, her brother Charles, now established as tutor to the Austrian court at Schönbrun, opened various influential doors for her, but she did not care for Viennese society and longed to travel as far afield as possible from the scenes of her tragic youth. She first chose Russia where, as the eternal, expatriate, indispensable English governess, she spent four lonely years. There, among a tempestuous, unruly family, she was an outcast again, always present but aloof and withdrawn. She became fond of one of her charges, a young girl who fell seriously ill, reminding her of her own loss of Allegra. Claire maintained a vigil alone at the dying child's bedside throughout her last night,

afterwards enduring with disgust the theatrical display occasioned
by the death and funeral. There were moonlight sledge-rides in the
snow, strawberry-picking picnics at her employer's country estate
outside Moscow, but Byron and Allegra always haunted her and she
was made miserable at a family dinner-party by a guest extolling
Byron's virtues. On New Year's Day 1827 she wrote unhappily in
her journal, 'I was frightened to think I had another year to run
like the latter,' although her exile was relieved by an occasional
letter from Mary containing an affectionate note from Percy.-
'Darling boy!' she confided to her journal, 'This made me gay the
whole day.'

No one guessed at her past as she doggedly tried to instil the
beauties of the English language, of which her lovers had been such
masters, into the uncomprehending Russians. But the English newspapers came her way and it was in Russia that she learned of
Byron's death. One of the subsequent books distressed her by its
portrayal of Shelley, and she wept alone in her room at the
poignancy of her recollections.

She was still an attractive young woman and men sought her
company. She took up music again and one of her suitors was a
young musician who gave her lessons. He must have reminded her
of Byron, for she used a phrase to describe him similar to the one
she had used for Byron : 'His countenance is very original.' But she
always disdained marriage and repulsed the Russians who tried to
flirt with her.

Shelley's bequest was not to be hers for some years and she was
compelled to earn her living by teaching the well-to-do. She taught
all over Europe – Nice, Dresden, Carlsbad and Pisa again, full of
sad memories of Allegra and Shelley. In London, teaching still, she
wrote of one of the dreary families who employed her, and of the
underpaid, thankless drudgery : 'The daughter is going to be married to a Genoese and must have an Italian lesson every day. . . .
that vile omnibus takes two hours to get to Richmond and the same
to come back and so with giving my lesson I am never back before
seven.' It was unrewarding work, the pupils being mostly uninterested in absorbing what she had to offer. Claire came to detest
them. She who had associated with philosophers and poets, who had
lived among the literate, was intellectually and emotionally starved.
She became nervous and edgy, and sudden noises startled her. She

dressed badly, was downtrodden and shabby, depressed by her lowly position in the prosperous families who employed her where, though she might be attractive, she had no opportunity to shine.

But in 1844, when she was forty-six years old, Sir Timothy Shelley died and Claire received Shelley's bequest of £12,000. Although she claimed that her brother was 'like me, immensely prudent', his advice on investment proved to be unwise, and Claire was compelled to continue teaching.

Always she clung to her connection with Mary Shelley and her son Percy, for she had often had the care of him as a small boy, and the Shelley family were as dear to her as her own. 'Love to dearest Percy,' she wrote, 'He must not buy any hearth-rug for his sitting-room for I have worked him one, roses of all colours except black . . . an emblem of his life, past present and future.' Sent to Harrow by Mary, the Percy whom Claire had known as a boy was now a very different person and, sadly, she could not be truly at ease with the family. Although invited to visit them at Field Place, Sussex, she would not go. Her streak of independence was far too strong to admit of anything which might be interpreted as toadying. Over-sensitive on this point, she seemed prickly, and Sir Percy did not care for her. Not unnaturally he resented his father's generous bequest and when, later, Claire applied to him for help, in exchange for some documents, he was far from cordial : 'Miss Clairmont wishes to sell me certain letters and papers. . . . The relations between Miss Clairmont and myself are not those of intimacy. . . . Miss Clairmont is no relation of mine. . . . Miss Clairmont being a stranger in the Shelley family received £12,000 from money raised upon the Shelley estates. . . . the sum above named ought to have satisfied the lady.'

As she aged, Claire turned to her brother's children for the affection she craved. Her niece Pauline, who shared her aunt's love of music, became attached to her. Claire became a Roman Catholic and lived in a Florentine convent for some years, but always the memory of her dead child haunted her. Never having seen the body of Allegra, she became obsessed with the idea that her daughter might still be alive somewhere, unknown to her, waiting to be claimed. It was the outcome of years of introverted brooding. When she was eighty years old she wrote to Trelawny on the subject. It had been nearly fifty years since he had heard from her, but the

circumstances of Allegra's death were still vivid to him and he tried
to reassure her. 'Now for your questions – Byron was greatly grieved
at the loss of Allegra. The remains could not be brought to Pisa –
the absurd quarantine laws prevented it. The body was inclosed in
lead . . . sent to England consigned to John Murray.' There was
little comfort there to assuage her aching heart.

She still had ten more years to live. 'In this life,' she wrote, 'one
dies of anguish many times before one really dies. And not the
promise of cycles and cycles of unbroken felicity could bribe or win
me to live over again.'

Later, in Florence, she lived at the rear of an old Palace, sharing
the quarters with several unattached females, a spry little old
personage of some distinction, her once-black hair transformed into
a cap of white curls. Music was still her great solace but she was
always reticent with those around her who were curious about her
tragic past and the two great poets whom she had loved.

Claire died in Florence in 1879, aged ninety, and was buried with
the little shawl of Shelley's she had treasured. She inscribed her own
bitter epitaph : 'In misery she spent her life expiating not only her
faults but her virtues.'

Teresa

'Be thou the rainbow to the storms of life.'

The Bride of Abydos (Canto II, Stanza 20)

The Contessa Teresa Guiccioli was one of the fourteen children of Count Ruggero Gamba, of an ancient, respected and cultured family of the Romagna province in Italy. The family lived in a decaying palace at Ravenna during the winter, driving by oxen-cart to their rustic home at Filetto for summers which were spent, united happily but impecuniously, in country pursuits.

Teresa's father, for an aristocratic, provincial Italian bowed down with the care of many daughters, had remarkably progressive views on women's education and Teresa was sent to the unusual convent school of San Chiara at Faenza, where several of her relatives were also pupils. Here in a family atmosphere, under the care of nuns, she absorbed a wide range of learning, supervised by the Abbess Madre Rampi. The school was later closed by the ecclesiastical authorities, who considered it a dangerous influence, teaching girls more than was thought wise or necessary. A contemporary of Teresa's at the school disliked her and considered her arrogant. When she left the convent, Teresa's education was continued under the supervision of Professor Paolo Costa who was also tutor to her brother Pietro. Under this learned man Teresa studied theology, philosophy, literature and languages. Her French was fluent and she became familiar with the great European thinkers. Dante was her hero and Costa taught her what she was later to learn for herself, that a poet personifies a nation's spirit.

By the time Teresa was eighteen years old, she was, despite her sheltered existence and lack of knowledge of life outside the province, a highly-literate young woman. She was also a sexually unawakened but voluptuously beautiful girl, whose head was filled with romantic literature and legend. Ravenna and the province of Romagna are as romantic as their names imply, with their histories of legendary lovers, their ancient palaces and mosaic-filled churches.

The Gamba family was not rich, and as was the custom in a family with many daughters, the eldest had to be sacrificed to the highest marital bidder. In Teresa's case, he quickly appeared on the scene. Count Alessandro Guiccioli may first have glimpsed Teresa through a convent grille. The middle-aged Count was looking for a third wife; according to Italian custom a virgin is desirable and they are best found chaste before they emerge from their convents. Count Guiccioli was, though in his late fifties, handsome, spry, the epitome of civilized urbanity and a practised seducer of pretty young women. He sported a fine head of red hair, probably dyed, and red whiskers.

Both his previous marriages had strange histories. The first Contessa Guiccioli had been older and was said to have been even more disagreeable than her outwardly suave husband. She had brought to the marriage a handsome dowry. Having acquired the Contessa Placidia, as she was called, and her wealth, the Count satisfied his other desires, peopling his Palazzo with young and comely housemaids whom he systematically seduced, grew tired of, and replaced with others. But one of these successive maids, Angelica Galliana proved permanently engaging, bearing him six illegitimate children, upon which his lawful Contessa protested and was immediately banished by her autocratic husband to one of his isolated country houses. Here the unhappy woman was prevailed upon to make a will in her husband's favour, soon after which she became ill and died. Her death was providential to the Count for he was deeply in debt, but he was not long in remarrying, taking advantage of his new wealth to choose for his second wife his former servant and the mother of his children. She in turn died when the eldest was twelve years old. On the night of her death the Count went to the theatre as usual.

By the time of his second wife's death the Count, mostly by tireless intrigue, had become not only rich but a considerable landowner. His lust for land was as strong and sustained as his other obsessions. He presented a front of respectability and attended church regularly, but he had at one time gambled and borrowed to such an extent that he had spent a period of time in a Rome gaol, soon after which the man supposedly responsible for his incarceration was found mysteriously stabbed by persons unknown.

The middle-aged landowner, despite his reputation for murder-ous intrigue, was considered to be an excellent match for Teresa. He inspected her carefully then made his offer which was gratefully accepted since the marriage would facilitate her sisters' chances in the marriage market. 'Her body is her only reality,' had written one of Teresa's convent companions and the Count Guiccioli doubtless found his young bride all that a practised voluptuary could wish, although his demands were at times repellent to Teresa and she complained of 'his *strange* habits'.

Aware that his prize possession should have an appropriate setting, he opulently decorated the Palazzo degli Osi in Ravenna for Teresa, and she drove about the town in an elegant blue and white coach drawn by six prancing black horses. At home, an elaborately costumed negro page waited on the new Contessa. Always smilingly good-natured, she was popular with the servants and attentively visited her step-children, of whom she was genuinely fond, in their convents and monasteries. Teresa became the docile young step-mother to seven children the eldest of whom was only a few years younger than herself.

The dowry Teresa's father struggled to raise was prudently invested by the Count, yielding a small regular sum for Teresa's personal use. Now and again, the Count grudgingly gave her a few extra *scudi*. During one of his frequent absences administering his estates, the young wife was left alone with only her old governess, a priest and servants for company and Teresa pined for her elderly husband. He had instilled in her his own frugal habits. 'My adorable husband,' she wrote to him, 'the evenings pass so dismally here,' adding proudly, 'I've still got the five scudi thou gavest me for a present and I hope when thou art home again thou wilt be pleased with my economy.' Teresa was not allowed even nominally to run her home. Discouraged by the Count's displeasure, she meekly wrote during another of his absences, 'I shan't take the risk of interfering in household matters unless you give me the sign.'

In April 1819 the couple were in Venice. Teresa, three months pregnant, was in mourning for the recent death of her mother and one of her sisters. The Count's addiction to the theatre was not to be denied and he paid his usual nightly visit, insisting on her accompanying him afterwards to a *conversazione* at the home of the Countess Benzoni, a noted Venetian hostess whom Byron had

likened to Lady Melbourne. Teresa was reluctant to go but dutifully accompanied her husband to the worldly salon where she
saw what she later described as 'a celestial apparition'. It was
Byron.

Teresa neither wrote, spoke nor read English and Byron was
unwilling to be introduced to her at the *conversazione*. Self-exiled
from England, he was in the midst of a prolonged bout of de-
bauchery in Venice and to him, emotionally bankrupt, one Italian
woman seemed very like another. But sitting beside Teresa, he discovered slowly that this beautiful girl was no ordinary, insipid,
convent-bred Italian but was possessed of a vivid intelligence with
which he could communicate. Both were more disturbed than they
thought possible, and on leaving the Palace that night Teresa was
aware of a new and mysterious element in her life.

A romantic woman can only write in romantic terms. 'I then felt
attracted to him by an irresistible force,' she recalled and Byron,
equally drawn to Teresa, arranged to see her the following day.
Their first assignation was planned with all the secrecy required in
the best love stories. 'An old boatman appeared with a note, in an
unknown gondola, and took me to Mylord's gondola, where he was
waiting. . . . I was strong enough to resist at that first encounter . . .
next day . . . my strength gave way.' Their passion was mutual,
instantaneous but impossible in their circumstances fully to indulge,
a factor which invariably intensifies the feelings aroused.

Teresa did not care for Venice; she was at heart a country girl
bred in the rich pine-forests bordering the Adriatic Sea in which she
was fond of bathing. She galloped her horses in an undisciplined
manner through the aromatic woods and before her marriage had
lived an outdoor life with her family, with shoots and picnics around
the rambling old palace, the doors and windows of which were
always hospitably open. By nature warm and extrovert, she was
surrounded by an unrestrainedly affectionate family. Venice, humid,
airless and artificial, did not appeal to Teresa: its decaying
splendour was, she wrote, 'without flowers, without trees, without
birds . . . pleased her so little . . . with its lugubrious gondolas instead
of her team of horses.' A Venice with Byron however, was different,
transformed for her into an 'abode of the very light of life, an
earthly paradise'.

In the ten short days they had together in Venice after their first meeting, the intoxicated but very young Teresa behaved with a carefree lack of inhibition, causing the whole of Venice, accustomed to more discreet amours, to chatter with excited gossip to which Teresa herself was completely oblivious. In a state of romantic euphoria Teresa wrote of herself at this time, 'Her spirit skimmed over the Venetian lagoons.' She heard only 'melodious sounds' and all she saw were 'smiles of a celestial countenance'. All her senses were heightened by being with Byron. 'Earthly Paradises cannot be expected to endure,' she wrote later after it was all over, but from the very beginning Teresa used all her intelligence to ensure that this romance should appear as perfect as any legend of her native Ravenna and last as long as her art could contrive. The prospect of imminent separation, for her husband was about to take her back to Ravenna, caused Teresa indiscreetly to invade Byron's opera box from which he was watching Rossini's *Othello*, and to stage a dramatic and publicly noted farewell scene.

Nurtured as she had been on the most romantic French literature, Teresa began to see herself playing a heroine's role with herself as a contemporary Beatrice. Her exaltation was so intense as to cause alarm. Her confidante and friend Fanny Silvestrini acted as a messenger between the lovers when Teresa wretchedly accompanied her husband back to the Romagna, but warned her affectionately, 'I beg you, dear Friend, to be circumspect and prudent, lest the intensity of your love betray you.' Reassuring the girl, she added, 'If by a man's words one may judge his heart . . . be certain of the love, the tenderness . . . He has sworn . . . you have made on him an impression that can *never* be erased.'

The very difficulties which beset the continuance of the affair provided a welcome challenge and added an adventurous spice to what had initially been so easy a conquest that Byron might quickly have tired of it. Teresa considered wild schemes for clandestine meetings, her ardour undampened by Fanny Silvestrini who counselled prudence: 'To meet in the theatre would certainly be an unwise step . . . You will give yourself away . . . the Town is small, the resources for two lovers are few.' But perfectly aware that Byron, whatever his protestations of love, would be incapable of celibacy, Teresa realized that she must somehow draw him to Ravenna, since the temptations of Venice were many and well-nigh irresistible. Fanny tried to calm her fears: *'He loves you with the most intense, most vivid and most fervent love* . . . he will come at any cost, he will come,' she assured Teresa.

But he did not come and Teresa was inconsolable. 'I realize that you are caught up in a great storm of passion . . . try to recover,' counselled Fanny, while Byron quickly became interested in a heavily-protected young Venetian girl, falling into the Grand Canal on his way to an assignation, and joining her dripping wet. It was during this period that he poured out to Augusta a passionate declaration of his unceasing love for her.

Three times Byron was on the point of going to Teresa and the latter, despairing of seeing her lover again, resorted to a strategic lack of communication. '*I cannot find words to describe to you his anxiety about* your silence,' wrote Fanny Silvestrini and shortly afterwards Byron left for Ravenna. 'The die is cast,' he wrote and Fanny cautioned Teresa again, 'Control yourself, for Mercy's sake, before your husband and the whole of Ravenna . . . do not lose your head.'

Byron knew he would be in some danger if he went to Ravenna with the avowed intention of continuing a love-affair with the wife of a Papal count of evil reputation. It was well known that Count Guiccioli was merciless and had caused already two men's violent deaths. And not only were the Italian men murderously inclined. Byron was warned against the tendency of jealous Italian females to murder their inconstant lovers. His decision was a calculated imprudence, an act of bravado in the face of a very real risk which was a considerable attraction.

In Ravenna, Teresa, having awaited Byron in a condition of unsatisfied longing and having him near her at last, became ill. Her family was tubercular and coughing and blood-spitting so common as scarcely to cause alarm. But Teresa's ailment, though she later attempted to conceal the fact was a well-timed though dangerously late miscarriage, of which Byron feared he might have been the cause. Teresa must have been bewailing her five months' pregnancy, which would not have increased her attraction for her lover. The late miscarriage rendered her at once slender and frail, temporarily unattainable and therefore immediately more desirable.

On the evening of his arrival at Ravenna, Byron went to the theatre to be met with the alarming news that Teresa was seriously ill and dying. The Count Guiccioli, also at the theatre and unaware that Byron was in Ravenna to resume a love-affair with his wife, courteously called on him in his theatre box and reassured him with better news of Teresa's health. The pretext for Byron's presence in Ravenna was its associations with past literary figures, Dante, Boccaccio and Dryden, together with the famous Byzantine mosaics and Byron dutifully made the rounds of the monuments while he impatiently awaited Teresa's recovery.

They were still apart in the middle of June, Byron exasperated by Teresa's teasing, poetic letters, the woman still maddeningly neither visible nor attainable. Provoked, he wrote recklessly, 'If trouble arises there is only one remedy, that is, to go away together. . . . Great love is necessary – and some courage. Have you enough?' It was a direct question and Teresa avoided answering it. She had embarked on a scheme to make Byron her *cavalier servente*, the ancient Italian custom whereby a young married woman attached to herself an escort of her own choosing : he would be discreet and attentive, the relationship usually of life-long duration and conducted with the complaisant older husband's consent. But Byron's invitation to elope flouted this convention which was dependent upon the woman's remaining in public her husband's faithful wife. Teresa realized, too, that if she did elope with Byron he might not remain hers for very long.

At last, Teresa recovered from her illness and she left her bed to drive out in a carriage with Byron, their first opportunity for private conversation since they had parted in Venice in April. Their idyll was resumed and Byron found he liked Ravenna now that the necessity to pretend an interest in its antiquities was gone. He responded to the wildness of its surroundings and its lack of pretension. He had his horses and, having always detested city parks in which only restrained cantering was possible, was able to give them full rein in the environs of the town, exploring the uncultivated and unknown forests.

Teresa was equally fond of riding, with a high-spirited disregard for all but the most uninhibited enjoyment of the air, the scenery and Byron's company. 'She can't guide her horse,' complained Byron exasperatedly, 'he runs after mine and tries to bite him, and then she begins screaming.' Teresa costumed herself operatically for her rides in the forest, 'in a high hat and sky-blue habit . . . both our grooms have the devil's own work to keep her from tumbling, or having her clothes torn off by the trees and thickets,' reported Byron. Teresa's memories dwelled mistily on strolls and rests, when the couple would recline together 'in the deep forest shade . . . under the great resinous pines . . . thyme and other scented herbs.' They made love insatiably whenever and wherever they could.

In her determined assumption of the mantle of romance, Teresa made herself, even to Byron, an embarrassingly absurd but enchanting and irresistible figure. Should Byron be tempted to stray from her side, Teresa dealt deftly with his wandering eye. A certain Geltruda attracted him at this time, but the watchful Teresa arranged for the distracting rival to be spirited away, and was careful to flirt herself, in order to keep Byron attentively at her side.

Teresa was the only woman in Byron's life who aroused him to jealousy. That summer, her freshness, vitality and ardour captivated his jaded appetite. Clever enough to wield her power over him, she stung him into writing delightfully jealous notes : worried by a persistent admirer in her opera box, he demanded an explanation of the man's presence, so tormented by Teresa's ogling of his rival that he was unable to concentrate on the play. Byron fumed and Teresa, entranced at his reaction to the feminine wiles she deployed, added a satisfied comment to one of Byron's furious notes, 'Billet de jalousie *magnifique – passioné – sublime* !' Pursuing her policy of alternately pleasing him and teasing him, she goaded Byron into a furiously reproachful note, 'I have no strength to bear a fresh torment every day . . . goodbye for ever,' adding with rare self-pity, '*Midnight*. My time for sleep before I knew you.'

The tragi-comedy, enacted against the Italian *mise-en-scène* of pine-woods and Palazzos and opera-boxes, had a quality as timelessly enchanting as the Mozart operas with which it had much in common. There could not be a more engaging heroine than Teresa with her thick auburn ringlets draping magnificently sculptured shoulders. She had dark blue eyes and perfect teeth. Byron teased her about her short, peasant legs, but this defect was hidden by the costume of the day, though the scarlet satin shoes she affected peeped coquettishly out beneath her skirts. The supporting characters filled out the cast with a perfection most librettists would envy. A villainous old husband, a fond father, a devoted *confidante*, priests and maids and black pages. And Byron for a hero ! No wonder Teresa cooed and chanted in her Romagnuola accent at a *conversazione*, 'Mio Byron!' She entertained him by her facility in turning a pretty sonnet praising wifely constancy to be sent to a niece on the verge of matrimony, whilst she herself was in the midst of a tempestuous illicit love affair.

The romantic trance in which Teresa and Byron were living, mutually excluding the rest of the world, could not last long. Both were indiscreet and though Teresa might write, 'At the theatre or at an assembly . . . it little mattered so long as they breathed the same air,' an observer wrote with foreboding, 'My Lord's love was becoming ever more intense, and more noticeable in a small town. The time chosen for his calls . . . coinciding with the business or siesta times of the husband, when the wife was most at leisure.' Count Guiccioli received an anoymous letter about his wife while errand boys celebrated the affair by singing a vulgar song about the now famous lovers.

Teresa's brother Pietro was in Rome and had not met Byron but wrote in alarm to his sister that the man she had described to him as an 'angel upon earth' had the most appalling reputation and had probably been a pirate. But Teresa defiantly replied, 'Why should I not love such a friend?' continuing with a passionate belief in the heart's laws, 'In loving Lord Byron as I love him, I do not think I am offending against the holy laws of God.' Teresa demanded to know why she should give Byron up. 'Is it because of what the world will say? But this World . . . I have already appraised; I have realized its vanity, its injustice, and its incapacity to fill a Heart and Soul that has any other than frivolous and vulgar needs. . . . And what would the World give me in return, to make up for the sacrifice that I should make . . . of his high intelligence – of his great soul. . . . If I never saw him again, there would be no Sun left in the sky for me.'

Early in August 1819, Count Guiccioli took his wife to Bologna. Hitherto he had been the complaisant husband, shrewdly observant, impeccably courteous but playing a waiting game. Byron wrote to Teresa from a vine-hung courtyard, delightedly recalling to her their recent past: '*Think*, my love, of *those* moments – delicious – *dangerous* – but happy . . . not only for the pleasure, more than ecstatic . . . but for the danger . . . The Hall! Those rooms! the open doors! . . . how many obstacles! . . . it has been the real triumph of love.' And once again they resorted to their varied and colourful messengers, priests, negro boys and the faithful Fanny.

Count Guiccioli had assiduously cultivated Byron. England was the wealthiest country in Europe and Lord Byron represented riches, position and political influence. Count Guiccioli was experienced in the hazards of Italian politics and sought to make use of Byron's obvious passion for his wife by asking Byron to have him appointed British Vice-Consul at Ravenna, thus gaining British protection should trouble arise. But though Byron wrote to John Murray to engage his help, this ludicrous appointment was wisely never made.

Teresa had mostly recovered her health since the miscarriage earlier in the year, but daily gallops through the forest and indulgence in the emotional exaltation of a very serious love affair had aggravated her tendency to consumption, which had already caused several early deaths in her family. In addition there were some worrying gynaecological symptoms which, together with her persistent cough, gave the lovers a pretext to travel to Venice to consult, on Byron's advice and with her husband's consent, a Dr Aglietti. It was probably not coincidental that Count Guiccioli borrowed several thousand francs from Byron before he and Teresa were able to depart with the Count's approval.

It was a journey embarked upon at the height of their love affair, and prolonged by Teresa into an idyll of some weeks. They paused en route to make a pilgrimage to Petrarch's grave under a late summer sky which Teresa lyrically described as 'made of sapphire and opal'. The romantic spell was unbroken by the noting, in a niche above the door of the ancient ruin, of the embalmed body of Petrarch's pet cat.

Byron and Teresa were already a subject for gossipy speculation in Venice where Count Guiccioli expected Teresa to take lodgings, but their stay was brief. Teresa was not so self-absorbed as to fail in her duty to visit her step-daughters in their convents before boldly going with Byron to a villa he had taken at La Mira, from which she wrote a prudently disarming letter to her husband. It was September and the weather, Teresa noted rapturously, reflecting the state of her heart and her relationship with Byron, was 'all serenity, softness and splendour'. The Count was plainly told, 'I am not in Venice but La Mira, where I've come by Aglietti's advice.' She had suffered from an unromantic attack of piles. But Byron, she assured her husband, was most attentive and she signed herself 'your most affectionate consort'.

From the arcadian charm of the Palazzo Foscari at La Mira she wrote to her husband again, unwisely mentioning her health only in a passing sentence surrounded by unguarded and ecstatic praise of Byron. She assured the Count she was not at all bored, for she had the numerous books Byron had procured for her and a piano which he delighted for her to play to him and then, she wrote, 'there is his company, which is more precious than all the rest together.' Such ecstatic happiness was more than the miserable Count could bear. He was not so much jealous of Byron as of his wife's luminous rapture. Byron was a little disturbed by the Count's lack of response to his cordial messages. 'In your last letter', reproved Teresa, 'there wasn't a good word for him.'

Teresa's father, Count Ruggero Gamba, now alarmed at Teresa's extended stay virtually alone with Byron, instructed his son-in-law, several years his senior, to remove his wife immediately from a very compromising situation. Byron had obligingly tried to put into effect Count Guiccioli's desire to be appointed British Vice-Consul at Ravenna, but had failed. The Count was also in Byron's debt financially but for the moment he did nothing despite his father-in-law's letter, merely writing complainingly to Teresa and telling her he would not fetch her yet. Teresa replied far from meekly, 'What am I to do in the meantime? I'm in a pretty fix. . . . I needed a man and an *amico* like Byron to cheer me up a little,' and once again her pen ran away imprudently, 'From now on I judge all men by him – the only person with whom I can live.' But to Byron she was always careful to preserve the aura of romantic unattainability that she recognized was necessary to a man like Byron. 'It was requisite for a woman to live in a sort of illusive atmosphere,' she later wrote, 'to appear somewhat like an immaterial being.' She was careful not to eat in his presence, since Annabella's hearty appetite had repelled him, and spent much of her time secluded in her own quarters.

Unwilling to sully an ideal and perfect love, Teresa steadfastly refused Byron's gifts. At La Mira he offered her a brooch and, mistress of the romantic gesture, she inserted a lock of her own auburn hair in it before returning it to Byron and was rewarded by seeing him hang it round his neck on a gold chain. She had at that time no knowledge of the English language, she and Byron spoke

Italian together, yet their mutual sympathy was such that they were
able to laugh together when she reminded him of Augusta and he
adopted in their letters the crosses he had formerly reserved for his
sister. 'There can be few crosses more holy for us than these,' he
wrote. It was the greatest possible compliment he could pay a
woman and it helped to cement an already enduring relationship.
But the faithful Fanny Silvestrini warned Teresa that her husband
was having her watched and that the interlude of seclusion and
peace and love must shortly end, for as autumn drew near the Count
was expected.

It was at La Mira and under Teresa's influence that Byron wrote
his 'Prophecy of Dante' which she copied for him. Little Allegra,
Claire Clairmont's daughter, came to stay. Teresa became fond of
the child and took a great interest in her, but nothing and nobody
had any real existence except Byron with whom she sat and talked
undistractingly. Fanny Silvestrini declared that he worked more
contentedly when Teresa was in sight and her lively chatter did not
intrude. During this idyllic period spent together Teresa's sympathy
elicited from Byron his version of the marriage to Annabella, his
love for Augusta and the thwarted political ambitions that had
resulted in his loathing of the English Establishment. Teresa calmly
accepted Byron's passion for Augusta as a not at all unnatural love,
and tenderly bundled Augusta's letters to her brother with silk
ribbon.

Under pressure from her father, Teresa contemplated a return to
Ravenna and her husband. The Count seemed in no hurry to have
her back and suggested that she should borrow another large sum
of money from Byron, whose reaction was to wager with his friends
that he would not only keep the money but also retain Teresa. But
finally Count Guiccioli wrote with a directive that his wife must be
relinquished together 'with all her linen'. Teresa and Byron again
prepared to part.

Her return to the marital home was conditional on an extraordinary set of regulations drawn up by the Count by which he
expected his wife to abide. Even by the standards of the time when
a wife was little more than her husband's chattel, they were autocratic, if not the product of severe megalomania. Teresa must forgo
most feminine pleasures such as variety of dress, and dedicate herself
to such 'household matters as come within her competence'. She

might be allowed to 'offer suggestions, or ask advice, but . . . not give orders'. It was indicated that 'inasmuch as she neglects the care of business and house,' her husband would retaliate by neglecting her. Strict times for conversation and music were outlined and special emphasis placed on the stricture that she be allowed as few visitors as possible and resign completely any desire to travel, a reference to Teresa's earlier request, on the pretext of a persistent cough, that she be allowed to tour the Italian lakes under Byron's escort. The final edict was, 'She shall be absolutely docile.'

The outraged young wife refused to sign the document and issued her own rebellious set of conditions with a contemptuous flourish, resulting in days of raging disagreement. The Count was unyield-ingly exigent, Teresa utterly immovable. With hauteur she insisted on having her horses, any visitors she chose and, furiously satirical, 'the right to pull the donkey's tail', but graciously agreed to read daily to her husband and drive out publicly together.

The enraged Count, in desperation at his inability to tame his intransigent young wife, unexpectedly begged Byron to intercede. With considerable difficulty, for Teresa was now ready to elope with him, Byron persuaded her, in the interests of her five unmarried sisters on whom such a flight would bring public disgrace, to stay. Teresa prepared to return to the Count's Palazzo at Ravenna, and finally tore herself away from Byron, her misery increased by his suffering from a delirious fever through which she had been nursing him devotedly.

Teresa wrote daily, but Byron came to the momentous decision that he must leave for England. He planned to take Allegra with him and Fanny offered to escort the child as far as Calais. On receipt of a farewell note from him, Teresa staged a magnificent dramatic scene, producing floods of despairing tears and finally retiring to her bed coughing blood. At this, the defeated Count relented and suggested that Byron should return to Ravenna. On the point of leaving, Byron expressed his relief. 'It is better to be with a woman I love, at the risk of assassination, than in a country where I neither like, nor am liked,' he wrote and was back in Ravenna for victorious Christmas Day celebrations, a ravishingly radiant Teresa at his side, and the whole of Ravenna sighing romantically over a love story which was already becoming legendary.

The Count obligingly offered Byron the second floor of his Palazzo and Byron, together with a menagerie which included a badger, a crane, dogs and monkeys, moved in. Bewildered Allegrina, as Teresa called her, was also of the household, driving out daily with Teresa whom she called her 'Mammina'. All appeared amicable but there were ominous undercurrents. Ignazio Guiccioli, the Count's eldest son, later wrote that his father systematically spied on the lovers and there was, as he watched his wife's radiance settle into a contented happiness, a price to be paid.

The Count had already extracted a certain amount of money from Byron and soon he was asking for more. As director of the Ravenna Theatre Committee, the Count wished to bring the celebrated but expensive diva Giuditta Pasta to sing there and Byron willingly subscribed £200 towards the project, only to find that the Count wished to take the credit for this act of patronage. In addition, Teresa had become over-confident and careless in the *ménage à trois*, spending more time in Byron's quarters than was discreet. 'So long as Guiccioli's avaricious and sordid mind nourished hopes of the Lord's guineas, there was no trouble,' wrote an observer, although Byron's refusal to fall in with the Count's plan that he should marry his twelve-year-old daughter offended him. Not only would this have secured the child's future, reasoned the Count, but he would also rent one of his Palazzos out to Byron and his child bride.

In April the Count took action. Byron was told that 'the visits he had once allowed had now become displeasing to him,' and Teresa was threatened with divorce. But the Countess had not been so imprudent as to deny the Count his marital rights. Although discovered almost *in flagrante delicto* by the Count's paid informer, Teresa had already admitted her liaison to her husband and he had neither objected nor ceased his own relations with her.

Teresa's grandmother was fortunately connected with the Pope and, supported by her family, she now petitioned for a legal separation, begging the Pope to command the Count to allow Teresa an income suitable to her position. Teresa's father was outraged and, for the first time aware of the degree of his son-in-law's villainy, expostulated to His Eminence the Cardinal Legate Rusconi that the Count had 'attempted, for vile financial considerations, to prostitute, sell and disgrace my daughter.' He challenged his son-in-law to a duel.

In mid-summer Byron wrote, 'There has not been such a row in the Romagna these three hundred years.' The region was aflame with gossip about the triangular drama being enacted in the Palazzo Guiccioli. The women were all sighs and swoons of envy and praise for the brave lovers; the men shrugged off Count Guiccioli's case as coming somewhat late in the day, 'after a year of toleration,' as Byron wrote. Totally captive, Byron committed himself irrevocably to Teresa : 'I am *now*, your lover friend and (when circumstances permit) your *husband*,' over which a jubilant Teresa wrote '*Promesse!!! d'être mon époux!!*' Since Lady Byron and Count Guiccioli were very much alive, however, their hopes of a future marriage were ill-founded and remote.

By mid-July the Pope had granted the request for a separation and Teresa, with the help of her father and brother, secretly packed and departed with them to her father's country home at Filetto, whilst her husband partook of his afternoon siesta. On awakening and finding that his wife had flown, leaving him only with her lover and his animals for company, the Count also departed and Byron was, apart from the servants and his zoo, alone in Ravenna.

Filetto was not far away, but Byron was unable to see Teresa alone, for the allowance of a hundred *scudi* a month from her husband was dependent on Teresa's chastity and Count Gamba and Pietro maintained constant chaperonage. Teresa kept the romance warm in her inimitable way; she would send Byron single roses, and he responded in style by kissing them. Unaccustomed to celibacy he wrote complainingly of her absence, rousing Teresa to unreasonable but natural jealousy of an ugly maidservant. It was at this time that Byron became part of Teresa's close and affectionate family circle. He was already fond of her many sisters, the youngest of whom was only two years old, and he frequently addressed Count Gamba as 'Papa'. This was to be Byron's only experience of uncomplicated family relationships. The fiery young Pietro with his wild ideas about liberty and revolution – what Byron called 'the very *poetry* of politics' – was especially attractive and in turn idolized Byron. There were pleasant outdoor parties, once to watch an eclipse of the sun; games of bowls and fishing afternoons on the river bank. Teresa had found another villa for Byron and Allegra nearer at hand, where Teresa was able to mother the child a little and help Byron with his work.

Teresa appeared content with this state of affairs but Byron distressed her by sending her a too-realistic French novel, depicting, he said, 'the misery unhallowed liaisons produce'. This evoked a torrent of reproach, for there were disturbing similarities between the book and her own love-affair. Teresa wrote him a long and stormily reproachful letter and Byron was contrite. 'Your flame-coloured hair and the head under it', he told her, are 'hotter than lava.' She preferred to read the French translations of Byron's works that he also sent her. These gave her greater insight into his character than did his conversation, she declared.

But by the end of October Count Guiccioli, desirous of reclaiming Teresa's allowance, was plotting, and threatening Teresa with confinement to a convent. As winter approached Teresa returned to Ravenna, where she resumed her role as Byron's amanuensis and inspiration. She told him quite plainly while he was working on a tragic epic that without love in it it would be insufferably tedious. Once again her unquenchable zest for romance triumphed over Byron's satirical streak and, smothering his sense of the ridiculous, he began 'Sardanapalus'. 'The sublime love of Myrrha was conceived that evening,' Teresa wrote.

Italy had been for some time in a state of political ferment. There had grown up a fervent revolutionary force intent on overthrowing the Italian monarchy, and Austrian domination. Inspired by the eleventh-century saint who had sacrificed wealth and position for a charcoal-burner's life in the forest, they called themselves the *corporazione de' Carbonari*. Rumours had reached the authorities that Byron was but fleetingly interested in the Contessa Guiccioli and that political agitation was his real motive in the Romagna, where Count Gamba and his son Pietro were prominent in the new movement. For some time Byron had been ceaselessly spied on; Teresa's father and brother were also under police surveillance. Even the seals on Byron's watch chain were interpreted as having some sinister political significance.

In the midst of rumbling revolutionary fervour, Teresa and Byron wrote and loved as unconcernedly as possible, while their lives in the Romagna were regularly punctuated by conspiracies, sudden arrests, assassinations and espionage. While Teresa had inspired Byron to write more romantically, he was privately expressing his political ideas in his journal. 'There must be a universal republic,' he wrote. The plottings erupted into a tragic farce of an encounter between Austrian troops and twice as many revolutionaries, most of whom fled, and on 18 July Pietro Gamba and his father were banished from Ravenna leaving Teresa with her younger sisters and Allegra, for whom she now arranged the fatal stay in the convent at Bagnacavallo.

As soon as Teresa was left unprotected, the ever-watchful Count Guiccioli seized his chance to demand her return or confinement to a convent, and she was thrown into a state of anguished indecision, distraught with the dread that if she left Byron she might never see him again. With difficulty Byron persuaded her that she must leave. From Faenza she wrote passionately of her tormented journey and sent him again a symbolically perfumed flower. Firmly but kindly, Byron rebuked her for a wild proposal to spend a day in Ravenna with him, and Teresa journeyed on to her father and brother in Florence. 'Teresa writes to me like a lunatic,' expostulated Byron.

They were not reunited until the autumn, by which time Shelley and his wife Mary were in Pisa, where Shelley had taken a house on Byron's behalf. Teresa had not met the Shelleys before, but she quickly came to a sensitive understanding of the poet's contemplative mysticism. 'Rather spirit than man,' wrote Teresa to Byron, and Shelley returned Teresa's sympathetic interest.

At Pisa Teresa impatiently awaited Byron's arrival from Ravenna where he inexplicably lingered. Her constant complaints irritated him, but he confessed to Augusta that his feelings for Teresa had mellowed into a conjugal affection, and he completed the circle at Pisa in late October. Never afterwards was Teresa to enjoy Byron's undivided attention. From now on she was to a degree an observer of a strange collection of expatriate intellectual eccentrics, a breed of which she had no previous experience. The unattractive and parasitic Hunts with their brood of dirty, undisciplined children arrived and the alarmingly piratical Trelawny loomed over the others.

Mary Shelley made the intellectual woman's mistake of underestimating the romantic female. She dismissed Teresa as 'a nice pretty girl', and Teresa was slightly awed by this *femme supérieure* who had already published several strange, unfeminine novels, the best known of which was *Frankenstein*, and who was now receiving daily lessons in Greek. Plaintively Teresa wondered if Byron would

love her more if she were to emulate Mary and become more of a
scholar, but she wisely contented herself with dictating to her lover
the course he should follow in writing 'Don Juan', which she had
earlier insisted he should discontinue, distressed by its extreme
cynicism. Once again, she emphasized, there must be more love
interest in his work, and Byron, with surprising docility, did as he
was told.

The winter was spent among the widening circle of English
literary figures gathered in Pisa around Byron and Shelley, but
Teresa kept herself aloof, confining herself to her private quarters
and driving out only with Mary Shelley. The following year was
doom-laden. Teresa had indiscreetly stayed with Byron at Leghorn
and word had reached the Count. Her allowance was thus endangered again, its cessation threatening her passionate independence, for, as always throughout her relationship with Byron, she
refused to accept money or gifts from him, or to be the kept woman
implied in the word 'mistress'. Yet her own family was too poor and
had too many others to support to help Teresa. Towards the end of
a humid Spring came the news of Allegra's fatal illness. Bulletins on
her progress were daily awaited, although neither Byron nor Teresa,
paralysed by the damp heat of Leghorn, travelled to see the child.
But when the final message came of her death and Byron was
stricken with silent grief, Teresa's practical sympathy came to the
fore : she attended to all the painful after-death details, the acceptance of death inherent in the Catholic religion and the Latin races
providing a comfort the self-punishing Byron could not experience.
Teresa supervised Allegra's embalming and the little body was
shipped to an embarrassed Harrow clergyman.

In spite of the Pope's evident sympathy for Teresa he could
scarcely ignore the obvious truth, and in July, 'in order to dissuade
the imprudent young woman', her allowance was suspended and a
sense of impending tragedy hung in the hot, heavy, summer atmosphere. There was, felt Teresa, an 'evil fate conspiring against our
peace'. At Pisa on 13 July a distraught Mary Shelley appeared in
the middle of the night looking for the missing Shelley, whose
drowned body was found five days later.

In Byron and Teresa's daily life there was little of its former
carefree passion and tranquillity, for the battening, thankless Hunts,
Leigh and his wife Marianne with their six children, were installed

in the Palazzo Lanfranchi, causing such chaos that Byron's bull dog guarded the upper floors from their depredations. Their coarse-living presence was a constant affront to Teresa's highly-cultivated elegance, their mode of living repellently ugly to her.

The political imbroglio in which all Italy was plunged had resulted in Count Gamba and Pietro being ordered to leave Pisa, their departure once again leaving Teresa totally dependent on Byron. The large party of expatriates embarked for yet another home at Lerici where Teresa's brother and father had found refuge and awaited her. Here the mood was elegiac. Teresa tried to comfort the grief-stricken Mary Shelley through the dark, turbulent months of winter during which Teresa was saddened by another death, that of her sister Caroline. Count Gamba tried to persuade Teresa to return to Ravenna to care for her remaining motherless sisters, an action he felt would materially assist in restoring her husband's allowance to her, but Teresa would not leave Byron.

'The eyes of the heart', she wrote afterwards, 'penetrate most mysteries.' Byron was already planning to go to Greece with Pietro but, lacking the courage to tell Teresa himself, he enlisted her brother's aid. Distraught with certain fatalism she cried, 'I know that we shall never see each other again,' and Byron, catching her sense of drama, told her she must write his life in Italy; in the 'fine style of San Chiara!' he added in a touching tribute to the elegant flourish of her pen. 'One does not write the life of a living man!' wept Teresa.

Byron left Teresa for Greece in July 1823, spending his last two hours alone with her. She was left with only Mary Shelley's unconsoling company, for Pietro, her loved younger brother, went with Byron. The following day Teresa and her father set off to try to return to the Romagna. Teresa was still only twenty-one years old. She knew it was the end of one life. 'I feel as if I were dying,' she wrote during the journey. At the frontier they were stopped and Count Gamba was seized and banished to Ferrara. Teresa was alone and without means but not without friends. She turned to her old professor Paolo Costa, from whom as a young girl, fresh from the convent, she had absorbed all the wisdom and philosophy endorsing her romantic attitude to life, and who had himself been exiled for his liberal opinions. Prevented from teaching at Bologna university he was earning a modest living by private tuition. Among his pupils

was the Count Guiccioli's eldest son, Ignazio, four years younger
than Teresa. The young man had inherited his father's passion for
the theatre and wished to become a dramatist. When a historical
verse play of his was later published, it was prefaced by a dedication to his beautiful stepmother.

Whilst at Bologna Teresa plunged into fresh studies in an effort
to assuage her fathomless sense of loss. Byron was conscience-
stricken, aware of the suffering he was causing her. However, he
wrote little and perfunctorily, often just a postscript at the foot of
Pietro's letters. The young man reassured his sister of Byron's faith-
fulness to her memory, but she who had been all fiery jealousy now
felt drained of feeling. In her letters she was unnaturally stoical.
Byron was pleased that she was studying English seriously at last
and Pietro wrote encouragingly, praising her progress in meta-
physics. Poor Teresa! Her tedious studies were poor solace for her
lost lover but with deliberate fatalism she applied herself to her set
task and in October both Byron and Pietro were writing anxiously,
Byron for the first time scolding her for her neglect. Teresa, who
had poured out her adoration in over 500 letters, was silenced by
the agony of his absence at war, the only adventurous pursuit the
history of man has shown to rival the lure of a sexual quarry. Teresa
laboured under a great sense of failure. She had given herself
unstintingly to the perfection of a great love-affair with her poet-
genius-lover. He had taken her gifts and had displayed a heartening
constancy but the alluring spectre of victory in Greece had defeated
her and she was now without hope.

Byron, who had always written to Teresa in Italian, now wrote at
her request in English for she told him she was becoming proficient
in it. So it was in his own language that Byron told her happily of
his sighting of a swallow. But the harbinger of spring foreshadowed
his death the following month.

Teresa's brother Pietro was able to write the necessary letters
announcing the news to others but, incapable of putting words on
paper to his sister, he left the British Consul at Ancona to inform
Professor Costa. Teresa's old tutor in turn was afraid that Teresa's
sanity would be affected and informed her husband the Count,
begging him to send her father. But the Count sent his eldest son,
Ignazio, and the eighteen-year-old boy broke the dreadful news
compassionately. In moments of high tragedy the true romantic

behaves with monumental dignity and Teresa was superbly calm in her grief. She had already said farewell to Byron and knew he would not return to her. In addition to losing Byron she was never to see Pietro again.

The following year Teresa, urged by her family, cautiously agreed to return to her apparently repentant husband. But the reunion was motivated by the Count's Machiavellian plot to trap Teresa in a compromising situation and drive her from him, thus causing her to forfeit her renewed allowance. In this vicious situation Teresa was virtually a prisoner with only the Count's children as allies, but she clung on while a statement was sent to the Vatican, as a result of which she was enabled finally to escape her husband five months after the mockery of a reconciliation.

The Count's son Ignazio confirmed that his father's subsequent frenzy was due not to the loss of his wife but to the obligation to continue her allowance which, to his further rage, had been increased. The sensitive Ignazio had also tried to escape his tyrannical father and wrote to Teresa, 'Now I see why . . . he came to destroy three wives . . . why no Friend has ever clasped his hand . . . why everybody hates him.' Teresa did not hate her husband in spite of his villainy. She wrote to him always in a spirit of compassion for the disease of his deeply-rooted unhappiness and loneliness, wishing him to be what a man of his nature could never be : content. Obsessively avaricious and selfish though he was, 'resentment', wrote Teresa, 'did not exist in my heart.' She never ceased to take a kindly interest in his welfare, writing most affectionately when his son died. When he suffered a cataract, she consulted distinguished oculists and anyone who might be able to help, while the half-blind old man, miserly and miserable, hobbled nightly to the playhouse, fascinated by the puppet-master's facility in pulling the strings in the marionette theatre. He seemed unable to endure Teresa's pity and his own inability to manipulate his escaped wife and truant children.

Following Byron's death it was inevitable that Teresa should become an interesting figure for the curious public, and she was conscious of her importance as the one enduring love in the life of literature's most romantic figure. It was a position she was proud of and which she used all her considerable arts to foster. Teresa was young still, but her life for many years after became a charade of romances with others who resembled, either physically or in spirit, the poet who had been the Paolo to her Francesca, the Dante to her Beatrice. The young man who was most to touch her heart was Henry Edward Fox, whom Byron had known as a boy. He was an appealing figure and resembled Byron in being handsome, lame and morbidly sensitive, but he had not that sensual streak or rebellious personality which had characterized Byron. Treated with cruel indifference by his mother Lady Holland, he was the begrudged heir, since his older brothers were illegitimate. Insecure and unhappily a fugitive, he met Teresa in Italy and immediately his boyish good looks and limp signalled to her the beginning of another legendary love-affair.

He was not attracted to her at first. Her pursuit of him was too candid and he did not care for her affectation of an ardour he did not share. But the reluctant young man found himself drawn to Teresa in spite of her sexuality which had initially repelled him, and their spasmodic, unsatisfactory liaison was to continue for some years. 'Poor Lord Byron,' wrote a weary Fox, 'I do not wonder at his going to Greece!' For Teresa was untiring in her efforts to romanticize the affair into a continuance of her earlier grand passion. The role of understudy is difficult and unrewarding and Teresa demanded more of him, emotionally and physically, than he could supply. Teresa subsequently had other lovers, but it was always Byron whom she sought and failed to find.

With her brother Vincenzo she paid the first of several annual visits to England in 1832, for she wished to make a pilgrimage to Newstead Abbey. While there she paid an emotional visit to the church at Hucknall Torkard, spending an hour closeted alone close to Byron's tomb. In London, as the guest of the socially dubious Lady Blessington, whom she had refused to meet when Byron and she had become acquainted in Italy, Teresa was once again a figure of romantic curiosity. Her clothes and Titian ringlets were unashamedly unfashionable in the modish drawing-rooms from which she gazed in sentimental nostalgia over the Hyde Park Byron had so detested; she aroused less romantic amusement by her sentimental singing at the piano.

But the worldly Countess of Blessington was among the few hostesses to receive Teresa. Mary Shelley, whose grief Teresa had shared in Italy and who in her turn had comforted Teresa on

Byron's departure for Greece and death, had changed and become irredeemably bourgeois. Shelley's widow, once with her husband an advocate of free love, and daughter of the woman who wrote *Vindication of the Rights of Women*, was living near Harrow with her son Percy, the heir to the baronetcy, a day-boy at Byron's old school. Terrified of losing her lately-acquired social position by receiving Byron's Italian mistress, she begged her not to call. Teresa was unaware of such niceties in the English code of behaviour and with her natural Mediterranean warmth went to Harrow nevertheless, visiting Allegra's grave and spending a day with Byron's tutor Dr Drury, but she and Mary did not meet again.

Augusta Leigh had always interested Teresa and it was with difficulty that Byron had dissuaded Teresa from writing embarrassingly affectionate letters to Augusta. John Murray now smoothed the way for an introduction and Teresa visited Augusta at St James's Palace, where they talked for several hours. Teresa may have expected a *femme fatale* and Augusta surprised her by her mousiness, although she retained an indefinable aura still. 'She is a very interesting person for me,' confessed Teresa to Lady Blessington after the meeting.

Teresa consulted John Murray about the sale of her precious hoard of Byron manuscripts. She was only prepared to part with 'the dear property' in order to raise a monument to Byron's memory in Ravenna near to the tomb of her other idol, Dante. The French poet Lamartine, who had sufficiently won Teresa's confidence in Rome for her to agree to his publishing their conversations about Byron, had betrayed her trust by suggesting in print that only a cripple could have written 'Don Juan'. Teresa was incensed. Whatever was the truth about his foot, she declared with immense charm, 'it was but one grace more.' Determined to preserve an untarnished romantic legend, she went to indefatigable lengths to perfect it, believing that the relationship should be hallowed for posterity as a pure, platonic love. She made innumerable erasures in the letters in her possession, obliterating unattractive references which were aesthetically displeasing to her and which might mar the image of the ideal love Teresa wished the world to see. The posthumous portrait of Byron which she supervised is poignant evidence of her feelings, a beautiful soulful-eyed, pale and full-lipped feminine face, without a spark of life.

Biographies and pamphlets increasingly appeared, Mrs Beecher-Stowe's articles published in an American journal causing Teresa much distress. She wrote and published her own story of Byron in which as, in the portrait, an impossibly ideal man was drawn. 'His nails were roseate as the shells of the ocean,' she rhapsodized, 'his lips were harmoniously perfect . . . his mouth . . . purely intellectual and divine . . . his sublime and noble brow . . . and that kind of supernatural light which seemed to surround him like a halo.' Below all the stylish phrases she revealed her awareness of Byron's political significance, the real reason for his self-exile. Indignantly she wrote of his hatred of his country and its hypocrisy, his passion for the truth, and his persecution.

In 1847 when Teresa was forty-five, she had lived alone for over twenty years. She now became the second wife of a childless widower, one of the richest men in France and a genial and loquacious senior politician. '*Je suis aristocrate*,' the passionate anti-monarchist Marquis de Boissy declared. Count Guiccioli had died seven years earlier, Teresa's father the year before, but Teresa had steadfastly rejected her persistent suitor. Finally she capitulated but drew up a table of conditions echoing her first husband's treatment of her. The enamoured Marquis signed the document unread, 'I shall be your lord and master in law,' he told her, 'your slave in fact.' As romantic a man as ever won the heart of a woman, Teresa's new husband took the greatest pride in his wife's former connection with Byron.

In Paris, in a palatial house the interior of which was designed as an operatic *mise en scène* with sparkling fountains and a large portrait of Byron importantly postioned, the Marquise de Boissy entertained liberally and happily, commoners, aristocrats and *littérateurs* together, her smiling husband at her side, seemingly content to play a supporting role to Teresa's romantic heroine. She took careful pains to present herself always as the woman Byron had loved, dressing her thinning hair forward over her forehead, her immaculately maintained *maquillage* preserving a youthful appearance.

'Always wear white for me,' the Marquis beseeched Teresa as he lay dying in the house Louis XV had presented to Madame Dubarry, two nuns praying by his bedside. Whereas Teresa had worn mourning for Byron, she thereafter always wore white.

11 Portrait of a lady in a mantilla, thought to be Medora Leigh. *Watercolour by Thomas Wageman.*

12 Countess Teresa Guiccioli aged eighteen. *After the painting by E. C. Woolf.*

13 Ada, Countess of Lovelace, Byron's daughter.
Painting by Margaret Carpenter.

Before her husband's death in 1866 she had become interested in spiritualism and had cultivated a friendship with the medium Daniel Dunglas Home through whom she regularly received spirit messages from Byron. Now she contentedly communicated with both men in their spirit world. 'I had the most perfect love for Lord Byron – the most perfect friendship for the Marquis de Boissy . . . they are together now, and are the best of friends,' she told a visiting worshipper at the shrine she had made peculiarly her own. Sitting on her Parisian terrace surrounded by gleaming silver and wild violets, amid murmuring fountains, she still played the part she had perfected – that of the fugitive wood-nymph captured by Lord Byron. She could be seen turning over with delicate fingers the precious keepsakes of a divinely blessed romantic past – a crimson-covered volume, a locket, scraps of cloth and a scattering of rose leaves and letters. These she would display to a privileged few in a sacred silence.

Once more Teresa went to England for a final farewell. During her time with Byron she had often presented him with a flower and she now left in his Cambridge rooms her last tribute, a handful of violets and a rosary.

After Teresa's death at Setimello in 1873, she was formally remembered by her countrymen for her devoted and practical work following a severe cholera outbreak in her native province of Romagna, but to the world and history she remains unforgettably Byron's last love. It was said of her 'None of her graces were free from art,' but it was an art which came from the heart.

The Next Generation

Medora

> 'Yet in my lineaments they trace
> Some features of my father's face.'
> *Parisina* (Stanza 13)

Elizabeth Medora Leigh was born in the spring of 1814, the Honourable Augusta Leigh's third daughter. A few days after the birth, Byron was at Six Mile Bottom to see the child he appeared to believe was his. He wrote to Lady Melbourne, 'Oh but it is not an ape, and it *is* worth while.' (A child of incest was superstitiously thought likely to be deformed.) The child was accepted as having been fathered by Colonel Leigh. A delightful child, she was known in the family as Elizabeth or Libby, but she preferred Medora, after one of the heroines in Byron's 'The Corsair', which was written at Newstead Abbey during the three weeks in January 1814 when Byron and the pregnant Augusta were snowbound there together. Medora was the third choice of name for the heroine of this poem. Originally she was Francesca. On 6 January she became Ginevra, nine days later Medora, which may be a contraction of the Spanish *'me adora'* meaning both 'she loves me' and 'he loves me'.

Augusta's husband never questioned his paternity and Medora grew up among her brothers and sisters, unaware that she might be the first of Byron's three daughters. Shortly after Byron married Annabella Milbanke, they were guests at the Milbanke family home in Leicestershire for several weeks. During that time, Augusta wrote to Annabella of Medora whom she and Byron sometimes called Mignonne, 'The likeness to Byron . . . makes her very good-humoured.' In another letter she wrote meaningfully, aware that it would be shown to Byron, 'Here comes *Medora*.'

A few weeks later the bridal pair were at Six Mile Bottom where Byron constantly asserted to his bride that he had been his half-sister's lover. His affection for the infant, less than a year old, was so openly displayed that Annabella innocently told Byron and Augusta that she wished Byron could be painted while looking at Medora. Thereupon Byron impulsively told his wife that he was Medora's father.

Eleven years later in 1826, Augusta, after surprisingly strong opposition from her husband, finally arranged the marriage of her daughter Georgiana, aged eighteen, to Henry Trevannion, a young, penniless Cornish connection of the Byron family, with whom Augusta had become infatuated. Augusta's great friend Mrs Thérèse Villiers, who was to play such an important part as a go-between with her equally intimate friend Lady Byron, later wrote to the latter, 'With respect to her [Augusta's] *fearless* opposition to Col. L. on the subject of Georgiana's marriage I have always had an ex-planatory version of *that* in my own mind, but being *solely* my own, I will not, even to you, commit to paper – though I would *tell* it to you.' Augusta and Henry Trevannion may have been lovers.

Medora and her mother were the only relatives present at the marriage. The young pair were penniless and without prospects and the marriage was only made possible by Augusta's appeal to Anna-bella for financial help. Lady Byron's assistance went further : she later lent the young couple, and the children who quickly followed the marriage, her mansion Bifrons[1] at Patrixbourne near Canter-bury, where Medora, now aged fifteen, joined her sister. According to Medora's narrative, 'The last admonitions I received from my mother . . . were to . . . please my brother-in-law.' She was urged not to cross him on account of his delicate health and extreme sensitivity, and she promised to do as her mother wished.

At Canterbury, three years after her marriage, Georgiana was pregnant with a third child[2] and far from well. Medora was left 'much alone with Mr Trevannion . . . thrown entirely upon him for society . . . with him both indoors and out, by day and night, and was frequently sent . . . into his bedroom on errands after everyone

[1] So called because of its double front. The mansion had belonged to the Rev. Edward Taylor who, according to rumour, discharged it as a gambling debt to the Prince Regent. The Prince Regent gave it to one of his mistresses, the Marchioness of Conyngham, to whose family the estate still belongs.
[2] Henry and Georgiana's daughter, Ada, was baptized at Patrixbourne on 28 June 1828.

else in the house had retired to rest.' Henry Trevannion 'took advantage of my youth and weakness,' continued Medora, 'and I found myself likely to become a mother.'

Medora declared that she had always disliked Henry Trevannion and had delighted in mocking him. Her seduction may have initially been, if Henry Trevannion was as sensitive as Augusta considered him, a form of revenge. Medora was said to resemble Byron as a child, and at fifteen she was a tall, dark-haired beauty, able to torment women and enchant men. Her brother-in-law was an unstable young sensualist, and Medora and Henry were prey to a mutual sexual attraction of such force that it was only to burn itself out eight years later.

Medora's condition at Canterbury was a cause of local gossip and it became apparent to a local clergyman, the Hon. and Rev. W. Eden, who told the new Lady Byron. Annabella was informed, Augusta was not.[3] Annabella, with Lord Byron was instrumental in sending the Trevannions and Medora across the Channel to Calais where Medora, 'in misery and anguish of mind . . . weak state of health', was delivered prematurely of a son who was left in the care of the doctor who attended her. Three months later the trio returned to London, the Trevannions staying with an aunt, Medora with her mother at her quarters in St James's Palace. The child, left behind in the care of a foster-mother, did not long survive.

Augusta, acutely conscious of her vulnerable social position and the precariousness of her finances, saw the desirability of launching Medora socially and tried to force the young girl, much against her will, into attending balls where she might be likely to attract the notice of eligible young men in society. Augusta was still unaware that her fifteen-year-old daughter had been seduced by her brother-in-law, much less that she had borne his child. It was about this time that the mentally retarded sister, Augusta, died, thus giving Medora a suitable excuse for avoiding the social activities into which she was pressed.

Medora was often alone in her mother's apartments while Augusta was occupied by her social round. Frequently visited by Henry Trevannion, she again became pregnant. Annabella later wrote to

[3] The new Lord Byron and his wife had quarrelled with Augusta Leigh on account of her inheritance.

Mrs Villiers that she was 'convinced . . . that after the birth of E's
first child . . . Mrs L was accessory to the continued criminality,' but
Augusta's letters written to Henry and Medora on the disclosure of
the state of affairs displayed genuine shock. Mrs Villiers wrote to
Annabella, 'After the birth of E's first child and when the second
was in progress . . . Mrs L was entirely ignorant of the criminality.'
The astute and curious Mrs Villiers laid verbal traps for her friend,
but Augusta did not fall into them and betray herself.

The Trevannions were about to go and live near Bath and,
according to Mrs Villiers, 'Elizabeth announced her determination
to go, assigning as her reason the intercourse she had with her
brother-in-law,' to whom she was now in total thrall. The weak-
willed Augusta forbade Medora to accompany the Trevannions to
Bath, upon which Medora staged a melodramatic scene, holding a
bottle of poison in her hand and threatening suicide if she could
not stay with Henry. Georgiana, who had suffered a good deal at
her young husband's hands, also declared that she wished Medora
to go with them as she feared her husband. The vacillating Augusta
could not but agree and the trio departed for the west country.

Colonel Leigh had displayed little interest in his wife and family
over the years but now Augusta was terrified that her husband
would learn the state of affairs at Bath where Medora, pregnant
with a second child, was staying with Henry and Georgiana. Henry's
treatment of his wife in the *ménage à trois* was so intolerable that
Georgiana constantly complained to her mother. Even then, Augusta
was too cowardly to approach her husband directly on the matter
and communicated with him through a third party. Perhaps aware
at last of the extent of Augusta's involvement with Byron, and
suspecting Medora's paternity, Col. Leigh finally travelled to Bath
and removed Medora to London. 'Colonel Leigh unexpectedly
arrived . . . preceded by an attorney and a sherriff's officer . . . in
a travelling carriage . . . a woman, intended to represent a lady's
maid, sat inside,' wrote Medora, and what followed 'was great
misery to me.'

It was at Bath that Georgiana and Henry had told Medora the
shattering news that Colonel Leigh was not her father. Though
George Leigh was not a man of integrity but a spendthrift and a
gambler, who had neglected his wife with disastrous results, Medora
was very fond of him and believed she was his favourite child.

Colonel Leigh's affection for Medora had caused him to act decisively in an effort to save her, an indication of Medora's great personal charm.

Before she left Bath, Medora had a few moments alone with Henry, who made her promise she would escape as soon as possible and elope with him. On going to her room to prepare for the journey, she found Georgiana greatly upset at the turn of events but the young wife promised Medora that she would try to obtain a divorce so that Henry and Medora could marry.[4]

Medora and Colonel Leigh set off in the carriage, Medora suffering some disillusion when the gambling Colonel's concern for his daughter evaporated at the first opportunity to cheat the turnpike with a bent coin. The party arrived at midnight in London where Colonel Leigh made Medora get out of the carriage. From Oxford Street they proceeded in a hackney cab to Lisson Grove where finally she was handed over to a Mrs Pullen.

Far from being, as she ardently hoped, rescued by the man she thought of as her father, Medora now found herself a prisoner, incarcerated in a room where 'the windows . . . were securely nailed and fastened down, and there were outside chains and bolts . . . to the door.' Although Colonel Leigh tried three times to visit her, Medora refused to see him. Her mother came only once and one of her aunts sent her several pious volumes, but the sixteen-year-old girl, awaiting the birth of her second child, who until she was fifteen had lived a close and happy family life with her brothers and sisters, would seem to have been largely abandoned.

Two weeks had passed in this solitary confinement when, apparently quite by chance, but probably with Georgiana's connivance, as she sat at the barred window looking out, Medora saw Henry Trevannion driving by with Georgiana and they exchanged glances. Thereafter Trevannion drove by nearly every day and Medora received secret letters from him hidden in her laundry. Trevannion bribed the woman in whose charge Medora had been placed and after four weeks' incarceration Mrs Pullen showed Medora how to remove the shackles fastening the door. Medora

[4] It was then against the law for a husband to marry his wife's sister. A divorce was not granted by the Ecclesiastical Court due to collusion between the parties.

seized her opportunity, put on her bonnet and walked out of the house to find Trevannion waiting for her. Secretly and speedily, the two made their escape.

They made their way to France and settled on the Normandy coast under the assumed names of Monsieur and Madame Aubin. Medora miscarried her second child and probably a third. 'Trevanion began to lose hope that I should ever bear a living child,' wrote Medora and they agreed to live apart, Medora informing her mother that she was about to enter a convent in Brittany.

Augusta agreed to allow her daughter sixty pounds a year and Medora entered the convent, but it was too late. In the convent Medora found she was 'once again likely to become a mother'. It was probably her fourth pregnancy and she was still under nineteen years old. 'The delicate state of my health . . . forbad the hope that the child would live,' she wrote, and with the kindly Abbess's permission she left the convent.

Her daughter Marie was born prematurely. Henry Trevannion was delighted and the three settled 'in an old chateau, in a secret and unfrequented spot . . . in great poverty, but as brother and sister.' Henry Trevannion appeared to reform; he 'at this time gave himself up wholly to religion and shooting', whilst Medora devoted herself to her now thriving child. But Augusta, who had for some time continued the allowance, came to hear of Medora's departure from the convent and 'under such circumstances I could not continue her allowance without considering myself accessory to her misconduct,' she wrote. Medora and Henry's problem was sheer subsistence; neither had any money at all nor prospects of any and Henry left for England on a begging mission. On his return, what she described as 'his passionate attachment' was renewed and he tried to revive relations with her, but Medora, now twenty-one, and absorbed in her child Marie, resisted him.

When Medora was twenty-four, the suffering and privation she had endured over the previous nine years began to take their toll; she fell seriously ill with consumption and appeared to be dying. Augusta wrote that she '*did all that was possible for me to do, to free her then and her child*' from the persistent Trevannion, for Medora and Henry were still together. A doctor who came to her rescue was kind to the friendless girl who, as she confided to him, had no one to turn to in a strange country. She implored his help in freeing her from Henry whose reformation had been short-lived. The sympathetic Dr Carrel's brother was a lawyer and Medora was advised to write to her aunt, Lady Chichester. On receipt of five pounds from her, she left Trevannion and with the three-year-old Marie settled in the nearby town of Pontivy.

Augusta took legal advice in an effort to rescue Medora, gave the doctor authority to act on her behalf and begged Medora to return to England. Monsieur Carrel, on the spot, fully realized the extent of Trevannion's power over Medora and wrote, 'As long as Mr H. Trevanion remained in the neighbourhood it was *impossible*.' Medora, too frail to endure any further emotional distress, repulsed her mother's desire to come to France, and she herself was too delicate to undertake the journey to England as Augusta wished. The distracted Augusta wrote to her. 'Dearest dear Libby – Your poor dear letter . . . has remained much longer unanswered than it ought to do – but I have been ill and I did not wish to answer it under the influence of extra depression.' Medora's letters were, she continued, 'most painfully distressing to me – first of all your health, on which subject I had been so sanguine, and then to think it has been made worse by distress of mind!' In answer to Medora's plea for money Augusta scarcely knew '*yet* what to answer to your *pecuniary* question : I feel all its justice and necessity, but am so situated that I can only say I *hope* to give you the £120 per annum . . . if I *can*!'

Augusta simply could not keep her promise. Mrs Villiers explained to a critical Lady Byron that 'the insanity and death of her daughter Augusta . . . debts and selfishness of her husband . . . disasters and misconduct of her Children . . . bad management . . . have obliged her to borrow money . . . and what ought to be her income, is consumed in interest for these loans.' Moreover, there were 'Georgiana Trevanion and her three growing up daughters! . . . deeply in debt . . . She is entitled to £100 per ann. since old Mr Trevanion's death – but has never received one farthing of that pittance.' Mrs Villiers later defended Augusta to Lady Byron : 'Her wishes and inclination led her to give hopes of more, the fault was in *that*, and not in the non-execution. . . . I see manifest proofs of poverty in and about her . . . her daughter Emily never goes about in society because she will not spend a farthing on good clothes when her sisters have no bread.'

Augusta confessed later, 'It is true that I sent her scanty sums –
but *I could not* send *more* . . . often driven to . . . painfully humiliating . . . borrowing what I have as yet been unable to repay.' She
detailed her responsibilities : 'Above the claims of my four other
children Georgey and hers have for the last six years been *wholly*
dependent on me, and . . . *it has been* difficult to save them from
absolute starvation.'

With no money and a child to support, Medora turned to the
French doctor and a furiously jealous Trevannion reported it to
Augusta, to whom the prospect of a possible marriage with a French
physician was worse than starvation. Mrs Villiers was more realistic
and told Annabella that it would be a blessing 'if Mr C., or even any
Tradesman, be he ever so low in the scale of society, had (knowing
her dreadful story) married Elizabeth.' However, Medora and the
French doctor did not marry.

In 1839 Augusta, straitened though her means were, hearing of
Medora's continuing ill-health and the probability that she would
not live long, tried to arrange a measure of security for Medora and
Marie. A Deed of Appointment was executed whereby on Augusta's
and Annabella's death, £3,000 would come to Medora to enable her
to provide for the child. The following year Medora, still destitute
in Pontivy with Marie, wrote again to her lawyer, Sir George
Stephen, begging him to help her sell her interest in her mother's
Deed, as her immediate need for money was urgent. News of
Medora, 'over whose cradle I had watched with peculiar feelings',
came to Annabella, Lady Byron. She could not possibly resist an
appeal to help Medora, whom she had known as an infant and
whom she believed to be Byron's daughter. The girl was less than
two years older than her own daughter, Ada. Philanthropic by
nature and wealthy enough to afford to be so, she was the sole
person to come to Medora's aid. She acted at once. Medora 'received
a most kind and affectionate letter from Lady Byron, and money,
with offers of protection for myself and child', and in August 1840
Annabella sent a doctor to France to escort Medora, who' willingly
and joyfully accepted these offers' and met Annabella at Tours.

Annabella's generosity to Medora exposed Augusta in an unfortunately unsympathetic light. All Annabella's moral indignation
at the aristocrats' lack of practical help for the destitute Medora
found expression when she wrote to Mrs Villiers that Medora 'was

exposed not only to severe suffering, but to the temptation of accepting assistance from wrong quarters,' a reference to the masculine help Medora enlisted when she could. A young mother in Medora's position was helpless in a society completely ruthless and dominated by predatory males. It was, unfortunately, unlikely that a man would offer help to a young woman encumbered with a child without asking a price, and the 'protection' often accepted by impoverished young women, who happened to be comely, was often their only recourse. The alternative was starvation and homelessness. In order to provide for her child, Medora went without food and was forced into neo-prostitution to retain a roof over their heads.

When Annabella and Medora met again, Medora's charm and frailty, gentleness and elegant manners aroused all Annabella's protective possessiveness. Once more, Lady Byron cast herself in the role of a guardian angel. Together with the small girl Marie, they went, as Annabella proposed, to Paris. Medora willingly agreed, eager to please in every way she could this extraordinarily beneficent lady who had suddenly appeared in her life. Annabella was unwell en route and they paused at Fontainebleau. It was here that Annabella told Medora the reason 'for *the deep interest she felt, and must ever feel*' for her. It was that 'Her husband had been my father,' although Annabella was later to write that Medora 'was unfortunately in possession of that fact before she was connected with me, and after much embarrassment from her allusions to it, I determined on admitting it.'

Medora wrote that she was 'willing and anxious, in any and every way . . . to prove both my gratitude and . . . repay by my affection and devotion any pain she must have felt for circumstances connected with my birth and her separation from Lord Byron.' Annabella told Medora that her 'only wish . . . was to provide for me . . . according to my rank in life.' But there was a price. Medora wrote that Annabella 'implored and sought my affection by every means . . . spoke of the comfort I would be to her, and of the necessity that I should be a devoted child to her.' Annabella wrote ardently to Lady Wilmot Horton of her 'increased conviction that there never was a case which had a stronger claim to assistance or where the assistance was . . . to be the means of . . . a continuance of good conduct. . . . I have declared myself responsible for E.L.'s safety and comfort.' Medora's health was still very poor and a cause for concern. 'By means of extreme care E.L. has escaped a dangerous illness this winter – but from time to time an absess forms in her chest – after it breaks she seems relieved,' reported Annabella. Medora's godmother, Lady Wilmot Horton, wrote from Brussels, referring to her own responsibility, 'The duties of that office in these days are not generally considered very strictly binding – that circumstance has I believe always caused her melancholy fate to prey upon me. . . . Was the report true of her having become R. Catholic . . . so likely to die, it is probably the best thing for her.'

Annabella made it clear that she would not sanction contact between the mother and daughter and wished Augusta to be kept in ignorance of Medora's semi-adoption. She now had an adoring, pliant young Byron at her feet at last, and they had continued in Paris for nearly a year when Ada, Annabella and Byron's daughter, now Countess of Lovelace, came to Paris with her husband; for the first time the two young women met, believing themselves to be half-sisters.

Medora wrote, 'I received kindness and promises from both, and was made to feel that I was to be Ada's sister in all things,' adding the phrase which presaged her future conduct, 'as I was really.' Ada was touched at Medora's devotion to her mother, and happy to have Medora's companionship. She was, she told Lady Byron, 'sure she is *genuinely* and disinterestedly attached to you,' but like her mother was anxious about Medora's delicacy and deteriorating health. 'Can she be saved think you?' she asked her mother, considering that her friendship for the girl 'may perhaps tend more towards keeping her alive than everything else could.' The two young women, totally opposite in temperament and upbringing, had become close friends.

The relationship between Annabella and Medora apparently prospered. Lady Byron took her to England the following year and showed her certain of Byron's letters relating to the separation which she thought might be useful in the Chancery suit yet to be heard. By means of the Chancery suit, Medora hoped to obtain possession of the deed of £3,000 made by Augusta. Sir George Stephen was acting for Medora with Annabella's support against Augusta, who felt that if the Deed were to be possessed by Medora and used to raise money its whole purpose, which was to secure Marie's future, would be endangered. The French doctor Monsieur Carrel was involved and so was Henry Trevannion. But now Medora, after years of travail, began to show signs of serious mental instability and Sir George Stephen her legal adviser found himself in the embarrassing position of having to call on the Earl of Lovelace, Ada's husband, to complain of certain statements in which Medora had seriously slandered him, insinuating that Sir George's sister-in-law was also his mistress. A distinguished lawyer, nephew of the reformer William Wilberforce, he took the trouble to write a long and, in view of the nature of Medora's slander, a very mild explanation of how he had come to assist his wife's two spinster sisters, the eldest of whom was a forty-two-year-old Brighton schoolmistress.

Mentally disturbed and physically frail, Medora became ill again, reluctantly incurring medical expenses which must be borne by Annabella, upon whom she was wholly dependent and the force of whose emotional blackmail was beginning to be irksome to her. Lady Byron told Medora that if she left her she would die and Medora's affection was sought by means of occasional small gifts and minor sums of money which the young woman was simply in no position to refuse. Generosity does not necessarily awaken love, nor is gratitude a prelude to affection. Medora was secure in Annabella's demanding grasp and her resentment at the many years' privation, which had resulted first in abject poverty and now in virtual captivity, became recriminatory and manic. If she were Byron's eldest though unacknowledged daughter, Annabella reasoned to Lady Wilmot Horton, 'E would have been entitled to [the fourth part of the sum] by an *equal* division of the Byron property amongst the Children . . . if the Testator's wishes had been regarded this child would have had the largest share.' Not only did Medora feel cheated of what she felt was her rightful inheritance, she was also made a further instrument in Lady Byron's revenge against Augusta.

The case against Augusta was settled out of court in June 1842. Augusta had collapsed and Annabella feared that the mental and physical strain of the previous two years had finally wrecked Medora's health and sanity. Medora was, as ever, in others' hands. She resented the fact that the case had been settled against her wishes and without any consultation with herself, the person most nearly affected; she also disagreed violently with the choice of the two trustees appointed to administer the Deed. She was still dependent upon Annabella, who became sadly disillusioned. Totally lacking in understanding of the girl in her care, she concluded that there were 'two holds on this character – Love of approbation and of money'. Under Lady Byron's wing, Medora had become used to a certain style of living, but her acceptance of it conflicted with her growingly frantic desire to be free of Lady Byron's confining bonds. She boldly told her so and declared her desire to return to France as soon as possible, arrogantly demanding the money from Annabella to enable her to go, for there was nobody else who could supply it.

Annabella, sensing Medora slipping away from her, was thus still able to exert a financial hold and told Medora that she would 'provide as Lord Byron would have done. . . . spoke of the necessity of my having a lady to live with me abroad.' Medora had no choice but to agree to Lady Byron's conditions, although she bridled and made it plain they were abhorrent to her. Nevertheless Lady Byron was obdurate : 'The provision which I have promised for your future maintenance . . . is irrevocably yours but I will not resign the control over its application. . . . Your wish to throw off that control . . . has convinced me more and more how little prudence you possess . . . when I promised *my protection* I meant it in the sense of watching over your interest to the end of my life.' However, sensing Medora's increasing hatred of her, Annabella appealed for compassion : 'Dearest E, Your future arrangements have occupied me much, though illness has prevented my discussing them . . . I fear to your annoyance . . . anxious to consult your wishes – but after some of your objections . . . it is not easy to find any plan which will be satisfactory to you as well as to me.' She assured Medora that her 'opinions and feelings . . . have never been *imposed* upon you . . . When you confided to me the welfare of yourself and child, you desired to be rescued from the evils and dangers of your isolated and unprotected position – to live retired and unknown.'

Medora was aware of her own physical frailty and, since medical opinion had some time earlier recommended a warmer climate, she decided to take Marie to live at Hyères in the south of France. Annabella was discouraged but wrote that she would still 'endeavour to find means of promoting . . . security and comfort.' She would pay the cost of the journey plus a yearly allowance of £150 and a nursemaid's wages.

To Ada the disconsolate Lady Byron poured out her misery at the approaching loss of Medora and Ada answered her mother's bitter cry with a calm assessment. Medora's opinion, said Ada, 'is that everyone (and you more especially) ought somehow to *make up* to her the fortune and position her Father destined for her,' and 'by as much as she considers is wanting to that end, will she consider herself wronged.' Ada reassured her mother that she considered her offer of money 'LIBERAL . . . many would think it *more* than *liberal*,' though she agreed that life in the south of France was likely to prove more costly than Brittany. Still, she argued, Annabella was giving Medora £30 more than she had considered sufficient.

The French lady's maid, Nathalie Beaurepaire, who was to accompany Medora had been engaged by Annabella and Ada. Her previous experience had been among the moneyed and once engaged she discovered that Medora was not the respectable widow she had been led to believe she would be serving, but that 'her life and past history were not such as she would wish,' as Medora herself put it. The maid's offhand treatment of her young mistress goaded Medora into suggesting that she should leave, an opportunity the maid declined, knowing that she was in a position likely to prove lucrative in the future. Thus was Medora once again delivered into the wrong hands. For the maid's husband was out of work and Medora was persuaded that a manservant was also necessary. With Annabella's grudging agreement, Nathalie's husband was engaged.

Hyères in the south of France had been decided upon but Medora had no idea of how accurately to assess her needs. Annabella's arrangements were that the quarterly allowance should be paid to the maid who would be required to submit accounts to Lady Byron of how the money was spent. Annabella would not 'agree to any contribution towards your maintenance . . . the whole charge or none – and when', she concluded sternly, 'you ask or receive money from anyone else . . . you annul our agreement.' Medora was to adopt the name she had used before, Madame Aubin, but Annabella cautioned her about its legal use – 'drafts and receipts must be in the name given in your passport' – warning her that 'to use a false name in transactions with Bankers is liable to a penalty . . . any person who could be trusted to deliver the money to you should be the medium of its transmission.' The only person was the maid and Annabella asked Medora, 'Do you trust Nathalie sufficiently?' Hence Annabella's stringent arrangements to prevent Medora escaping only served to bind her more tightly to the rascally pair of servants. The Medora who so passionately longed for independence was even more securely held.

Before she left England Annabella wrote her a letter full of puzzled reproach, elegiac in its dignified acceptance of Medora's failure to offer what was most desired – love. 'I suffered myself to believe that you . . . were able to love me – But I ought not to have let you deceive yourself and me . . . and should not have accepted your . . . affection. . . . I will endeavour to forget.'

The plans for Medora's departure went forward with an obstructive Annabella overseeing the arrangements. Medora wrote that she wished to take the Southampton boat but Annabella objected and wrote to Ada that Medora had often 'assured me she could not bear so long a passage . . . and to go by *Rouen* and Paris . . . I think she might die of the voyage,' while to Medora she sent an agitated letter giving her meticulous instructions as to the route she should take to Dover. Unknown to Annabella, there was a French officer Medora wished to meet in Paris whom she hoped would propose what she most longed for – a respectable marriage.

A few days before Medora left England she went to London and unexpectedly caught a glimpse of her mother as she was crossing Montagu Square from York Street. They had been estranged ever since the court case over the Deed and breathlessly Medora wrote to Annabella of the shabby, genteel mother whom she was never to see again, escorted by a squalid servant. 'I instantly recognized her . . . she shuffles along . . . & looks WICKED.' The gratified Annabella wrote back to Medora to tell her that she was 'nearer my heart than ever'. Medora in her farewell letter to Annabella addressed her as 'Dearest Pip', the pet name only Byron had used for Annabella : 'I have come up today early on purpose to get you a daguerrotype done of me . . . as little ugly as possible . . . I have had the little yellow smelling bottle you gave me filled with salts . . . & it never quits me,' but before Medora and Marie left the country her mood of grateful and fond affection had changed again.

They departed on 22 July after a day punctuated by hysterical scenes of frenzied recrimination on Medora's part. Ada who was with her wrote later to her mother that she 'at first refused the forty pounds I offered her for travelling expenses but finally clutched the bank-notes with a sort of contemptuous eagerness and impatient haughtiness !' Medora threatened to throw herself 'down the throat of the first man she could get hold of to marry . . . And then came all sorts of vituperations . . . some so really *ridiculous*, that one could scarcely feel otherwise than inclined to laugh.' Ada was too kind to laugh outright, and observed that the distraught Medora was 'subject to fits of extreme coldness and trembling'. Nevertheless Medora was eating well and Ada concluded calmly, 'She will not die at present, in my opinion.'

Ada's tranquillity in the face of Medora's appalling behaviour enabled them to part friends, but Ada's husband took a different attitude and wrote to Annabella in relief at Medora's departure : 'a curious compound – very unsatisfactory to deal with . . . She cannot bear dependence . . . she may escape . . . by marrying and then find herself in the power of a bad man.' Ada undertook to help Medora again should she be needed, and wrote to her mother, 'She is such a fool to stand in her own light; with that great tall childish figure of hers too.'

Annabella's stringent arrangements meant that Medora, Marie and the servants were short of money on their way through France. Unfortunately the French officer Medora was expecting to meet did not then materialize. After three days' travelling they arrived at Hyères penniless. Lady Byron had promised to spare nothing which would restore Medora's health and, wrote Medora, 'wished me to get masters for Marie's education; to hire carriages, & c., . . . and would send me books.' But her beneficence was doled out in small amounts to the maid, and only on receipt of favourable accounts from Nathalie, devices which served only to enrage Medora further. Moreover, Annabella, the mathematician, was unable to understand the lack of simple numeracy in others less well versed in rendering accounts. Neither Medora nor the French servants could understand what was required of them or carry out her instructions. By December they were very short of money and were forced to rent a cheaper house, while an exasperated Annabella was incapable of keeping the situation under control from a distance. Medora claimed that she never saw the letters which passed from Annabella to Beaurepaire, indeed, 'having had no control whatsoever over the money paid for my maintenance . . . neither ever having clearly understood its application', she could not 'explain it'. The servants were untrustworthy and Medora was obliged to borrow from them. Annabella decided that Beaurepaire must be dismissed but when Medora attempted to discharge him he merely laughed and told Medora of 'his devotion . . . and his intention of sooner than leaving . . . to stay for nothing.'

Medora had also asked Annabella for an additional twenty pounds a year for Marie's education. Her devotion to the child was total and passionate, a fact in her favour which Annabella duly noted, but she had become so sensitive to Annabella's possessiveness that when the latter sent a letter addressed solely to the child, Medora wrote a stinging reproof. Annabella, apologizing, wrote back, 'As to your alarm . . . I don't know what was in it . . . and if I did wrong in directing it to *Marie* I beg your Mamaship's pardon.'

Medora was once more desperate for money and was urged by the servants, who still pretended undying devotion to their mistress, to travel to Paris and there enlist the aid of the distinguished lawyer Monsieur Berryer, who had earlier helped her. To this end the whole party travelled north again, thus breaking the condition Annabella had made that financial help would only be forthcoming if it should remain Medora's sole source of income. Annabella wrote long-sufferingly to Medora, 'If you are not ill . . . I do not understand how anyone with either heart or conscience can act towards me as you do,' and withdrew her promise of an increase in the allowance due on Medora's approaching twenty-ninth birthday. She recalled Medora's birthday the year before when they had been together: 'Am I to believe that your tears and your tenderness were feigned? – I cannot do so,' she wrote in anguish, 'I must first hear from yourself that you were playing upon my affection. . . . Tell me then at once . . . that I may know whether I am still as I have been, Yours.' Medora had told Annabella of the projected trip to Paris but had presented Annabella with a *fait accompli*. 'You must be greatly improved in health,' wrote Annabella caustically, on being informed, and warned her friend Selina Doyle, then in Paris, that she 'could not recommend . . . Miss Doyle . . . to have any intercourse with her'. Wearily Lady Byron concluded, 'As to my pounds . . . they will only follow many others into the vortex of that family.'

In Paris Medora and the servants took lodgings, while accusations and recriminations flew back and forth between Annabella, Medora, the lawyer and the servants. In spite of Annabella's warning, the Beaurepaires obtained several sums of money from Selina Doyle and

Medora's escape to Paris gave her a euphoric sense of power which was reinforced by the lawyer's ready interest.

In May Lady Byron sent to Paris her emissary, a Dr King, with a proposal that Medora should unreservedly resign control over herself and her child to Lady Byron. This Medora instantly rejected and told Dr King that he could leave Paris immediately, for she would on no account agree. Dr King was the proprietor of a lunatic asylum in Sussex and though not informed of what Annabella called *'the secret'* of Medora's believed paternity, he medically examined Medora as, some years earlier, a doctor had examined Byron, and came to a not dissimilar conclusion. She was pronounced to be 'of sound mind'. Lord Lovelace asked Dr King his opinion of the French lawyer, for Annabella had confided to her son-in-law her doubts about Berryer's relationship with Medora, but Dr King's view was that 'Berryer had interested himself out of pure feeling and sympathy', and that all Medora suffered from was 'a certain self-sufficient, unmanageable spirit, too proud and self-willed to submit to any control whatever.' She was a true Byron.

After consultation, Dr King came up with a generous offer to Medora of £300 a year from Lady Byron, but again it was abso-lutely conditional upon her signature and complete surrender. Medora again arrogantly rejected it. 'Sign, sign, you great fool!' urged the doctor but he left Paris the next day, his mission unful-filled.

Prior to her departure from England Medora had deposited a box of papers with Lady Byron, including her mother's Deed which she was now advised by the lawyer to obtain. Annabella's lawyer refused to send the document, Annabella was too ill to travel herself and Medora too frail to go to London. Once again Nathalie Beaurepaire stepped in. Medora hesitated but gave her 'having little choice . . . an order authorising her to receive the box of papers . . . entrusted her with a letter . . . the name and direction of my family in case she should be in difficulties.' Medora recounted that the servants now 'behaved most insolently. Every day my misery increased.' The letters Nathalie sent from England indicated that she was behaving with gross duplicity and the alarmed Medora consulted Mr Bulwer of the British Embassy at Paris, who advised her that it was vital to prevent Nathalie from obtaining possession of the document.

At this point, a Captain de Bathe[5] arrived in Paris from the south of France where he had met Medora as Madame Aubin and, knowing nothing of her history, had been attracted by her charm. It was decided that Medora should travel to England and, if possible after all that had passed, appeal to Lady Byron in a conciliatory manner. The gallant captain agreed to bear the cost and escort Medora to London.

Medora's obsession with her supposed paternity dominated her actions at this time and she poured out her tragic story to all whom she met. An alarmed Sir George Stephen wrote to the Earl of Lovelace that Medora 'disclosed to a stranger the *whole* of her parentage . . . utterly lost to all sense of feeling and delicacy . . . she has a secret by aid of which she may extort money . . . where will be the end of it?'

In spite of Dr King's contrary opinion, Annabella decided that Medora's behaviour must be due to partial madness and determined to sever all contact with her 'and no longer to pay to *her* the annuity', arranging to help her anonymously if possible. Sir George Stephen gave it as his opinion that '£100 per ann. . . . is the very extent of all that good feeling . . . can require. Ten times [more] . . . would not satisfy her . . . men in my profession know . . . some people . . . can only be kept in order by the uncertainty of their means, and . . . Miss Leigh is one of them.'

Annabella was willing to allow '£150 per ann. to be placed in the hands of Trustees . . . provided the Deed be not sold,' and on the condition 'she do not return to a life of vice'. A few days later the Earl of Lovelace wrote to his mother-in-law, 'As for Mrs L. the only thing for her is suicide or flight,' for Medora, accompanied, protected and supported by Captain de Bath, was in London where she 'obtained by law the absolute control over the Deed.' She thus frustrated the furious Lady Byron who was placed, she wrote, 'in a most disadvantageous position. . . . I was a Guardian *without power.*'

Determined to withhold any further financial help from Medora, Annabella wrote, 'Her forfeiture of my protection consists . . . in 1st. Not having lived *retired* and *unknown* . . . endeavouring to excite the interest of Strangers, and divulging her real name. 2nd. In

[5] A Sir James de Bathe had been a friend of Byron's at Harrow.

adopting another Protector instead of myself.' Medora's godmother, Lady Wilmot Horton, pointed out to Annabella that '*If* she *could prove* herself to be a Natural Child . . . she would forfeit all her *rights*. . . . a Natural Child has no right. . . . it would invalidate even the Deed.' Medora by her conduct had alienated all sympathy and was endangering herself legally.

In London, helped by Monsieur Berryer and Captain de Bathe, she wrote to all her relatives, frenziedly applying for help, accusing Annabella of deceit and Augusta of avarice, feeling herself sacrificed to her family's desire to conceal her supposed paternity. The servants were actively blackmailing Medora's relatives. Annabella, who intended helping Medora, still 'carefully concealed the intention on my part of supplying the funds – as then the Beaurepaire would *adhere*.' 'Should Nathalie hint at any of E's revelations,' Annabella's defence would be an appearance of incomprehension. The Earl of Lovelace expressed anxiety 'as to the incredibility of the story . . . Berryer's taking her up may authenticate it,' but Sir George reassured, 'The story will be deemed incredible, and from *her* lips the raving of insanity.'

Pleading on behalf of Medora, Berryer the French lawyer had written to Annabella, 'Miss Leigh has revealed to me all her life's misfortunes . . . the sad circumstances surrounding her birth and that of her daughter . . . her poor health . . . the insufficiency of her income . . . her situation which could not but cause very great interest . . . her purity and nobility . . . she wishes for naught but to live modestly . . . solely devoted to her child . . . in a retreat of her choice . . . to be able to educate her dear daughter . . . I can confirm that the £150 was entirely insufficient . . . for herself, her child and for Nathalie Beaurepaire . . . I am convinced', the lawyer concluded with an emotional flourish, 'that you would suffer great distress if Miss Leigh were driven to desperation.'

By June the Beaurepaires and Medora between them were wreaking havoc among the Byrons, Leighs and Chichesters. Medora went so far as to imply that Annabella's motive in helping her initially had been to conceal her origin. Another gentleman friend of Medora, a Mr T. Smith, now appeared on the scene to plead her cause. Annabella ascertained that 'Mr S. was a person of respectability . . . formerly Secretary to the Chief of Justice at Corfu.' While stationed there he had been in the company of Byron for a period of some days. His intention was to mediate between Medora and Lady Byron, apologizing for Medora's appalling behaviour which he believed to be the result of ignorance and the French servants' villainy. It was to him and at his persuasion that Medora confided her written story, compiled at this time, although she was often too ill to write. The diplomatic Mr Smith saw Sir George Stephen who assured Annabella 'of his determination to make her absolute submission the indispensable condition of his mediating on her behalf . . . he has made himself acquainted with *everything*.'

The Beaurepaires were still hanging on, the grievance for which they demanded compensation being the original misrepresentation of Medora as a widow, and Dr Lushington advised Lady Byron that 'should Beaurepaire bring an action . . . Lady Lovelace and Miss L would be examined . . . the case would terminate favourably.' The prospect of another Court case was appalling and Dr Lushington recommended surrender. It was essential, '*in writing to fix the price of the loss of two characters*.'

Medora meanwhile wrote out a statement 'a brief sketch of a long life of misery and sorrow', copies of which were sent to numerous relatives in the hope of succour but the Duke of Leeds's ten pounds was the only result. Medora, desperate and unwell, acknowledged her uncle's gift from lodgings at '8, Church Row, Old St Pancras' in a long, incoherent outpouring of her history. She was, she told him, 'ruined at the age of fifteen . . . by those whose duty it was . . . to protect me.' She had acquired 'a taste for delicacies &c, my broken health required and which money alone can procure.' She had learned of 'the infamy of the mother, once so dearly loved, that I owed my birth to incest and adultery.' She found herself placed by Annabella, she wrote, 'in a position not to be endured, dependent on servants over whom I had no control, unable to have what was necessary for my health, and refused what my child's education required. . . . in the endeavours I have made to save myself . . . have found destitution.'

Three times, Medora maintained, she had begged Lady Byron's forgiveness. All she had was Augusta's Deed, 'the sole provision made for me out of the large property she received from my father – and her brother – Lord Byron.' She was anxious, she told her uncle, 'to give every proof of the truth . . . which is known to those alike respected and respectable . . . almost a stranger as I am to your Grace . . . beg you to consider my desolate and destitute position.' She signed herself 'most gratefully Your Grace's Obedient humble servant, E.M.Leigh.'

Medora was turned away from her mother's door and wrote to her the next day, 'My mother, the motive that led me last night to seek what I . . . hoped to be spared, to meet once more, you, I so tenderly loved, was not . . . to accuse you and reproach you, nor . . . to awaken your pity, for the misery I owe alone to you. Since I was made to understand you could never have loved me, the child of your guilt . . . a sacrifice to be made to those you feared . . . I have expected and sought nothing from you.' She was, she wrote, 'now compelled to seek aid . . . once more remind you I am *your child* . . . could I have felt I was writing to a mother, I would have said much, now I can only beg you by the memory of my father, the brother to whom you . . . owe all – no longer to forget and neglect . . . Your child Elizabeth Medora Leigh.'

Medora applied to her cousin, the Hon. William Osborne, 'When I was a happy child, you used to be kind and good-natured to me . . . I am in suffering and misery, will you refuse me what I am compelled to ask . . . aid and protection? I am sure you will not.' To her other cousin, the Hon. D'Arcy Osborne, she wrote, 'I have thought that, though so many long years have gone by since we met, you will not . . . refuse to befriend, one you were once fond of; – destitute, alone in the world . . . if I am mistaken in so thinking, forgive this application from your cousin Elizabeth Medora Leigh.'

Her letters were ignored.

In December 1844 Sir George Stephen informed Annabella that he had no more news of Medora : 'It is impossible not to infer that she has found other resources.'

Medora had. Earlier that year, her piteous pleas for help from her family ignored, she had found another benefactor and had borrowed £500 from a Captain Hugh Cossart Baker on the security of the Deed. It was a legally drawn indenture and interest on Captain Baker's loan was paid regularly for three years, after which it ceased, the capital still owing. Towards the end of that year, Medora and Marie left England for the last time, once again bound for the south of France. She was now thirty, and Marie ten years old.

The list of military gentlemen who had befriended Medora came to an end with her marriage to a retired French officer in St Afrique, and in 1848 when she was thirty-four she gave birth to another child, a son named Elie. A year later, her slight frame exhausted and wasted, she died. The news reached her family through her lawyer to whom her daughter, Marie, now aged fourteen, had communicated the news. 'What is to become of the unfortunate child?' asked Lady Wilmot Horton of Annabella. Abandoned by all her family, Medora's children and widower were befriended by an elderly, retired French army officer, G. de Warroquier, who told Lady Byron, 'Do not judge her harshly. . . . God has claimed her at last.'

Ada

'Her thoughts were theorems.'

Don Juan (Canto I, Stanza 13)

Augusta Ada Byron was born in London on Sunday, 10 December 1815. From the moment of her conception, probably at the Lodge, Six Mile Bottom, near Newmarket, where her parents Lord and Lady Byron were on a wedding visit to Byron's half-sister Augusta, her mother was subject to the severest trials. During this extraordinary triangular visit Byron made it plain that he preferred the company of his half-sister. Annabella wrote of evenings when she went to bed alone, and later she told how 'Once or twice . . . I heard the freezing sound of heartless professions.' Throughout the rest of Annabella's pregnancy, which was spent in Piccadilly Terrace, Byron's behaviour was so alarming that she had to be guarded by day and night.

The expectation of an heir caused Byron to display occasional concern for Annabella, who was in mourning for her uncle, and a kind letter from him surprised Annabella and made 'young Pip', as the expected child was referred to, quicken. Annabella ended her letters to Byron 'A-da', a form of 'adieu' echoed later in their choice of name for the child. Byron declared his intention of leaving the country the moment the child was born, 'because a woman always loves her child better than her husband.'

Annabella was an only child, born late in life to Lady Milbanke who took a consuming interest in the forthcoming birth of her first grandchild. 'I very *highly approve* of your engaging Mr Le Mann,' she wrote to her daughter, 'in preference to any of the fashionable Accoucheurs as really it is not a business of *fashion* but of *Nature* . . . you will get through without more than the necessary sufferings. . . . I trust that the first cry of a fine Child will cause you to forget them, as the Sweet Sound of yours did me.'

The Milbankes were provincial and practical. They did not move in fashionable society, which Annabella considered intellectually beneath her. Annabella's mother recalled 'the *surprise* excited by my chusing to stay in the Country' for Annabella's birth, engaging a local doctor to be in attendance, rather than going to London and having 'some other *fine* man . . . not *half* so *attentive*. . . . Croft, the fashionable man . . . people continued to place confidence in, even after he became *deranged* . . . a very *Vile Man* . . . attending the Duchess of Devonshire and keeping her *Secrets*.' Another popular medical man of the day was indebted, Lady Milbanke declared, 'for his introduction to the fashionable world from attending Moll Raffle abroad, for which the Marquis of Wellesley gave him an immense sum.' 'Pray let little *Pip* . . . have handsome apparel, as well as *Mamma*,' generously instructed Lady Milbanke to her daughter, offering to foot the bill, 'as I shall have pleasure in decorating the little Byron.' And Lady Milbanke's pride in her daughter's splendid marriage was such that she sold some of the family jewels in order to pay for a romantic portrait of her celebratedly handsome son-in-law to be painted by Phillips. It showed Byron in Albanian costume.

Byron's fondness for animals added to Annabella's trials. Not only was his huge Newfoundland dog in Piccadilly but also his pet parrot, who more than once attacked Annabella's foot, causing Byron to dash out of the room and hurl the parrot and the cage through the window into the area below. His financial affairs were in such disorder that bailiffs were constantly coming and going, and the prospect of making Lady Milbanke, whom he greatly disliked, a grandmother, was the only thing which lightened his gloom. The Milbankes too were in financial distress, with Annabella's father on the brink of a debtor's prison.

Such were the stresses and strains attendant upon Lady Byron during her pregnancy. As her confinement drew near she was aware of increasing concern on all sides about financial matters; Augusta was a disturbing presence, and Byron's growing violence such that she feared for his sanity. During Annabella's labour Byron frenziedly hurled objects about in another room and sent word to Annabella that her seriously ill mother had died. A few hours before the birth Byron told his wife that he hoped she would die and the child too. Should the child live he would curse it, he told her. Augusta Leigh, Mrs Clermont, Byron's valet Fletcher and George Byron all believed that after the birth she would be in considerable danger if left in the house alone with him. Told of his child's birth, the new father looked at it and asked his wife, 'The child *was* born dead wasn't it?'

Augusta Ada Byron, despite this tumult, grew up possessed of a notably calm temperament. The child was called Augusta, after her aunt, and Ada, a name Byron admired and had chosen because it had commonly occurred in his family during the Plantagenet reign. At first she was known as Augusta junior, for Byron fancied a resemblance to his sister, who was invited to be a godmother.

Five days after Ada's birth Annabella was writing of her resolve to separate from Byron, telling her mother she would be pleased when Ada could be consigned to her grandmother. Byron's earlier violence had subsided into a cold withdrawal and early in January Annabella received a curt note from her husband. As her mother had asked her to Kirkby, he wrote, 'There you can be for the present . . . the sooner you can fix the day the better . . . The child will of course accompany you.' Annabella had been advised that a trial separation was desirable and answered that she would arrange to leave as early as possible. On the day before their departure Annabella took the month-old infant for Byron to see, in what was to be a final farewell.

But the separation was supposedly only temporary and Annabella wrote Byron cheerfully affectionate letters informing him of Ada's progress. En route to her family home she wrote, 'Dearest B . . . the child is quite well, and the best of Travellers . . . Ada's love to you with mine.' From Kirkby she wrote fondly again, telling Byron that the 'little angel' was flourishing in the fresh Leicestershire air. Annabella herself was more relaxed and she continued, '*Miss* finds her provisions increased, & fattens thereon.'

Ada was left in her doting grandmother's care while Annabella, preoccupied with the legal tangle of the separation proceedings, joined her father in London. Desiring reunion with Byron, and terrified that she might lose Ada, whom Byron was determined not to relinquish, she suffered great emotional stress at this time. Unknown to Byron, she and her father arranged for a bill in Chancery which made Ada a Ward of Court. The sinister Mrs Clermont had been left in Piccadilly, reporting on affairs there to her mistress, and Byron's feelings about her exploded in a set of verses which, when published in a Tory newspaper, caused a considerable stir in political circles, for Mrs Clermont, as we have seen, was rather more than a family retainer.

On her marriage, Annabella's fortune of £20,000 became the property of the husband, and when her uncle Lord Wentworth died during her pregnancy his will was 'so worded as to place the property, when inherited' by Annabella '*wholly in my husband's power*'. During the summer, while Byron, Annabella and Augusta were awaiting Ada's birth, Byron wrote his will, making Augusta and her children his sole inheritors and making no provision whatever for his wife and daughter. Although she was secure in the knowledge that Ada's future interests were well-protected,[1] for the present Annabella was forced to ask Byron to provide for her. 'I could not have maintained myself and my child properly for less than £500,' she wrote. Her father's financial embarrassment precluded any help from her parents.

The Deed of Separation was signed by Byron and Annabella in April 1815, by which time the name Augusta had been dropped and the four-month-old child was known as Ada. Obsessed by the idea that Annabella was planning to take Ada abroad, Byron repeatedly tried to exercise his paternal authority, even threatening litigation : 'Remember I require an explicit promise that Ada shall on no consideration quit the country. . . . By all that is most sacred, there is no measure which I will not take to prevent it.' Annabella replied distantly through Augusta, with whom she was in constant touch, that she had never had any such intention, but Byron was not satisfied and Annabella was forced to issue a formal declaration : 'There never has existed, nor does there exist, the remotest intention of removing Miss Byron out of the Kingdom.'

Eager for news of Ada, Byron wrote from the continent, constantly asking through his sister for news of his infant daughter. Pride of paternity in most men rests with legitimate offspring. Byron sent a parcel of presents to Augusta to share out among her children. He did not single out any of Augusta's children but mentioned Ada three times, telling Augusta that he wished Ada to have a ball and a crystal necklace and that she was to give Ada 'anything else you may like to add for her – the love !'

---

[1] £16,000 had been secured by the marriage settlement, to go to Ada on Byron's death.

Annabella had settled for the moment in 'Lowestoffe' with Ada. They stayed in the small house for some months, and there in Lowestoft, fronting the cold North Sea, attended by several servants and a nursemaid, the child grew strong, flourishing in the bracing East Anglian air on a protein diet, 'sucking beef and mutton in a bag . . . so good-humoured that it will be a very agreeable companion.'

On Ada's first birthday Annabella wrote some verses for her daughter, an elegy for her own lost hopes. These were sent to her confidante Mrs Villiers with a warning not to suppose that Annabella longed for Ada to be with her father. 'I consider her as *fatherless*,' she wrote. But during a visit to Madame de Stael, Byron's own poem about his daughter was openly displayed to Annabella. In these verses Byron wrote that he believed his daughter would be taught to hate him and Annabella appealed 'to all who have ever heard me speak of him, and still more to my own heart, to witness that there has been no moment when I have remembered injury otherwise than affectionately and sorrowfully.'

Lady Noel, however, could not forgive Byron his treatment of her daughter, and Ada was often in her care as Annabella began the restless wanderings which took her all over England. Ada's grandmother decreed that Ada, whilst a child, should know nothing of her father, making a stipulation in her will that Ada should not be shown his portrait until she was twenty-one.

When Ada was two years old Newstead Abbey was sold to Colonel Wildman for £94,000; Ada was not to visit it until the year before her death. Annabella began to write her life story especially for Ada, fearing that other, more romantically inclined persons, whose view of Byron was unhampered by the experience of marriage to the poet, would influence her daughter. Byron meanwhile wrote to Augusta of 'the eternal war . . . which I foresee about . . . Ada,' and in 1817 he informed her gloomily of the imminent birth of his child by Claire Clairmont, the child he came dearly to love, feeling she might be a comfort to him in his old age since Ada was denied him.

Ada, conceived and born amid scenes of turbulence and distress, grew up a quiet scholar. She did not appear to resemble her father but displayed great powers of concentration, singleness of purpose and an extraordinary intellectual vigour. Byron continued to communicate with his wife, commenting that their 'domestic affairs . . .

have now . . . nearly made a tour of Europe . . . been discussed in
most of its languages, to as little purpose as in our own,' and always
pleading for news of his daughter, of whom he heard nothing for
months at a time. He wished the four-year-old child to start learning
Italian and asked for a portrait of 'Miss Byron' to be painted by his
favourite Holmes, whom he also wished to paint Augusta. Shortly
after Ada's fifth birthday Annabella firmly declined to read Byron's
proffered memoirs, considering 'the publication or circulation of
such a composition at any time . . . prejudicial to Ada's future happiness.' Byron sent Augusta a few locks of his hair asking her to
'select the *best-behaved* curls, and set them in a golden locket for
Ada my daughter,' and ordering an inscription to be engraved round
the locket, '*Il sangue non i mai acqua*,'[2] the Italian version of blood
is thicker than water. He hoped that Ada would wear it, desiring her
to know at least of his existence.

When Ada was eight, Byron was in Greece and wrote wistfully
again to his sister, wishing she 'could obtain from Lady B some
account of Ada's disposition, habits, studies, moral tendencies, and
temper, as well as her personal appearance.' Except for the miniature drawn five years earlier he had no idea what she looked like
and craved to 'form some notion of her character, and what way
her dispositions or indispositions ought to be treated.' He promised
he would not interfere with Lady Byron's plans for their daughter.
'Is she imaginative?' he asked Augusta. 'Is she social or solitary;
taciturn or talkative, fond of reading or otherwise, and what is her
tic? . . . her foible – is she passionate?' He hoped 'the Gods have
made her anything save poetical . . . enough to have one such fool
in the family.' His hopes were realized. Ada preferred prose to
poetry and her 'tic' was mathematics, 'chiefly exercised in connection
with her mechanical ingenuity'. Lord Byron's eight-year-old daughter was absorbed in constructing ships and boats. Byron responded
to this information with passionate interest : Ada's 'tendencies very
nearly resemble my *own* at a similar age . . . Strange as it may seem
. . . her preference for *prose* . . . *was* and indeed *is* mine (for I hate
reading verse, and always did.' Delightedly he told Augusta he
'never invented anything but *boats – ships*.' A recent severe illness
he had suffered appeared to be epilepsy, he told Augusta, and

[2] Literally, 'Blood is not water.'

anxiously asked her to warn Annabella to consult a doctor in case Ada should be affected. A few months later Byron was dead.

Annabella wrote to Mrs Villiers of the effect the news had on his daughter : 'Ada shed large tears . . . It is a great comfort to me that I have never had to give her a painful impression of her father.' The fiercely hostile Lady Noel had died the previous year and Annabella was now free to speak of Byron to his daughter. The following year Sir Ralph Noel died and Ada became her mother's sole charge.

A governess was engaged and, together with a woman friend, Annabella and Ada travelled extensively in Europe. They spent a year touring Holland, Germany and Italy. Annabella had discerned a talent for drawing in the child and at Genoa arranged for Ada to take lessons from a Signor Isola, whose services Byron had employed. Ada was nearly eleven and displayed an independence of mind which was encouraged by her mother's liberal views. She did not care for her governess nor did she share the romantic attraction for the sea that both Byron and Annabella enjoyed. On Ada's first sight of the ocean she commented shortly, 'I don't like it. It is so like my governess.' They travelled back through Switzerland and here Annabella took Ada to visit Emmanuel de Fellenberg, disciple of the practical Christian, Henry Pestalozzi. Both men had been pioneer educationists generations in advance of their time. The well-born de Fellenberg, destined for politics but fired by Pestalozzi's ideals, had established a school at Hofwyl dedicated to the education of all classes of boys by training through physical activities. His theories impressed Annabella to such an extent that she put them into practice later in her life.

To mark Ada's fifteenth birthday Augusta sent her niece a birthday present. 'I could not resist sending her some little token of my remembrance. I selected a Prayer-book . . . in two volumes . . . had them nicely bound, and *Ada*, in Old English characters, engraved on the back . . . directed "to the Hon. Miss Byron, with every kind and affectionate wish".' Cautiously Augusta wrote over this, 'With Lady Byron's permission . . . In another outside envelope directed to them to Lady B, sent them booked by post,' but Annabella did not care for the gift and the disappointed Augusta concluded, 'and have never heard one word since.'

At sixteen Ada's governess was replaced by Dr King, an academic friend of Annabella, who offered to tutor Ada. He took the post at

£300 a year. 'He is just the person to work out my ignorance,' wrote Ada.

Annabella was pleased with Ada's progress under Dr King's tutelage. 'There are no weeds in her mind,' she wrote proudly, but Ada was incurably untidy. Excessively tidy habits may conceal mental disorder, but in Ada this was reversed, her husband later complaining of her chronic untidiness. Already the sixteen-year-old had read widely. 'She has taught herself part of Paisley's *Geometry*,' wrote Annabella, 'which she especially enjoyed.' But all this intellectual stimulus had not always agreeable results as far as Annabella was concerned. Ada boldly challenged her mother's ideas with unanswerable logic, until even Annabella was bewildered and complained. It also resulted in a breakdown, for a mysterious illness struck Ada when she was sixteen, her body and mind suffering from severe overstrain. Dr King was dismissed. 'Everyone laments the interruption of her education,' wrote Annabella, adding wisely, 'whilst I observe its progress.'

The male tutor was replaced by a Miss Lawrence and from her Ada, still unable to walk without crutches, absorbed the growingly popular religious principle of Unitarianism. Miss Lawrence had run a school of her own at Liverpool. The dominating feature of her religion, an off-shoot of Congregationalism, was the rejection of the mystery of the Trinity : 'The essence of God is one, not in kind but in number.' Priestly, the famous scientist and discoverer of oxygen had been a dedicated Unitarian in the late 1700s, which fact appealed to Ada the mathematician. Many Unitarians of the time were gifted intellectually; they were practical Christians, deeply interested in democracy and social progress.

Miss Lawrence impressed Lady Byron by her new teaching methods. In advance of her time, she used linked square boxes which were subdivided, and had to be filled according to subject, detail and interest. 'The squares were gradually filled up', observed Miss Lawrence, 'as the knowledge enlarged.'

Miss Lawrence was but one among Annabella's circle of idealistic and distinguished friends, who helped to influence Ada towards Unitarianism. William Frend had established the first Sunday-school at Madingley near Cambridge. Unorthodox and hot-headed, he had abandoned the established church for the pursuit of a more practical Christianity. 'This odd, imperious man, warm-hearted, . . . instilled his freedom of thought' into Ada, resulting in the girl's distrust of the established church, its dogmas and its clergy.

These educational and religious influences, colourless, cheerless and provincial, were fostered by Annabella, whose horror of the feckless aristocratic attitude to religion and life determined her daughter's and, in turn, her grandson's academic and social education.

Annabella's desire to reform the English upper-class educational system was largely inspired by Byron's experiences at Harrow and confirmed by her friendship with William Frend. She wrote, 'Castes are as much the disgrace of England as of Hindustan.' Her overwhelming abhorrence of the Public Schools caused her to thunder, 'The outcry against these evils is beginning.' To Ada, as to her mother, the upper classes were always to be inferior.

The finer things of life were not neglected entirely by the zealous Annabella in favour of her efforts to develop Ada's social conscience. Byron expressed a wish that Ada should study music and she learned to play the violin, practising tirelessly and preferring to walk round a room playing for hours rather than stop playing to go outdoors for necessary exercise. She also played the guitar and that more romantic instrument moved Annabella to recall Byron's tenderer moments. 'More than music haunts the air . . . Is it a spirit . . . touches thus my heart?' she wrote privately. Ada was later to foresee the possibility of computerized music : in her commentary on Babbage's innovatory analytical machine, she wrote : 'Supposing that the fundamental relations of pitched sounds in the science of harmony and musical composition were susceptible of such expression and adaptations, the engine might compose elaborate and scientific pieces of music, of any degree of complexity.'

The 'singular girl', as she was described by the popular red-haired Irish woman writer Mrs Jameson, was introduced to her father's poetry in her late teens. 'Read to Ada the beautiful lines on Greece in *The Giaour* and the *Fare thee well,*' wrote Annabella, recording that the critical Ada was 'With the first highly pleased, from its *effusion of feeling* character, the second she thought laboured and inferior in pathos.' At such an impressionable age a considerable but concealed interest in her father was naturally aroused, although it did not appear to extend to his poetry. Although all Byron's poetry was available to Ada in the drawing-room at Fordhook in Hampshire where they lived for a time, Lady Byron was astonished and disappointed at Ada's apparent lack of interest. Byron's daughter was silent and secretive about her instinctive perception of the truth about her father.

When her daughter was eighteen, the philanthropic Lady Byron put aside her social conscience and presented Miss Byron at Court. Annabella wrote that 'the young Lioness . . . was drest in white satin & tulle & c.' Still not very robust physically, it was feared that the presentation would exhaust Ada, but fortunately she only had to stand for fifteen minutes. Neither mother nor daughter took pleasure in such frivolities as fashionable costume but Annabella wrote, 'I find myself obliged to give more thought to these matters [balldresses] . . . in order to prevent *her* from being called upon to do so.' It was wearying work. 'I cannot help wishing *the Season over*,' Annabella wrote. Ada, unused to Court life though she was, was neither awed nor impressed but was a detached observer, entertained by her first sight of such august personages as the Duke of Wellington, Talleyrand and the Duke of Orleans. She reported to her mother about these eminent persons that 'she liked the straightforwardness of the first,' – Talleyrand she thought simian but the Duke's Gallic charm delighted her.

From a life of provincial dullness and serious study Miss Byron emerged a bright butterfly who enjoyed the brilliant social scene. 'She is going to the Court Ball on the 17th,' wrote Annabella during the season of 1833. 'The expectation of hearing the Band, and of seeing some distinguished persons, makes her look forward to it with pleasure.' But Annabella feared that Ada's enjoyment might be spoiled by the excessive public interest which the name Byron still generated. Ada appeared to be unconscious of public curiosity, however, and danced energetically all night long in spite of Annabella's anxiety about her possible fatigue. 'They who dance with temperance will be likely to pray with more pleasure,' observed Annabella solemnly, deciding that archery would be a more suitable exercise and furnishing her garden with a target for Ada's use. Ada's sense of the ridiculous was roused to helpless laughter by operatic convention. On being taken to hear the celebrated Giuditta Pasta, the greatest diva of the day, for whom Bellini wrote *Norma* and *La Sonnambula*, in the role of Donizetti's *Ana Bolena*, Ada found the work irresistibly comic and refused to take it seriously.

The following season her interest in mathematics reasserted itself. Another of her tutors had been Dr Augustus de Morgan, whose wife Sophia was William Frend's daughter. Sophia wrote that Ada's 'greatest delight was to go to the Mechanics Institute to hear the first of Dr Dionysus Lardner's lectures on the difference engine. . . . While the rest of the party gazed at this beautiful instrument with the same sort of expression and feeling that some savages are said to have shown on first seeing a looking glass or hearing a gun, Miss Byron, young as she was, understood its working and saw the great beauty of the invention.' The engine was the invention of Charles Babbage whom Ada met at this time and with whom she was to be associated for the rest of her life. During the same season Annabella took Ada to the Doncaster races in the misguided expectation that seeing the wagering English, rich and poor, enjoying the sport of kings would horrify Ada as it did Annabella, who deplored 'the risk to man and beast . . . desperate gambling.' The excitement of race-course life and gambling, however, were intoxicating and Ada's reaction was exactly the opposite to that so ardently hoped for by her mother. Combined with the limitless mathematical visions inspired by Babbage's machine, it was later to have catastrophic results. Deciding that her daughter should see the harsh realities of working-class conditions, Annabella took Ada in 1833 on a tour of industrial centres, visiting a ribbon factory at Coventry, the Derbyshire potters and other Midland towns, but Ada ignored the people, fascinated by the machinery. 'Science has thrown its net over me,' she was later to write, 'and has fairly ensnared the fairy or whatever she is.'

At Fordhook, the season over, she pursued her studies, delving deeply into astronomy and writing mundane letters for her ailing mother. 'Mama is again so very unwell that she cannot write. . . . she therefore wishes me to tell you that Mr Craig was obliged to have the benches & c. made last week.' She began a serious correspondence with the brilliant and indomitable Mrs Somerville, who regretted that so little attention was paid to Lady Byron's considerable abilities, although the daughter seemed more brilliant than the mother. Now aged fifty-four, she had survived a horrendous childhood during which at nine years old, she was sent to a criminally rigorous boarding school where she recalled being 'enclosed in stiff stays with a steel busk in front while . . . bands drew my shoulders back till the shoulder-blades met. . . . a steel rod, with a semi-circle which went under my chin, was clasped to the steel busk in my stays.' Persistently defiant in the face of her friends and family who strongly disapproved, she was almost completely self-taught, continuing through life to be not only a powerful and exploring intellect but also 'an excellent judge of a well-dressed *déjeuner* and of choice old sherry,' and a devoted wife and mother. Somerville College, Oxford was named after her and her library of books reposes at Girton College, Cambridge.

Ada's attraction for Mrs Somerville was not wholly intellectual. She had visited Italy some years earlier and had gained an unforgettable glimpse of Byron, who strikingly resembled her own brother, an impression confirmed by her husband. Anna Jameson wrote of a visit to Lady Byron and Ada about this time. The former gave her the impression of 'something blighted to the very heart's core . . . Ada is a frank, natural fine-hearted girl . . . not handsome now, but likely to become a very fine woman.'

In 1835 when Ada was twenty, she became engaged to William, 8th Lord King, later created Earl of Lovelace. The courtship was formal and she was 'My dear Miss Byron' until ten days before their wedding on the 8 July, when ardour prompted the bridegroom to risk addressing her as 'My dearest Ada'. Augusta was still *persona non grata* in the immediate family and Ada's husband was warned he must have no dealings whatever with Byron's sister.

Ada and her husband preferred a country life to London. Ada absorbed herself in books concerning mathematics, astronomy and mechanics but soon she was also occupied with the cares of motherhood, for the first of her three children was born two years after her marriage. Nature had endowed her with little maternal instinct. Her husband was autocratic and dedicated to practising his self-taught gifts as an engineer and architect. He designed himself a Somerset home, built on a hillside at Ashley Combe. Neither appeared to show much understanding of children, though Lady Byron's influence on her son-in-law was considerable and under her aegis a school for working-class children was started at Ockham Park. Their eldest son, named after the grandfather he had never known, Byron, rebelled against the conventional career mapped out for him by his father, rejected his family and ran away to sea as John Okey. He died while still a young man.

A frequent guest of Ada, both in London at her home in St James's Square and at Ockham Park and Ashley Combe, was her intellectual mentor Charles Babbage, inventor of the first calculating machine. It was written of Ada that 'eagerly she sought the acquaintance of all who were distinguished in science, art and literature.'[3] None did she cultivate more genuinely than Babbage and the much older mathematician in his turn was entranced by the beautiful young Countess, whose mind had such brilliant potential; he addressed her first as Lady Lovelace but she soon became his 'ladyfairy'. Lord Lovelace was proud of his wife's intellectual superiority and was as welcoming to Babbage as was Ada herself. During Ada's first pregnancy she was preoccupied with a mathematical puzzle and told Babbage she was trying 'to find courage enough to take to pieces one of the wooden crosses, though even with the other before me I doubt if I have the ingenuity to put it together again.' Guided by the demands of calculus and ignoring biology, her husband wrote on Ada's behalf inviting Babbage to spend Easter with them, Ada having a list of mathematical queries to put to her mentor.

After the birth of her second child, Anne Isabella, named after Lady Byron and shortened for a time as in her namesake to Annabella, Ada wrote to Babbage, 'You may possibly have heard of the very tedious and suffering illness . . . since a Miss King has been added to our family. . . . I am now to all appearances perfectly well again, and am in fact most wonderfully improved, yet . . . still far from being really strong.' To Ada, her daughter's birth and her own subsequent severe illness were but a tiresome interruption of her eagerly pursued studies, and she was impatient at not being able to invite Babbage as often as she would have liked. Babbage told Ada, 'I think your taste for mathematics is so decided that it ought not to be checked.'

In 1839 Babbage was again invited to spend Easter with Lord and Lady Lovelace. Ada flattered the mathematician, telling him, 'When alone, the pleasure of monopolizing you is so great; when in company, you make the company so *tenfold* agreeable, that I cannot choose between them. I can only say that we wish to see you at *all* times, and as much as possible. . . . I much wish to have you here, and talk with you. . . . to-day I have been working much at *mathe-*

---

[3] Albany Fonblanque, ed. of *The Examiner*.

matics . . . I must show you a certain book called my mathematical scrap-book,' and complaining that a stay of several days was shamefully short.

The widower found Ada irresistible. She instructed Babbage one icy January to take the train to Weybridge where he would be met by an open carriage. It was likely to be extremely cold, and she advised him that warm outer clothing would be essential. Everybody was out of doors ice-skating and as Ada had acquired the necessary ability, the middle-aged mathematician was invited to bring ice skates and join in the pastime. He could not refuse.

Babbage, who had fathered eight children by a wife whom in all other respects he unthinkingly neglected, harboured a respectful but romantic attachment to Ada. When she wrote asking him to find her a tutor to help further her studies he regretted his failure to find one but told her that he had several times been to see a popular romantic play then showing in London, called *Love*, the title of which he pointedly underlined.

Early in 1841, when her youngest child was two years old, Ada received a long letter from her mother, who was then in Paris staying in the Rue de Rivoli where she had taken Medora Leigh under her wing. In this difficult letter she revealed Byron's believed paternity of Medora. But Ada surprised Annabella by writing to her from St James's Square that she was 'not in the least *astonished* . . . in fact you merely *confirm* what I have for *years and years* felt scarcely a doubt about.' Tactfully Ada had not mentioned the subject to her mother. She explained that she 'should have considered it most improper in me to hint to you that I in any way suspected.' Ada's letter severely discomposed Annabella, who was left guiltily wondering whether in some unguarded moment she might have suggested the idea to her daughter. She agreed that 'there was a remote reference to the fact' in the poems but concluded philosophically that 'the truth always makes itself felt, at least to persons of a certain kind of intellect.' She had wished, she wrote 'to leave your Father's aberrations sufficiently indistinct to enable you still to contemplate his memory with a sort of gratification.' Ada replied that she could not 'recall the precise moment or circumstance which *first* suggested . . . the miserable events . . . remember *several* which have confirmed and strengthened the impression . . . some years at least. – perhaps six, seven, or eight if not more, since that

impression . . . very distinctly traced out.' It was about eight years
earlier, when Ada was fifteen, that her mother first read Byron's
verses to her. In her own solitary way and undetected, Ada had
read Byron's poetry. Intelligent and percipient, although living a
sheltered unworldly existence, she had drawn over the ensuing years
her own conclusions.

But the possibility of Medora's being the tangible result of
Byron's love affair with his half-sister she had not suspected. 'The
notion would not naturally occur,' she wrote to her mother in
March, 'because Mrs L., being married at the time, it might not
have been easy to prove . . . or . . . feel any degree of certainty about
it.' Annabella revealed as little as she need, always protective of Byron
to his daughter, but Ada could not help wondering how her mother
'came ever to suspect anything so monstrous. The natural intimacy
and familiarity of a Brother and Sister certainly could not suggest
it to any but a very depraved and vicious mind, which *yours*', wrote
Ada, 'assuredly was not.' Perceptively she concluded that she could
not 'help fancying that *he* himself must have given you some very
clear hints of it.'

The result of the opening up of the past between mother and
daughter was an invitation to Paris for Ada to meet her supposed
half-sister Medora and her small daughter Marie. The following
month Ada, accompanied by her husband, travelled to France.
Annabella's friend Mrs de Morgan was there and described Medora
at that time as 'excessively slim; her face – like Lady Lovelace's –
had a strong family likeness to Lord Byron,' though Ada was shorter
than Medora. Physical resemblances there may have been but in
character they were complete opposites. Medora's thin, nervous
restlessness, allied to a consciousness of being foredoomed, gave her
an air of theatrical tragedy – the personal drama that she was herself enacting. She found a perfect foil in the calm friendship of the
quietly humorous Ada.

The Medora melodrama continued for several years, Ada remaining relatively uninvolved on the fringes of the affair, concerned at
her mother's distress but maintaining a calm and affectionate attitude towards Medora. In London before again departing for France,
Medora and Marie were guests of Lord and Lady Lovelace in St
James's Square and there was free intercourse between the two
young families. Medora wrote of one occasion, 'Ada's visit gave me

GREAT pleasure yesterday; tomorrow the children come to me & Thursday she and Lord L–.' These were farewell meetings and Ada, unlike her mother, made no emotional demands on Medora who had repulsed the possessive Annabella.

But during the final meeting Ada was subjected to a hysterical outpouring of recriminatory abuse by Medora. 'The last half-hour I was there,' reported Ada to her mother, 'I was compelled to hear a discourse on the bitterness of dependence.' This rose to such heights of absurd paranoia that Ada's sense of humour overcame her and she wrote, 'I can't help laughing after all.' Medora's daughter Marie, then aged ten, never forgot her calm, kind aunt Ada and when in later years she devoted herself to good works in Paris, she called herself Miss Ada Leigh, founding the 'Ada Leigh Homes' there.[4]

Ada afterwards wrote Medora a long letter from her home at Ockham Park. Kindly meant, it merely emphasized to Medora the hopelessness of her position and her detested dependence upon Annabella :

> . . . My dear Elizabeth, do for one moment reflect on what your position *was*, when my mother rescued you from a state of abject misery and poverty ! *She*, on whom of all people in the world you have *least* natural claim ! At the time, you were living in degradation and wretchedness in Brittany ! . . . here is a *person*; on whom you have *less* than *no* natural claim whatever; . . . has . . . incurred large law-expenses for you; paid for Marie's education in England; Made you elegant and valuable gifts; placed about you a maid very superior . . . offered you the use of a carriage . . . When I, some time ago, began to treat you as an intimate and valued friend and relative, not only from my own inclination, but from my mother's direct encouragement . . . it never occurred to my interesting disposition that affection and kindness would develop pride and ingratitude . . . you are on the brink of destruction . . . I am anxious to make a last effort towards saving one whom I cannot look on with indifference . . . You have but *one* course to pursue – submission to your benefactress . . . What motive *can* my Mother ever have had or now have, regarding you, save disinterested affection? . . . do not make *me* regret . . . Remember what you were in Paris – Grateful for *any* countenance from me. You had scarcely dared hope it. Remember too

---

[4] The Ada Leigh Homes do not now exist. Marie later married the Bishop of Toronto, John T. Lewis, DD, LLD.

that there *are* circumstances, disgraceful circumstances, connected with your *birth and your position* . . . Remains of the feelings I had for you dictate this step.

Ada did not relinquish her mathematical studies and her children were often under Annabella's occasionally reluctant care; Lady Byron had to suffer her two grandchildren enthusiastically brushing her long hair. Few touching family scenes as this appear to be associated with Ada. Her enjoyment of motherhood was noticeably less than her enthusiasm for calculation and Ralph was handed over to his grandmother Lady Byron when he was nine years old, providing ready material for her practical experiment in educational reform. Ralph, to his later unhappiness, was not sent to Public School and found himself something of an outcast at Cambridge. Ada's life seemed to be lived totally insulated from the outside world in a highly-ordered private bubble of intellectual exploration. She appeared to have no qualms about her mother, who was not always equal to the task of caring for a lively adolescent boy. Annabella wrote a tired, grandmotherly note to Ada when Ralph was twelve years old, 'As to Ralph, you are welcome to extend *my* Holidays. They do me good . . . I am only Serva Servorum,' and to a friend, 'You will pity the sorrows of a poor old Granny when you think of my having *unaided by any human being*, to manage such a big thing as he is.'

Emerging occasionally from her absorption in mathematics, Ada struck a romantic note, wrote a later Countess of Lovelace, when 'she appeared at a Queen's Ball clad in a semi-Oriental dress, evidently meant to impersonate one of Byron's heroines. Her hair in long dark plaits, and woven and tied with pearls, hung to her waist. Descriptions of this unusual garb passed rapidly in whispers from ear to ear, and in the course of the evening the whole company managed to file past the sofa on which she sat, pretending to talk to each other, but with sharp eyes fixed on every detail of the strange and picturesque figure.'

Ada's discovery of her father's portrait, hidden under a dark curtain for many years by the express order of his mother-in-law, made a profound impression and another deeper one was made by her visit to Newstead Abbey. When, some years later, the Contessa Teresa Guiccioli visited the Abbey, Colonel Wildman recalled

Ada's stay there on his invitation, for they had met in London.

As Lady Lovelace was looking at the library one morning, the Colonel took a book of poems and read out a poem with all the force of the soul and heart. Lady Lovelace, in rapture with this poem, asked the name of its writer. 'There he is' said the Colonel, pointing to a portrait of Byron . . . Lady Lovelace remained stupefied and, from that moment, a kind of revolution took place in her feelings towards her father. 'Do not think, Colonel', she said, 'that it is affectation in me to declare that I have been brought up in complete ignorance of all that concerned my father.'

From that moment an enthusiasm for her father filled her whole soul. She shut herself up for hours in the rooms which he had inhabited and which were still filled with the things which he had used. . . . She chose to sleep in the apartments which were most particularly hallowed by the reminiscences of her father, and appeared never to have been happier than during this stay at Newstead, absorbed as she had become for the first time in all the glory of him whose tenderness for her had been so carefully concealed from her. . . . Everything told of her father's renown and nothing could replace it. All these feelings so possessed her that she wrote to Colonel Wildman to beg that she might be buried next to her illustrious father.[5]

Byron had prophesied to Teresa that 'Ada's mother may have enjoyed the smiles of her youth and childhood, but the tears of her maturer age shall be for me!'[6] This visit to Newstead Abbey was climactic and a letter to Lady Byron on the subject caused an estrangement between mother and daughter for a time.

In the early years of Ada's friendship with Charles Babbage, Ada was decidedly subservient to him. Her letters displayed an awe and admiration which soothed the ego of a man whose advanced ideas were not recognized by the Establishment of the day. He foresaw the uses which could be made of explosives in underwater warfare, anticipated the use of stage lighting and invented the useful little tinkling cash trolley running on overhead wires which was to become such a feature of shops everywhere. Ada wrote to him in 1841,

[5], [6] Teresa Guiccioli, *Lord Byron, jugé par les témoins de sa vie* (Paris, 1868), trans. H. E. H. Jerningham (*My Recollections of Lord Byron, and those of eyewitnesses of his life*), London, 1869.

'I scarcely dare so exalt myself as to hope however humbly, that I can ever be intellectually worthy to attempt serving you.'

When she was twenty-six, the gambling instinct which had lain dormant in her, together with her passion for calculation, began to bear dangerous fruit. She conceived her great idea, influenced by Charles Babbage's paper, published while she was still a child, *Some Questions connected with Games of Chance*. She only hinted to Babbage about her purpose, 'I am very anxious to talk to you. I will give you a hint on *what*. It strikes me that at some future time . . . *my head* may be made by you subservient to some of *your* purposes and plans . . . it is on this that I wish to speak most seriously to you.' The following month Ada wrote again on the subject, 'I am more determined than ever in my future plans; and I have quite made up my mind that nothing must be suffered to interfere with them . . . great good may be the results to *both* of us, and I suspect that the idea (which by the by is one that I believe I have long entertained in a vague and crude form) was one of those happy instincts which do occur to one sometimes so unaccountably and fortunately.'

Meanwhile, however, Ada's brain was occupied with the massive project of translating the distinguished French mathematician General Menabrea's work about Babbage's engine, *Notices sur la Machine Analytique*. Babbage suggested she should add some comments of her own and Ada embarked on this work with energy and enthusiasm, her Notes eventually extending to three times the length of the original work. To be Ada's admiring mentor was one thing, to dare to alter, however trivially, one of her Notes was another, and the 'lady fairy' told Babbage sharply, 'I cannot endure another person to meddle with my sentences.' The distinguished mathematician was amazed at his pupil's virtuosity and wrote, 'I am very reluctant to return the admirable and philosophic view of the Anal-Engine . . . the more I read your notes the more surprised I am at them.' Ada's obsession with ultimate abstraction was based on the belief that 'It is through Mathematics . . . alone we can adequately express the great facts of the natural world.'

Ada's husband Lord Lovelace assisted her with an interest and admiration rare in husbands of clever women. 'Lord L is at this moment kindly *inking it all* over for me,' wrote Ada on completing tables and diagrams, and he made himself useful in other ways:

'Lord L has put up . . . all that belongs to Note H,' Ada reported happily; 'He is quite enchanted with the *beauty* and *symmetry* of the table and diagram.' Ada's husband was sufficiently proud of his 'sweet bird' as he called her to defy the convention of the time and have her sign her work 'translated by A.A.L.' Once Lord Lovelace remarked admiringly to Ada 'What a General you would make!', a remark relayed by a proud Ada to Babbage, adding, 'It is well for the world . . . that I have not taken it into my head to deal with sword, poison and intrigue, in the place of x,y,z.'

The monumental work demanded great tenacity. 'You cannot conceive the trouble I have had with the trigonometrical Note E,' wrote Ada. 'In fact no one but me, I really believe, would have doggedly stuck to it, as I have been doing, in all its wearing minutiae.' When she arrived at an impasse she took refuge in riding her horse round the countryside. Later on, mentally exhausted, she wrote, 'I can neither talk, write, nor think common sense. And yet I feel more like a *fairy* than ever . . . Yours, Addlepate.'

Finally she wrote with satisfaction and delight of the finished work which had fully occupied her mind for two years, 'To say the truth, I *am* rather *amazed* at . . . the really masterly nature of the style and its superiority to that of the memoir itself.' Ada enchanted her husband by her reactions, 'I have made Lord L. laugh much by the dryness with which I remarked "Well, I am very much satisfied with this first child of mine. He is an uncommonly fine baby".' Babbage had dared to tamper again with her work but now she was inclined to be amiably tolerant. 'You will be amused and somewhat triumphant, perhaps,' she wrote, 'when I own that I entirely approve your alteration to my footnote.'

General Menabrea was astonished at finding his mathematical memoir 'not only accurately translated, but with interesting scientific commentaries added to it, by an unknown author whose initials he could not connect with any of the mathematicians of the day,'[7] and was even more amazed to discover that the initials A.A.L. belonged to Byron's daughter.

In Ada's Note G she cautioned future generations against over-dependence on the calculating machine, which 'has no pretensions whatever to *originate* anything,' and in spite of her semi-mystical

[7] Letter from the Prince de Polignac to Lady Anne King.

attitude to mathematics, she was aware of its dependence on the
human element, that the machine could only 'do whatever *we know
how to order it* to perform.'

The translation and annotation successfully published, Ada could
now give the whole of her mind to devising and developing her idea
for an infallible system for betting and winning on race-horses. In
her association with Babbage she was now the dominant partner and
made her own stringent conditions : 'I want to know whether if I
continue to work *on* or *about* your great subject, you will undertake
to abide wholly by the judgement of myself. . . . If I am expected
to be able to lay before you in the course of a year or two, explicit
and honourable propositions for *consulting your engine*,' Babbage
must devote himself entirely to the project. She conceded that 'the
influence of *ambition & fame*' spurred her on : 'No living soul was
more imbued with it than myself. . . . I certainly would not deceive
myself or others by pretending that it is other than a very important
motive & ingredient to my character and nature.' In her realm of
exalted ideas, she had lost all touch with reality and was convinced
that she was guided by divine power. 'I wish to add my mite towards *expounding* and interpreting the Almighty and His laws and
works. . . . It is for you to decide,' she told Babbage, 'I wonder if
you will choose to retain the lady fairy in your service or not?' Byron
had first called Ada's mother 'Princess of Parallellograms', although
later she was his Mathematical Medea; Ada was proving to be
Babbage's Enchantress of Number. 'You are a brave man', she told
him, 'to give yourself wholly up to Fairy-guidance! . . . I advise you
to allow yourself to be unresistingly bewitched, neck & crop, out and
out, whole seas over, by that curious little being!' The advice was
unnecessary; he was, as he signed himself, 'Ever, my fair Inter-
pre*tress*, Your faithful Slave, C.Babbage.'

It has been suggested that Ada and Babbage used the word 'book'
in their correspondence as a code for the system they devised in an
effort to bet profitably on horse-racing.[8] Lord Lovelace was an
admiring and ready assistant, Babbage doing all the fetching and
carrying and practical work in an activity which must be kept completely secret. Babbage was made use of in other ways by his Enchantress. In 1845 Ada asked him to see one of Augusta Leigh's sons,

[8] Maboth Moseley, *Irascible Genius* (Hutchinson, 1964).

'who wants to sell me a rifle & a pair of pistols which he declares to have been my father's.' But her visions of success soared to dangerous heights, and she was convinced of her kinship with another world. 'That brain of mine is something more than merely mortal, as time will show,' she wrote to Babbage after one of her periodic and serious illnesses, 'if only my breathing and some other etceteras do not make too rapid a progress *towards* instead of from *mortality.* . . . Before ten years are over, the Devil's in it if I haven't sucked out some of the life-blood from the mysteries of *this* universe & in a way that no purely mortal lips or brains could do.'

Ada confided to Babbage, 'No-one knows what almost *awful* energy and power lie yet undeveloped in that *wiry* little system of mind.' Already this physically frail woman, who hid what Professor Morgan described as a 'power of thinking . . . utterly out of the common way', was beyond help. She was inextricably involved in her gambling activities, to which she devoted all her considerable energies. She wrote to Babbage, 'I am working very hard for you, like the Devil in fact; (which perhaps I *am*).' Charles Babbage was now in total thrall to his 'lady-fairy', who was euphoric : 'I am in good spirits, for I hope another year will *really* make me something of an *Analyst*. The more I study the more irresistable do I feel my genius for it to be. I do *not* believe that my father was (or ever could have been) such a poet as I shall be an *Analyst* and Metaphysician, for with me the two go together indissolubly.'

Already Professor de Morgan had warned her mother that 'All women who have published mathematics . . . wrestled with difficulties and shown a man's strength in getting over them' risked destruction, for 'the very great tension of mind . . . is beyond the strength of a woman's physical power. . . . as always happens, the whole of the thoughts are continually and entirely concentrated upon them, the struggle between the mind and the body will begin.' These were prophetic words.

By 1848 Ada, unknown to her family, was seriously in debt and writing to Babbage, 'I want you to *complete* something; especially if the something is likely to produce silver and golden somethings.' Babbage also needed money, for the Government had refused to continue to finance the refinement of his engine and his attempts to market game-playing automata which would play noughts and crosses had failed. References to 'the book' continued throughout their correspondence, Wednesday seeming to have been the most important day of the week for their activities.

It was on a Wednesday that Edward Bulwer Lytton failed to keep an appointment in London with Ada, for they had become acquainted. Bulwer Lytton had made his home at Knebworth House a gathering place for the most important figures of the day. Ada had written to him, 'I am desirous of seeing you, because I have a plan to propose to you,' and on receipt of Bulwer's excuse for his non-appearance, she indignantly but good-naturedly replied 'You asked *me* if I ever prayed! I will ask *you* . . . if *you* ever *swear?* . . . swearing, is in my opinion, not only hygienical but even a little *scriptural* – provided it be developed with *taste* & *elegance.*' To Bulwer she stated her philosophy of life : 'We ought to concentrate into *it* all the good & kindness that we can . . . a mutual *tolerance* & sympathy . . . what else is (enlightened) Christianity itself?' A few days later she added, 'Pray do not conceive that I am a mere con-glomeration of *logic* & of lines & triangles! Oh dear no! I am *religiously sceptical,* and *conscientiously unbelieving* . . . I certainly must have been born *very* wicked for I *think* & *feel* myself always *so very good.*'

One of Ada's strange traits was an exaggerated fondness for dogs and birds, which formed yet another bond between Ada and Bab-bage, their letters becoming full of ludicrously affectionate refer-ences to parrots and thrushes and starlings. On one occasion the death of a favourite bird caused Ada such distress that Babbage was despatched to London with the corpse and instructions to discover the cause of death. After three days' anxious consultations it was pronounced to have died from over-feeding and ten days later the bird, stuffed on Ada's instructions, was returned to her.

In November 1850 Ada wrote to Babbage a letter purporting to be about her illness but probably referring to the dire state of her finances : 'The invalid is certainly *better* . . . but the health is so utterly broken at present . . . some very thorough measures must be pursued or all power of getting any livelihood in any *way* whatso-ever will be at an end.' Her compulsive betting had reached the point where Lord Lovelace had finally become disillusioned, but Ada, success always just beyond her reach, persisted in the belief that she could not fail. 'In her desperate need of money she pawned the family jewels, and then implored the help of her mother in redeeming them, and in concealing the whole of the transaction from her husband. Lady Byron redeemed the jewels at the cost of a large sum, she also paid other debts, and she kept her unhappy daughter's secret.'[9]

Ada had also confided in the Irish authoress Mrs Anna Jameson more fully than in her mother, and this was considered a treacherous act by Lady Byron, who had lent the writer considerable sums of money. Annabella was outraged again to find how little she was loved by her own daughter; 'to love and be loved' had ever been her unfulfilled wish. Mother and daughter had been estranged since Ada's emotional visit to Newstead Abbey, which had aroused all her latent feeling for the father she had never known.

In 1852 Ada was found to be suffering from cancer. As she lay dying, to her physical agony was added mental anguish, for she was 'in the toils of an unscrupulous gang of betting men. . . . to extricate herself from their clutches . . . a humiliating and well nigh impossible task.'[10] On her death-bed, she named Babbage executor of her will, instructing him to pay off one of her servants, Mary Wilson, who had earlier been Babbage's maid and doubtless in the confidence of both in their betting activities. The maid had probably been more than that to the lonely widower, intellectually and spiritually enamoured of his Fairy-Countess who yet remained unattainable. Annabella, when she was inevitably applied to for the money, once more dipped into her fortunately ample purse and discharged another's debt yet again.

In great pain and dying, Ada was reunited with her mother, who stayed with her until the end, a devotional book by her side. 'Only the last few minutes were entirely free from pain,' wrote Lord Lovelace; 'the spirit passed away into its final rest so easily that we were not for some time aware she was gone.'

Ada died on 27 November 1852, aged thirty-six, her father's age at his death, and by her own desire was buried in the Byron family vault at Hucknall Torkard beside her father. In spite of her expressed unbelief, she turned to the New Testament and the Epistle according to St James for the epitaph she chose to be inscribed on her monument:

[9] Mary, Countess of Lovelace.
[10] Countess of Lovelace.

And the prayer of faith shall save the sick,
And the Lord shall raise him up;
And if he have committed sins,
They shall be forgiven him.

Appendix

A NEW CANTO

CAROLINE LAMB

I'm sick of fame – I'm gorged with it – so full
I almost could regret the happier hour
When northern oracles proclaimed me dull,
Grieving my Lord should so mistake his power –
E'en they, who now my consequence would lull,
And vaunt they hail'd and nurs'd the opening flower,
Vile cheats! He knew not, impudent Reviewer,
Clear spring of Helicon from common sewer.

'Tis said they killed the gentle soul'd Montgomery –
I'll swear, they did not shed for him a tear!
He had not spirit to revenge their mummery,
Nor lordly purse to print and persevere.
I measured stings with 'em – a method summary –
Not that I doubt their penitence sincere;
And I've a fancy running in my head
They'll like; or so by some it will be said.

When doomsday comes, St Paul's will be on fire –
I should not wonder if we live to see it –
Of us, proof pickles, Heaven must rather tire,
And want a reckoning – if so, so be it –
Only about the Cupola, or higher,
If there's a place unoccupied, give me it –
To catch, before I touch my sinner's salary,
The first grand crackle in the whispering gallery.

The ball comes tumbling in a lively crash,
And splits the pavement up, and shakes the shops,
Teeth chatter, china dances, spreads the flash,
The omnium falls, the Bank of England stops;
Loyal and radical, discreet and rash,
Each on his knees in tribulation flops;
The Regent raves (Moore chuckling at his pain)
And sends about for Ministers in vain.

The roaring streamers flap, red flakes are shot
This way and that, the town is a volcano –
And yells are heard, like those provoked by Lot,
Some, of the Smithfield sort, and some *soprano*;
Some holy water seek, the font is hot,
And fizzing in a tea-kettle *piano*.
Now bring your magistrates, with yeomen back'd,
Bawls Belial, and read the Riot-Act! –

The Peak of Derbyshire goes to and fro;
Like drunken sot the Monument is reeling;
Now fierce and fiercer comes the furious glow,
The planets, like a juggler's ball, are wheeling:
I am a graceless poet as you know,
Yet I would not wish to wound a proper feeling,
Nor hint you'd hear, from saints in agitation,
The *lapsis linguae* of an execration.

Mark yon bright beauty, in her tragic airs,
How her clear white the mighty smother tinges!
Delicious chaos! that such beauty bares! –
And now those eyes outstretch their silken fringes,
Staring bewildered – and anon she tears
Her raven tresses ere the wide flame singes –
Oh! would she feel as I could do, and cherish
One wild forgetful rapture, ere all perish! –

Who would be vain? Fair maids and ugly men
Together rush, the dainty and the shabby,
(No gallantry will soothe ye, ladies, then)
High dames, the wandering beggar and her *babby*,
In motley agony, a desperate train,
Flocking to holy places like the Abbey,
Till the black volumes, closing o'er them, scowl,
Muffling for ever, curse, and shriek, and howl.

A woman then may rail, nor would I stint her;
Her griefs, poor soul, are past redress in law –
And if this matter happen in the winter,
There'll be at Petersburgh a sudden thaw,
And Alexander's palace, every splinter
Burn, Christmas like and merry, though the jaw
Of its imperial master take to trembling,
As when the French were quartered in the Cremlin.

Rare doings in the North! as trickle down
Primeval snows, and white bears swash and caper,
And Bernadotte, that swaggerer of renown,
To Bonaparte again might hold a taper.
Ay, truckle to him, cap in hand or crown,
To save his distance from the sturdy vapour.
Napoleon, too, will he look blank and paly?
He hung the citizens of Moscow gaily –

He made a gallant youth his darkling prey,
Nor e'er would massacre or murder mince,
And yet I fear, on this important day
To see the hero pitifully wince:
Go, yield him up to Beelzebub, and say,
Pray treat him like a gentleman and prince.
I doubt him thorough-bred he's not a true one,
A blood-hound spaniel-crossed and no Don Juan.

Death-watches now, in every baking wall, tick
Faster and faster, till they tick no more,
And Norway's copper-mines about the Baltic
Swell, heave, and rumble with their boiling ore,
Like some griped giant's motion peristaltic,
Then burst, and to the sea vast gutters pour;
And as the waters with the fire-stream curl,
Zooks! what a whizzing, roaring, sweltering whirl!

Lo! the great deep laid bare, tremendous yawning,
Its scalding waves retiring from the shore,
Affrighted whales on dry land sudden spawning,
And small fish fry where fish ne'er fried before.
No Christian eye shall see another dawning —
The Turkish infidel may now restore
His wives to liberty, and, ere to Hell he go,
Roll in the bottom of the Archipelago!

And now, ye coward sinners (I'm a bold one,
Scorning all here, nor caring for hereafter,
A radical, stubborn, and an old one)
Behold! each riding on a burning rafter,
The devils (in my arms I long to fold one)
Splitting their blue and brazen sides with laughter,
Play at snapdragons, in their merry fits,
O'er some conventicle for hypocrites.

Ay, serve the skulkers with their looks so meek,
As they've, no doubt, served lobsters in their time,
(Poor *blacks*! no Wilberforce for them can speak,
Pleading their colour is their only crime,)
Trundle them all to bubble and to squeak —
No doubt they shut their ears against my rhyme,
Yet sneak, rank elders, fearful of denials,
To pick Susannahs up in Seven Dials.

Brave fiends! for usurers and misers melt
And make a hell broth of their cursed gold:
On all who mock at want they never felt,
On all whose consciences are bought and sold,
E'en as on me, be stern damnation dealt,
And lawyers, damn them all — the blood runs cold,
That man should deal with misery, to mock it,
And filch an only shilling from its pocket.

Ay, damn them all, a deep damnation wait
On all such callous, crooked hopeless souls!
Ne'er mince the matter to discriminate,
But let the devil strike them from the Rolls:
'Twill cheer their clients to behold their fate,
And round their bonfires dance in merry shoals.
Some poor men's tales I've heard upon my journies,
Would make a bishop long to roast attornies.

Perhaps the thing may take another turn,
And one smart shock may split the world in two,
And I in Italy, you soon may learn,
On t'other half am reeling far from you.
No doubt 'twould split, where first it ought to burn,
Across some city, that its sins should rue,
Some wicked capital, for instance, Paris,
And stop the melodrames from Mr Harris.

Save London, none is wickeder, or bigger;
An odious place too, in these modern times,
Small incomes, runaways, and swindlers eager
To fleece and dash; and then their quacks and mimes,
Their morals lax, and literary rigours,
Their prim censuras, and their gendered rhymes —
Mine never could abide their statutes critical,
They'd call them neutral or hermaphroditical.

True, their poor Play-wrights (truth, I speak with pain)
Yield ours a picking, and I beg their pardon —
'Tis needless — down must come poor Drury Lane,
And, scarcely less poor, down come Covent Garden:
If we must blaze, no squabbles will remain
That Actors' hearts against each other harden —
Committees, creditors, all wrapped up in flames,
That leave no joke for Horace Smith or James.

In rebus modus est: whene'er I write
I mean to rhapsodize, and nothing more —
If, some poor nervous souls my Muse affright,
I might a strain of consolation pour, —
Talk of the spotless spirits, snowy white,
Which, newly clad, refreshing graves restore,
And silvery wreaths of glory round them curl'd,
Serenely rise above the blazing world.

Free, bursting from his mound of lively green,
Wing'd light as zephyr of the rosy morn,
The poor man smiling on the proud is seen,
With something of a mild forgiving scorn —
The marbled proud one, haply with the mean,
Sole on his prayer of intercession borne:
Upward in peal harmonious they move,
Soft as the midnight tide of hallow'd love.

The rich humane, who with their common clay
Divided graciously, distinguished few;
Good Christians, who had slept their wrongs away,
In peace with this life, and the next in view;
Strugglers with tyrant passion and its prey,
Love's single-hearted victims, sacred, true,
Who, when dishonour's path alone could save,
Bore a pure pang to an untimely grave.

Blest they, who wear the vital spirit out,
Even thus, degrading not the holy fire,
Nor bear a prostituted sense about,
The misery of never quench'd desire,
Still quench'd, still kindling, every thought devout
Lost in the changeful torment – portion dire! –
Return we to our heaven, our fire and smoke,
Though now you may begin to take the joke!

What joke? – my verses – mine, and all beside,
Wild, foolish tales of Italy and Spain,
The gushing shrieks, the bubbling squeaks, the bride
Of nature, blue-eyed, black-eyed, and her swain.
Kissing in grottoes, near the moon-lit tide,
Though to all men of common sense 'tis plain,
Except for rampart and amphibious brute,
Such damp and drizzly places would not suit.

Mad world! for fame we rant, call names, and fight –
I scorn it heartily, yet love to dazzle it,
Dark intellects by day, as shops by night,
All with a bright, new speculative gas lit.
Wars the blue vapour with the oil-fed light,
Hot sputter Blackwood, Jeffrey, Giffard, Hazlitt –
The Muse runs madder, and, as mine may tell,
Like a loose comet, mingles Heaven and Hell.

You shall have more of her another time,
Since gulled you will be with our flights poetic,
Our eight, and ten, and twenty feet sublime,
Our maudlin, hey-down-derrified pathetic.
For my part, though I'm doomed to write in rhyme,
To read it would be worse than an emetic –
But something must be done to cure the spleen,
And keep my name in capitals, like Kean.

Sources and Bibliography

Airlie, Mabell, Countess of, *In Whig Society 1775–1818* (Hodder and Stoughton, 1921).

———, ———————, *Lady Palmerston and Her Times*, 2 Vols (Hodder and Stoughton, 1922).

Ashley Collection, British Museum.

Beecher-Stowe, Harriet, *Lady Byron Vindicated* (Boston, 1870).

Bessborough, Earl of, *Lady Byron and her Family Circle* (John Murray, 1940).

—————, ———, *Letters of Georgiana, Duchess of Devonshire* (John Murray, 1955).

Bickley, Francis, *Diaries of Sylvester Douglas, Lord Glenbervie* (Constable, 1928).

Blyth, Henry, *Caro – The Fatal Passion* (Hart-Davis, 1972).

Brailsford, Henry N., *Shelley, Godwin and Their Circle* (Oxford University Press, 1951).

Bulwer, Rosina, *Unpublished Letters of Lady Bulwer Lytton to A.E. Chalon R.A.* (London, Eveleigh Nash, 1914).

Bulwer Lytton, Edward, Correspondence, Hertfordshire Records Office.

Burney, Fanny, *Diary and Letters of Madame d'Arblay (1778–1840)* (London, 1842-6).

Byron, George Gordon, Lord, *Letters and Journals*, ed. Rowland E. Prothero (London, 1898-1901).

———, ———————, *Correspondence* (chiefly with Lady Melbourne), ed. John Murray (John Murray, 1922).

———, ———————, *Complete Poems*, ed. E. H. Coleridge (London, 1898-1904).

———, ———————, *Letters and Journals*, Vols I and II, ed. Leslie A. Marchand (John Murray, 1973).

Cavendish, Georgiana, Duchess of Devonshire, *The Sylph* (Dublin, 1779).

Cecil, Lord David, *Melbourne* (Constable, 1939).

Disraeli, Benjamin, *Venetia* (London, 1837).

Dowden, Edward, *Life of Shelley* (London, 1886).

Drinkwater, John, *Pilgrim of Eternity* (Hodder and Stoughton, 1925).

Elwin, Malcolm, *Lord Byron's Wife* (Macdonald, 1962).

——, ———, *The Noels and the Milbankes* (John Murray, 1967).

Erdman, David V., 'Byron and the New Force of the People', *Keats-Shelley Journal*, Vol. XI (Winter, 1962), USA.

——, ———, 'Lord Byron as Rinaldo', PMLA, Vol. LVII (March, 1942), USA.

——, ———, 'Byron and Revolt in England', *Science and Society*, Vol. XI (Summer, 1947), USA.

Erskine, Mrs Steuart (ed.), *Anna Jameson: Letters and Friendships, 1812–1860* (London, T. Fisher Unwin, 1915).

Forman, Buxton H. (ed.), *Letters of Edward John Trelawny* (London, Henry Froude, 1910).

Foster, Vere, *The Two Duchesses* (London, 1898).

Fox, Henry, *Journal of the Hon. H.E. Fox, 1818–1830*, ed. Earl of Ilchester (London, Thornton Butterworth, 1923).

Godwin, William, *The Elopement of P.B. Shelley and Mary Godwin* (Boston?, 1911).

Gower, Henrietta Elizabeth Leveson, *Hary-o. The Letters of Lady Harriet Cavendish, 1796–1809*, ed. Sir George Leveson Gower (John Murray, 1940, 1940).

——, ——————————, *Letters of Harriet, Countess Granville, 1810–1845*, ed. Hon. F. Leveson Gower (London, 1894).

Gower, Granville Leveson, Earl Granville, *Private Correspondence of Earl Granville*, ed. Castalia, Countess Granville (John Murray, 1916).

Gray, Austin K., *Teresa* (Harrap, 1948).

Grebanier, Bernard, *The Uninhibited Byron* (Peter Owen, 1971).

Grylls, R. Glynn, *Claire Clairmont* (John Murray, 1939).

——, ———, *Mary Shelley* (Oxford University Press, 1938).

——, ———, *Trelawny* (Constable, 1950).

——, ———, *William Godwin and His World* (Odhams Press, 1953).

Guiccioli, Ignazio, Marchese, *Gli Stati di Blois: dramma storico* (Rome, 1938).

Guiccioli, Teresa, Countess, *Lord Byron, jugé par les témoins de sa vie* (Paris, 1868), trans. H. E. H. Jerningham, *My Recollections of Lord Byron, and those of eyewitnesses of his life* (London, 1869).

Huscher, Herbert, 'The Clairmont Enigma', *Keats-Shelley Memorial Bulletin*, XI (1960).

————, ————, 'Charles Gaulis Clairmont', *Keats-Shelley Memorial Bulletin*, VIII (1957).

————, ————, 'Claire Clairmont's Lost Russian Journal', *Keats-Shelley Memorial Bulletin*, VI (1954).

Ingpen, R. E., *Shelley in England* (Kegan, Paul and Co., 1917).

Jenkins, Elizabeth, *Lady Caroline Lamb* (Gollancz, 1932).

Jones, F. L. (ed.), *Letters of Percy Bysshe Shelley* (Clarendon Press, 1964).

Knight, Frida, *University Rebel* (Gollancz, 1971).

Knight, G. Wilson, *Lord Byron's Marriage. The Evidence of Asterisks* (Macmillan, 1957).

Lamb Papers, Hertfordshire Records Office.

Lamb, Lady Caroline, *Glenarvon* (London, 1816).

————, ————————, *Graham Hamilton* (London, 1822).

————, ————————, *Ada Reis* (London, 1823).

Langley-Moore, Doris, *The Late Lord Byron. Posthumous Dramas* (John Murray, 1961).

————————————, ————, 'Byron, Leigh Hunt and the Shelleys', *Keats-Shelley Memorial Bulletin*, X (1959).

Lean, E. Tangye, *The Napoleonists* (Oxford University Press, 1970).

Lovelace, Earl of, *Astarte. A Fragment of the Truth Concerning George Gordon, Sixth Lord Byron*, ed. Mary, Countess Lovelace (Privately printed, 1921).

————, ————, *Lady Noel Byron and the Leighs* (Privately printed, 1887).

Lovelace, Mary, Countess of, *Ralph, Earl of Lovelace. A Memoir* (London, Christophers, 1920).

Mackay, Charles, *Elizabeth Medora Leigh. An Autobiography* (New York, 1869).

Marchand Leslie A., 'Trelawny on the Death of Shelley', *Keats-Shelley Memorial Bulletin*, IV (1951).

Massingham, H. J., *The Friend of Shelley. A Memoir of Edward John Trelawny* (London, Cobden-Sanderson, 1930).

Mayne, Ethel Colburn, *Life and Letters of Anne Isabella, Lady Byron* (Constable, 1929).

McGann, Jerome, 'Byron, Teresa and Sardanapalus', *Keats-Shelley Memorial Bulletin*, XVIII (1967).

Montgomery, Henry, *Unitarian Minister* (Belfast, 1841).

Moore, Thomas, *Letters and Journals of Lord Byron with Notices of His Life* (London, 1830).

Morgan, Lady, *Memoirs*, 2 Vols (London, 1862).

Moseley, Maboth, *Irascible Genius. The Life of Charles Babbage* (Hutchinson, 1964).

Origo, Iris, *Allegra* (London, L. and J. Woolf, 1935).

——, ——, *The Last Attachment* (Collins, 1962).

Panshanger Papers, Hertfordshire Records Office.

Papendiek, Mrs, *Court and Private Life in the Time of Queen Charlotte* (London, 1887).

Paston, George and Quennell, Peter, '*To Lord Byron*'. *Feminine Profiles* (John Murray, 1939).

Ponsonby, Sir John, *The Ponsonby Family* (London, Medici Society, 1929).

Robertson, Lorraine, 'Journal and Notebooks of Claire Clairmont', *Keats-Shelley Memorial Bulletin*, IV (1951).

Roe-Byron Collection, Newstead Abbey.

Smith, Mary R. D., *Recollections of Two Distinguished Persons* (Philadelphia, 1878).

Somerville, Martha, *Personal Recollections of Mary Somerville* (London, 1873).

Stanhope, Philip Henry, 5th Lord, *Notes of Conversations with the Duke of Wellington, 1831–1851* (London, 1888).

Steele, Mrs Elizabeth, *The Memoirs of Sophia Baddeley* (London, 1787).

Stuart, D. M., *Dearest Bess* (Methuen, 1955).

Thomas, Clara, *Love and Work Enough. The Life of Anna Jameson* (Macdonald, 1967).

Thornbury, Life of Turner (London, 1862).

Wyndham, Charles, *Letter from the Earl of Egremont* (London, 1763).

Wyndham, Maud Mary, *Correspondence of Sarah Spencer, Lady Lyttelton* (John Murray, 1912).

————, ————, *Chronicles of the Eighteenth Century* (Hodder and Stoughton, 1924).

Index

DATE DUE

11.08 '87			
DEC 1 5 1989			
1 5 1990			
GAYLORD			PRINTED IN U.S.A.